Human Rights and Climate Change

A Review of the International Legal Dimensions

Siobhan McInerney-Lankford, Mac Darrow, and Lavanya Rajamani

THE WORLD BANK
Washington, D.C.

1 2 3 4   13 12 11 10

ISBN: 978-0-8213-8720-7
eISBN: 978-0-8213-8723-8
DOI: 10.1596/978-0-8213-8720-7

Library of Congress Cataloging-in-Publication Data

Human rights and climate change : a review of the international legal dimensions.
    p. cm.
Includes bibliographical references and index.
ISBN 978-0-8213-8720-7 (alk. paper)
1. Climatic changes--Law and legislation. 2. Global warming--Law and legislation. 3. Human rights. I. World Bank.
K3585.5.H86 2011
344.04'6--dc22

2010053496

Contents

Foreword

The World Bank Study *Human Rights and Climate Change: A Review of the International Law Issues* provides a comprehensive and current review of the legal and policy frameworks governing the interface of human rights and climate change. The Study includes a conceptual overview of the link between climate impacts and human rights, focused on the relevant legal obligations underpinning the international law frameworks governing both human rights and climate change. As such it makes a significant contribution to the global debate on climate change and human rights by offering a comprehensive analysis of the international legal dimensions of this intersection. The Study helps advance an understanding of what is meant, in legal and policy terms, by the human rights impacts of climate change through examples of specific substantive rights. It gives a legal and theoretic perspective on the connection between human rights and climate change along three dimensions: first, human rights may affect the enjoyment of human rights. Second, measures to address human rights may impact the realization of rights and third, that human rights have potential relevance to policy and operational responses to climate change, and may promote resilience to climate change, including in developing countries in a way that may help sustainable development. Beyond a rigorous legal review and analysis however, the Study also contributes insights on the potential operational implications of the links between human rights and climate change in a diverse range of areas including policy measures, legal accountability, technology transfer and the potential role of the private sector.

The Study represents a timely and substantive contribution to an area that has been the subject of sustained attention in recent years, particularly in developing countries. This Study effectively consolidates knowledge from the fields of international human rights law, international law governing climate change and international environmental law, building on the existing work of the UN Office of the High Commissioner on Human Rights, the UN Human Rights Council and the International Council on Human Rights Policy. Although it maintains a legal focus, the Study has benefited from the input of a host of international experts from other disciplines as well.

The Trust Fund on Environmentally and Socially Sustainable Development (TFESSD) provided financial support for the publication of this Study and the research upon which it is based: this Study is part of an ongoing Trust Fund activity on the *Use of International Law to Address Social Impacts of Climate Change.* This publication has been reviewed and recommended for publication by the Legal Vice Presidency Research and Editorial Board and the Legal Vice Presidency is pleased to support its publication on an area of its broader initiative on knowledge and research. Moreover, since 2010 the management of the Trust Fund activity on the *Use of International Law to Address Social Impacts of Climate Change* has been integrated into the Nordic Trust Fund on Human Rights managed out of Operations Policy and Country Services Vice Presidency (OPCS). As such, OPCS is pleased to join in support of the publication of this Study as part of the Bank's knowledge and learning activities on human rights.

Hassane Cisse,
Deputy General Counsel
Knowledge and Research
Legal Vice Presidency
The World Bank

R. Kyle Peters,
Director
Strategy and Country Services
Operations Policy & Country Services
The World Bank

Abstract

This Study explores arguments about the impact of climate change on human rights, examining the international legal frameworks governing human rights and climate change and identifying the relevant synergies and tensions between them. It considers arguments about (i) the human rights impacts of climate change at a macro level and how these impacts are spread disparately across countries; (ii) how climate change impacts human rights enjoyment within states and the equity and discrimination dimensions of those disparate impacts; and (iii) the role of international legal frameworks and mechanisms, including human rights instruments, particularly in the context of supporting developing countries' adaptation efforts.

The Study surveys the interface of human rights and climate change from the perspective of public international law. It builds upon the work that has been carried out on this interface by reviewing the legal issues it raises and complementing existing analyses by providing a comprehensive legal overview of the area and a focus on obligations upon States and other actors connected with climate change. The objective has therefore been to contribute to the global debate on climate change and human rights by offering a review of the legal dimensions of this interface as well as a survey of the sources of public international law potentially relevant to climate change and human rights in order to facilitate an understanding of what is meant, in legal terms, by "human rights impacts of climate change" and help identify ways in which international law can respond to this interaction. This is a complex and dynamically evolving legal and policy landscape and this study aims to capture its most salient features insofar as they appear at present.

The Study employs the following three-part conceptual understanding of the links between human rights and climate change. First, climate change may affect the enjoyment of human rights: this is explored in Chapter II and draws from the existing work of the United Nations (UN) Office of the High Commissioner for Human Rights (OHCHR), the UN Human Rights Council and the International Council on Human Rights Policy. Second, measures to address climate change may impact the realization of human rights. This is a subset of the discussion of "impacts" targeting "secondary" human rights impacts of measures aimed at addressing climate change. Third, human rights have relevance to policy and operational responses to climate change, such that human rights obligations (both substantive and procedural) may be relevant to the design and implementation of effective responses to climate change, particularly in relation to adaptation and to some extent also to mitigation. Human rights may also have a role in promoting resilience to climate change and may reinforce sustainable development goals.

The Study includes a number of approaches from connecting climate change to specific human rights impacts under international human rights law, to tracing the applicable sources of law and surveying identifiable obligations under international human rights law and international environmental law. The Study reviews how human rights law addresses environmental protection in substantive and procedural terms focusing in particular on the advances made in the latter through the jurisprudence of regional human rights bodies for example. The Study considers also how environmental protection has been extended to regulate private as well as public action. Following from this is a discussion of the application of human rights to climate change, including an outline of the various ways in which human rights can be seen to "add value" to the discourse, including the use of human rights legal framework as a tool for helping analyse climate impacts and determining appropriate policy responses. The Study includes a summary analysis of principles and precepts of international human rights law and multilateral environmental agreements (MEA) to consider their compatibility in conceptual terms. It concludes with a short review of potential operational implications and areas for further research. Among these new issues in human rights and climate change is the role of the private sector in addressing the challenges identified and complementing the efforts of governments: this is particularly apt in light of the increased recognition of the emerging roles of both public and private sector actors in relation to human rights.

Acknowledgments

This Study was commissioned by the Environmental and International Law unit of the World Bank Legal Department (LEGEN) as part of a research project funded by the World Bank Trust Fund on Environmentally and Socially Sustainable Development (TFESSD) for FY09. The Study was produced under the direction of Siobhán McInerney-Lankford, Task Team Leader for the TFESSD Project on *The Use of International Law to Address Social Impacts of Climate Change* and includes the combined work of Mac Darrow (UN OHCHR, writing in a personal capacity) and Lavanya Rajamani (Centre for Policy Research, New Delhi). Charles Di Leva, Chief Counsel ESSD & International Law (LEGEN) was responsible for the overall supervision of the project.

Thanks are due to John Knox for substantive input on chapters IV and VI in particular and to Saskia Zandieh, Kanhu Charan Pradhan, Lakshmi Mathew and Vrinda Maheshwari for valuable research assistance at various stages of the project. Thanks are due also to Ed Anderson, Milan Brahmbhatt, Ed Cameron, Rachel Davis, Angus Friday, Ulrik Halsteen, Stephen Humphreys, Robin Mearns, Alberto Ninio, Robert Ondhowe, Hans-Otto Sano, Martin Schoenberg, Michael Toman, Hanneke Van Tilburg, Xueman Wang, and Vanessa Zimmerman for their comments on earlier drafts and their inputs and participation during the international workshop held at World Bank headquarters in May 2009 to debate the initial findings of this work. The authors are grateful to the World Bank Law Library for support of the research: particular thanks are due to Laura Lalime-Mowry, Christian Jimenez Tomas and Kimberly Erin O'Connor. Special thanks are due to Anna Socrates for outstanding editorial assistance with the final drafts of this Study.

The authors are grateful to the Trust Fund on Environmentally and Socially Sustainable Development (TFESSD) which provided financial support for the publication of this Study and the research upon which it is based. Thanks are due to the LEGVP Research and Editorial Board* which reviewed and recommended this Study for publication.

The findings, interpretations, and conclusions expressed in this Study are those of the authors and do not necessarily reflect the views of the Executive Directors of the World Bank or the governments they represent. This Study should not be understood to be linked to any World Bank policies, operations or positions related to the subject areas it covers. The last revision of this Study was completed in September 2010.

*Hassane Cisse, Editor-in-Chief, Kenneth Mwenda, Alberto Ninio (Chairs); Christina Biebesheimer, Charles Di Leva, Laurence Laulio, Siobhán McInerney-Lankford, Vikram Raghavan, Kishor Uprety and Vijay Tata, Members.

Acronyms and Abbreviations

ABA	American Bar Association
CAT	Convention against Torture and other Cruel, Inhuman or Degrading Treatment of Punishment
CBDR	Common But Differentiated Responsibilities
CDM	Clean Development Mechanism
CESCR	Committee on Economic, Social and Cultural Rights
CEDAW	Convention on Elimination of All Forms of Discrimination against Women
CER	Certified Emissions Reductions
COP	Conference of Parties
CRC	Convention on the Rights of the Child
CRC-AC	Optional Protocol to the Convention of the Rights of the Child on the Involvement of Children in Armed Conflicts
CRC-SC	Optional Protocol to the Convention of the Rights of the Child on the Sale of Children, Child Prostitution and Child Pornography
CRPD	Convention on the Rights of Persons with Disabilities
DFID	Department for International Development
DIHR	Danish Institute for Human Rights
EC	European Commission
ECtHR	European Court on Human Rights
ECHR	European Convention on Human Rights and Fundamental Freedoms
ECOSOC	Economic and Social Council
EGTT	Expert Group on Technology Transfer
EIA	Environmental Impact Assessment
EPA	Environmental Protection Agency
EU	European Union
FDI	Foreign Direct Investment
GDP	Gross Domestic Product
GHG	Greenhouse Gas
IACHR	Inter-American Commission on Human Rights
IBLF	International Business Leaders Forum
IBRD	International Bank for Reconstruction and Development
ICC	Inuit Circumpolar Conference
ICCPR	International Covenant on Civil and Political Rights
ICERD	International Convention on the Elimination on All Forms of Racial Discrimination
ICESCR	International Covenant on Economic, Social and Cultural Rights
ICJ	International Court of Justice

ICRMW	International Convention on the Protection of the Rights of All Migrant Workers and Members of their Families
IDA	International Development Association
IFC	International Finance Corporation
ILC	International Law Commission
ILO	International Labour Organization
IOM	International Organization for Migration
IPCC	Intergovernmental Panel on Climate Change
KILM	Key Indicators of the Labour Market
KJAS	Kenya Joint Assistance Strategy
LDCs	Least Developed Countries
MDGs	Millennium Development Goals
MEA	Multilateral Environmental Agreement
MWC	Migrant Workers Convention
NATO	North Atlantic Treaty Organization
NGO	Non-governmental organization
OHCHR	Office of the High Commissioner for Human Rights
PCIJ	Permanent Court of International Justice
PRS	Poverty Reduction Strategies
REDD	Reduced Emissions from Deforestation and Degradation
RBAs	Rights-Based Approaches
SSA	Sub-Saharan Africa
SBI	Subsidiary Body for Implementation
SBSTA	Subsidiary Body for Scientific and Technological Advice
SRSG	Special Representative of the UN Secretary General on Business and Human Rights
TNC	Transnational Corporation
UDHR	Universal Declaration of Human Rights
UN	United Nations
UNCLOS	United Nations Convention on the Law of the Sea
UNDP	United Nations Development Programme
UNEP	United Nations Environment Programme
UNESCO	United Nations Educational, Scientific and Cultural Organization
UNFCCC	United Nations Framework Convention on Climate Change
UNGC	United Nations Global Compact
UNHCR	United Nations High Commissioner for Refugees
UNHRC	United Nations Human Rights Council
UNICEF	United Nations Children's Fund
US	United States
WDR	World Development Report
WHO	World Health Organization
WTO	World Trade Organization

CHAPTER 1

Introduction

Climate Change: A Defining Human Development Challenge for the 21st Century[1]

The issue of climate change has captured global attention like few other causes. From relative obscurity in the late 1980s when it was first discussed in the UN General Assembly,[2] it has come to be characterized as "the defining human development challenge for the 21st century."[3]

The Fourth Assessment Report of the Intergovernmental Panel on Climate Change (IPCC), released in 2007, warned that the warming of the climate system is unequivocal and accelerating.[4] The global average temperature has increased by 0.74 degrees centigrade in the last century constituting the largest and fastest warming trend in the history of the Earth.[5] It is predicted to increase by 1.8 to 6.4 degrees centigrade.[6] Climate change will, among other impacts, increase the severity of droughts, land degradation and desertification, the intensity of floods and tropical cyclones, the incidence of malaria and heat-related mortality, and decrease crop yield and food security.[7] There is also increasing certainty that, as the climate system warms, poorer nations, and the poorest within them, will be the worst affected.[8] Of some concern is the fact that, in the short span of time since release of the IPCC report, there is growing evidence that its conclusions underestimated both the scale and pace of global warming.[9]

Climate change is expected to have profound impacts on human development.[10] The Human Development Report notes that climate change is hampering efforts to deliver the MDG promise, and that failure to address the climate change problem will consign the poorest 40% of the world's population – 2.6 billion people – "to a future of diminished opportunity."[11] Two degrees centigrade represents the threshold at which rapid reversals in human development become difficult to avoid.[12] The Stern Review provides authoritative guidance on the likely impacts of climate change on development in developing countries.[13] It records, for instance, that the cost of climate change in India and South East Asia could be as high as 9-13% loss in gross domestic product (GDP) by 2100 as compared to what could have been achieved in a world without climate change.[14] In an updated analysis in 2009, Stern remarked that "[t]he magnitude of risks involved in climate change is vastly greater than, for instance, the disruption that would be caused to people were the Western financial system to collapse."[15] The adverse impacts are likely to be compounded for those countries worst hit by the global economic and financial crises, putting vulnerable communities under additional stress and limiting the resources for mitigation, adaptation and clean technology transfer.[16]

It seems likely that the climate impacts documented by the IPCC and the Stern Review will undermine the realization of a range of internationally recognised human rights, and indeed in many parts of the world the damage is already evident. Yet it is only recently that human rights have entered the discourse on the climate change problem.[17] As will be discussed in more depth below, an explicit concern for human rights within this context could bring value in a number of ways, such as placing the individual at the centre of inquiry, drawing attention to the impacts that climate change have (actually and prospectively) on the realization of a range of human rights that are protected by law, buttressing vulnerable communities' and countries' claims for international assistance, and helping to empower the most marginalised groups and strengthening accountability for delivery on adaptation measures through a focus on obligations. The reluctance to consider the human rights dimensions of climate change thus far can, to some extent, as some scholars have suggested, be traced to disciplinary path-dependence.[18] That is, climate discourse has originated and remained the purview of physical scientists and has only recently entered the social science discourse. As such, the climate negotiations have adopted consensus-driven, welfare-based solutions with an economic orientation, and largely ignored parallel developments in the human rights arena.[19] The practice of human rights has, for its part, been historically dominated by lawyers, and only relatively recently gained the attention of economists and other social scientists.

Against this backdrop, this paper seeks, in a schematic way, to explore:

- The key tenets, principles and premises of the conceptual and legal frameworks relating to human rights and multilateral environmental agreements (MEAs),[20] and their relevance in the context of climate change discourse, regulation and action;
- The human rights impacts of climate change, including the human rights impacts of action to combat climate change;
- The relevant sources of public international law relevant to climate change and human rights, and in that connection, the typologies, content and boundaries of legal obligations under each regime;
- Key features of the human rights legal and institutional framework at regional and national levels, in addition to the global level, relevant to how the challenge of climate change is framed and to how mitigation and adaptation measures might be pursued;
- The compatibility of action to protect human rights and address climate change; and
- The distinctiveness and so-called "value-added" of an approach to climate change based upon human rights, entailing, among other things, using the human rights legal framework as a tool for helping analyse climate impacts and determining appropriate policy responses.

The International Climate Change Regime

A problem of this magnitude warrants swift cooperative action from the international community. To date, however, scientific studies show that the emission reduction commitments made by states have been inadequate (in that they are objectively insufficient to effectively address climate change)[21] and inadequately implemented (in that numerous countries are not on track to meet their commitments).[22] There are significant barriers to effective collective action on climate change. Vast differences exist between countries in terms of contributions to the stock of carbon in the atmosphere, industrial advancement and wealth, nature of emissions use, and climate vulnerabilities. Poverty is increasing in some parts of the world, along with persistent inequalities within and between countries.[23] There is a marked reluctance in many polities and societies to modify existing lifestyles and development pathways, and opinion is divided on the promise of technological solutions to complex climate change problems.

Operating within these constraints, states have over the past two decades established an international legal regime, albeit an evolving one, to address climate change and its impacts. The United Nations Framework Convention on Climate Change (UNFCCC)[24] and its Kyoto Protocol[25] constitute the international community's first significant steps forward to collectively address these concerns. These instruments have attracted near-universal adherence. Their basic purpose is to set in place an international legal framework for common but differentiated responsibility for the reduction of greenhouse gas (GHG) emissions, and support for national adaptation efforts with a particular concern for the special needs of developing[26] and vulnerable countries, including Least Developed Countries (LDCs) and low-lying states.

The UNFCCC's framework divides its member states in two major groups bearing different obligations. The first frameworks comprises the so-called "Annex-I countries," which are mainly developed, industrialized countries historically responsible for most GHG emissions, which are accordingly subject to emissions reductions targets. "Non-Annex-I" countries constitute the remainder, which include "developing countries" (a broad and undifferentiated category including countries as diverse as China, Singapore, Argentina, India, Mali and Tuvalu) as well as the Least Developed Countries (LDCs) which receive special assistance. The Conference of Parties (COP) is the UNFCCC's chief decision-making body.[27] The Kyoto Protocol, which was adopted in 1997 and entered into force in 2005, sets legally binding obligations on its 187 member states[28] including binding limits on GHG emissions for Annex-I countries during the first commitment period of 2008-2012 (as distinct from the UNFCCC which only "encouraged" mitigation and adaptation measures). States must furnish specific information on emissions and emission reduction measures, and the Kyoto Protocol provides a range of mechanisms to facilitate this, namely a "joint implementation mechanism," an international emissions trading system, and the so-called Clean Development Mechanism (CDM),[29] to be discussed in more depth later.

Unlike the international human rights regime, the UNFCCC and the Kyoto Protocol do not include express provisions for remedial measures for individuals or communities in light of a particular environmental harm. However, subsequent agreements have called for consideration of the social and economic consequences of response measures as well as enhanced international cooperation.[30] Notably, at the Thirteenth Session of the Conference of the Parties to the UNFCCC, the Bali Action Plan was adopted "to launch a comprehensive process to enable the full, effective and sustained implementation of the Convention through long-term cooperative action..."[31] The intention had been to reach an agreed outcome leading to the adoption of a decision at the COP 15 in Copenhagen in December 2009. Instead, the conference produced a non-binding political declaration "the Copenhagen Accord," negotiated by 28 states, which was intended to bridge the differences among parties while covering the pillars agreed in Bali.[32] A number of international funds have been established to support national adaptation in developing countries.[33] As critical as these and related agreements are, however, the slow pace of international negotiations and continuing political and economic differences between industrialized and developing countries make for, at best, a very cautious assessment of the potential for this legal regime to ward against the more damaging – yet entirely foreseeable – climate harm scenarios.[34]

The International Human Rights Regime

Human rights are universal legal guarantees protecting individuals and to some extent groups against actions and omissions that interfere with fundamental freedoms, entitlements and human dignity. Human rights law obliges governments (principally) and other duty-bearers to do certain things and prevents them from doing others.[35] There are many different conceptions of human rights, drawing from different political philosophies, ethical principles and normative justifications. Contemporary international articulations of human rights owe much to the liberal traditions of the European Enlightenment, protecting the individual from unwarranted interference by the state, as well as to natural law and dignitarian philosophical influences.[36] The idea, or ideal, of universality[37] and the notion that universally valid rights may be located "beyond law and history,"[38] dependent upon no more than our inherent dignity and common humanity, are central tenets of the international human rights discourse.

All states have ratified at least one of the nine core international human rights treaties,[39] and most have ratified several, covering rights of all kinds – economic, social, cultural, civil, and political. The two foundational human rights treaties, the International Covenant on Civil and Political Rights (ICCPR)[40] and the International Covenant on Economic, Social and Cultural Rights (ICESCR)[41] have 164 and 160 parties respectively. The Convention on the Rights of the Child (CRC)[42] has 191 states parties. The major emitters of GHGs are party to all three of these, with the exceptions of China, which has signed but not ratified the ICCPR, and the United States (U.S.), which has signed but not ratified the ICESCR or CRC.[43] The statements of rights in the human rights treaties are elaborated further by international expert bodies called "treaty bodies," which review states parties' periodic reports on their compliance with their substantive treaty obligations, decide individual claims of state non-compliance,[44] carry out investigations (in some cases),[45] and publish General Comments or other interpretive statements clarifying the meaning of various rights in light of evolving law and practice.[46]

Regional and national courts and tribunals occupy an important place in the scheme of human rights protection. Most national constitutions contain lists of human rights protections. General definitions at the global level are thereby translated into specific legal obligations and policy stipulations at the national level. The most significant and well established regional human rights mechanisms are the European Convention on Human Rights, the American Convention on Human Rights, and the African Charter on Human and Peoples' Rights.[47] Each of these agreements has at least one body with particular responsibility for interpreting it and reviewing states parties' compliance: the European Court of Human Rights, the Inter-American Commission and Court of Human Rights, and the African Commission and Court on Human and Peoples' Rights.[48] The European system is reinforced by the European Union (EU) Charter on Fundamental

Rights, although the legal status of the Charter and the scope of its application beyond the strict boundaries of the implementation of EU law remain unclear.[49]

These regional treaties recognise an extensive range of civil and political rights, including rights to life, liberty, freedom of expression, religion, movement and residence, and respect for privacy, family, and home.[50] In addition, the three regional treaties, but not the ICCPR, recognise a right to property.[51] Socio-economic rights are also protected by these regional systems, although the European and Inter-American systems have separate agreements for this purpose: the European Social Charter[52] and the Protocol of San Salvador to the American Convention.[53] By contrast, the African Charter incorporates socio-economic rights, as well as group rights, directly.[54] These treaties recognize and protect rights to work, to social security, to an adequate standard of living, including adequate food, clothing and housing, to the highest attainable standard of health, to education, to take part in cultural life, and to enjoy the benefits of scientific progress.[55] Uniquely, the Protocol of San Salvador includes a "right to live in a healthy environment" in its list of economic, social, and cultural rights.[56] The EU Charter on Fundamental Rights also reflects environmental protection objectives.[57] However, beyond the caveats expressed above concerning the Charter's legal status, environmental protection is listed under "Title IV: Solidarity," rather than Title V on individual rights, and taken in the context of the Charter as a whole can probably be understood as a policy objective of the EU rather than a putative human right.[58]

In contrast to international, African and many national experiences, the European and American regional courts do not have jurisdiction or direct authority to make binding determinations on economic, social, and cultural rights claims.[59] Nevertheless the latter courts are increasingly giving effect to socio-economic rights indirectly, by means of interpretation and enforcement of civil and political rights guarantees. Socio-economic rights are also promoted at the regional level through periodic review of national reports and, in the case of the European Social Charter, an optional complaints procedure.[60]

Human rights treaties impose several kinds of obligations on their parties. The ICCPR, for instance, requires each of its parties "to respect and to ensure to all individuals within its territory and subject to its jurisdiction the rights recognized in the present Covenant."[61] The term "respect" has been interpreted to require the state to avoid violating the rights itself,[62] but the obligation to *ensure* the right requires that the state do more than merely avoid direct violation. It requires affirmative action to secure the right, or make it safe from loss or interference, including from private actors.[63] The Human Rights Committee, the body of independent experts charged with monitoring implementation of the Covenant, has stated:

> The article 2, paragraph 1, obligations are binding on States [Parties] and do not, as such, have direct horizontal effect as a matter of international law. The Covenant cannot be viewed as a substitute for domestic criminal or civil law. However the positive obligations on States Parties to ensure Covenant rights will only be fully discharged if individuals are protected by the State, not just against violations of Covenant rights by its agents, but also against acts committed by private persons or entities that would impair the enjoyment of Covenant rights in so far as they are amenable to application between private persons or entities.[64]

The ICESCR requires each of its parties "to take steps, individually and through international assistance and co-operation, especially economic and technical, to the maximum of its available resources, with a view to achieving progressively the full realization of the rights recognized in the present Covenant by all appropriate means, including particularly the adoption of legislative measures." This language obviously gives states more discretion as to how to meet their obligations, and contemplates that, to some degree, the rights will be met through progressive realization rather than immediately. But this does not prevent legal obligations from being defined with a reasonable degree of precision, as the relevant treaty body – the Committee on Economic, Social and Cultural Rights (CESCR) – has made clear. First, while recognising that socioeconomic rights cannot be realised overnight, states must take immediate, concrete and targeted steps towards the realisation of the rights in question. Second, states must be able to show that they are using the maximum extent of available resources towards the realisation of the rights. Third, a certain number of obligations are of immediate effect, whatever the resource constraints, including an obligation not to discriminate between different groups of people in terms of the laws, plans, policies and resources committed to the realisation of the various rights.[65] States must also ensure essential minimum levels of protection of socio-economic rights, meaning that states should prioritise the basic survival needs of all.[66] Finally, according to the understanding of the Committee, states have an obligation to ensure against retrogression in the existing levels of human rights protection. For example, having made free primary education compulsory and available to all, states should not introduce school fees, nor should governments cut taxes that are needed to fund those services.[67]

Some of the General Comments of the CESCR have influenced others in thinking about the nature of state duties in this area. In addition to the duties to *respect* rights themselves and to *protect* them from interference by private actors, the Committee has also described a duty to *fulfil* rights, which requires the state to adopt appropriate positive measures towards the full realization of the rights. For example, the Committee has said that states have a duty to *respect* the right to food by not taking measures that would restrict individuals' existing access to food; they have a duty to *protect* the right by ensuring that private actors do not deprive individuals of their access to food, and they have a duty to *fulfil* the right by strengthening people's ability to obtain food security and providing food directly to those who are unable to enjoy their right to food by the means at their own disposal.[68] The CESCR has called the first of these duties to fulfil the duty to *facilitate*, and the second the duty to *provide*. It later added a third sub-duty of the duty to fulfil, the duty to *promote*.[69] National courts world-wide, along with certain regional tribunals, have shown an increasing inclination to adjudicate and enforce legal obligations of the kinds outlined above, whether or not based explicitly upon the ICESCR.[70] Most of these cases concern findings of violations of government to "respect" human rights, or implement existing policies or laws already on the statute books, and to "protect" human rights.[71] However courts in appropriate cases have also shown a willingness to enforce obligations of a positive kind, including failure to legislate, protect, institute appropriate planning, or otherwise take sufficient steps to realise the right concerned.[72] There is also a rich comparative jurisprudence on claims for equality rights,[73] and courts in certain jurisdictions have adjudicated claims connected with a failure of states to provide essential minimum levels of social services.[74]

While some rights belong to all human beings, others are held by individuals as members of a group, or held by a group itself. Both of the UN Covenants, as well as the American and European Conventions and the African Charter, prohibit discrimination by states on the basis of race, gender, and religion, among other grounds,[75] and other human rights treaties elaborate rights not to be discriminated against on racial grounds and rights of women not to be discriminated against on the basis of their gender.[76] In addition, members of certain groups enjoy rights in addition to the right not to be discriminated against. For example, Article 27 of the ICCPR states that persons belonging to ethnic, religious, or linguistic minorities "shall not be denied the right, in community with the other members of their group, to enjoy their own culture, to profess and practise their own religion, or to use their own language."[77] Finally, the ICCPR and ICESCR recognize one right held by a group itself: the right to self-determination of a people.[78] Of the regional agreements, only the African Charter includes peoples' rights, including the right to self-determination and "the right to a general satisfactory environment favourable to … [a people's] development."[79]

While the textual formulations of human rights in international treaties are generally broad, enabling interpretation and implementation in evolving circumstances and diverse national settings, the substantive contours and content of many human rights obligations are increasingly proving amenable to precise elaboration. The socio-economic rights obligations described above – in particular the obligation not to discriminate, the obligation to ensure "essential minimum levels" of rights, the obligation to avoid retrogression in the existing levels of enjoyment of rights, and procedural obligations to be discussed in Part IV – are critical in illuminating the transmission channels and legal principles through which the specific human rights entitlements of individuals and groups can be violated through government action or neglect in the climate change context. Correspondingly, this framework of obligations brings a sharper legal focus to our analysis of the so-called value-added of human rights in the context of climate change, by fleshing out how human rights criteria can strengthen the framework for decision-making and trade-offs in the climate change context, and buttress recommendations for "human rights thresholds" as will shortly be seen.

Finally, it is worth underscoring that, while the UNFCCC treaty regime is addressed to a quintessentially global problem based upon the principle of reciprocity between participating states (e.g. Article 7 UNFCCC), international human rights law principally concerns the responsibilities of states towards individuals within their own territory or effective control.[80] This is so notwithstanding the fact that both treaty regimes create mutual or common rights and obligations, unless they give rise to self-executing obligations, and that it is only when they are given effect to in domestic law that they may create state responsibilities towards individuals.

The foregoing raises complex questions, begging clear or categorical answers, to which the discipline of law is appropriately just one of many addressees. More detailed discussion from a legal perspective is offered in Parts IV and V below. However, for the general purposes of this discussion, the term "extra-territoriality" (or extra-territorial, in adjectival form) refers to the question of whether, and legal grounds upon which, a state's obligations under international human rights law can be said to extend to individuals *not* within that state's territory or effective control. As will be seen, the legal foundations for these obligations appear to be strongest when framed in negative terms, such as duties of non-interference or avoidance of harm to persons located elsewhere. However, some argue that international law could be viewed to be evolving towards supporting "extra-territorial" obligations to provide positive assistance to others in some circumstances, and obligations to cooperate internationally to address the human rights implications of global problems such as climate change. In this respect it is important to recognise that, whether or not it is possible to show a legal *duty* of a state to regulate with extra-territorial effect, states are certainly *permitted* to do so, provided they can establish one of the accepted bases of legal jurisdiction and subject to an overriding requirement of reasonableness – including if they are engaged in the extra-territorial protection of human rights.[81]

Linking Climate Impacts to Human Rights

Although the UNFCCC seeks to "protect the climate system for the benefit of present and future generations of humankind," it is not designed to provide human rights protections, humanitarian aid or redress to individuals or communities consequent upon environmental harms. The UNFCCC is instead an agreement between states to "anticipate, prevent or minimize the causes of climate change and mitigate its adverse effects."[82] The nascent interest in human rights in the climate change context can perhaps be attributed to some degree to a widely felt frustrations with the pace and directions of multilateral diplomacy.[83] Consensus-driven welfare-based approaches stand in uneasy relief, in the eyes of many, against the very tangible climate change harms already evident in many countries. The slow progress of international negotiations seems increasingly out of step with scientific knowledge and the pace of climate change itself.

Much of the recent interest in the human rights dimensions of climate change has been sparked by the plight of the Inuit[84] and the Small Island States, at the frontlines, albeit different ones, of climate change. In their 2005 petition before the Inter-American Commission on Human Rights the Inuit claimed that the impacts of climate change could be attributed to acts and omissions of the U.S., and violated their fundamental human rights – in particular the rights to the benefits of culture, to property, to the preservation of health, life, physical integrity, security, and a means of subsistence, and to residence, movement, and inviolability of the home.[85] These rights, it was argued, were protected under several international human rights instruments, including the American Declaration of the Rights and Duties of Man.[86] The Commission declined to review the merits of the petition, stating that the "information provided does not enable us to determine whether the alleged facts would tend to characterize a violation of rights protected by the American Declaration."[87] Although the Inuit Petition did not fare well before the Commission, it drew attention to the links between climate change and human rights and led to a "Hearing of a General Nature" on human rights and global warming.[88] The Hearing was held on March 1, 2007, and featured testimonies from the Chair of the Inuit Circumpolar Conference (ICC) and its lawyers but not representatives of the U.S.[89] The Commission has taken no further action, but the ICC petition did generate considerable debate in the academic literature.[90]

In the climate negotiations, indigenous groups more generally have delivered strong statements on the impacts of climate change on indigenous peoples' health, society, culture and well-being.[91] Indigenous peoples' organizations have been admitted to the Convention process as non-governmental organizations (NGOs), with constituency status.[92] The Permanent Forum on Indigenous Issues under the Economic and Social Council (ECOSOC) at its second session recommended the establishment of an *ad hoc* open-ended working group on indigenous peoples and climate change,[93] which did not come to pass.[94] In its seventh session of April and May 2008, dedicated to climate change, the Forum recommended that the Declaration on the Rights of Indigenous Peoples serve as a "key and binding framework" in efforts to curb climate change, and that the human rights-based approach guide the design and implementation of local, national, regional, and global climate policies and projects.[95]

Meanwhile, the Small Island States, and the Maldives in particular, launched a campaign to link climate change and human rights. Representatives of Small Island Developing States met in November 2007 to adopt the *Male' Declaration on the Human Dimension of Global Climate Change*, requesting, *inter alia* that the UN Human Rights Council convene a debate on climate change and human rights.[96] The Council adopted a Resolution tabled by Maldives titled *Human Rights and Climate Change* in March 2008 that requested the OHCHR to conduct a detailed analytical study on the relationship between climate change and human rights.[97] The OHCHR published its study in January 2009.[98] The study argued that climate change threatens the enjoyment of a wide spectrum of human rights, including rights to life, health, food, water, housing, and self-determination. It fell short of finding that climate change necessarily or categorically *violates* human rights,[99] but it did conclude that states have obligations under human rights law to address climate change. After considering the report, the Human Rights Council decided by consensus in March 2009 to hear a panel discussion on the topic at its June 2009 session, and encouraged its Special Procedures mandate-holders to consider the implications of climate change for the human rights within their mandates.[100]

In a similar vein, in the Americas, Argentina drafted and tabled a resolution on human rights and climate change which was adopted by the General Assembly of the Organization of American States in June 2008. The Resolution instructs the Inter-American Commission on Human Rights to "determine the possible existence of a link between adverse effects of climate change and the full enjoyment of human rights." [101] Argentina expressed concern that the inequitable impacts of climate change will place an undue strain on vulnerable states that will need to introduce climate policies and measures to ensure that they meet their human rights obligations.[102]

Yet a review of the politics of human rights in the international negotiations on climate change does not yield straightforward answers. On the one hand, a total of eighty-eight UN member states from various regions supported the Human Rights Council's consensus resolution 10/4 (2009), encouraging greater involvement by human rights expert bodies in the UNFCCC process.[103] Co-sponsoring states, particularly those most immediately threatened by climate change, typically underscore the importance of human rights in highlighting the human face and impacts of climate change, as part of a legal or moral claim for strengthened international mitigation commitments and adaptation support from wealthier countries and major emitters. Yet explicit human rights arguments have yet to gain traction to any appreciable extent within the climate change negotiations under the UNFCCC framework. While a number of states have raised explicit human rights arguments in the latter context, a revised negotiating text for the outcome document for the fifteenth Conference of the Parties (COP 15) released following the Bonn climate change talks in June 2009 contained only two relatively modest explicit human rights references.[104]

This seems to reflect differences of view between states (and regional and other groupings of states) on the so-called value-added of human rights in the climate change context, the comparative weight and focus to be given to human rights obligations within and beyond national borders, and perhaps also perceptions in various quarters that human rights might risk overloading an already fragile climate change agenda. Human rights have sometimes been characterised as a source of mistrust between developing and industrialised countries, with certain developing countries expressing concern at human rights being used as a way of either preventing their development (should binding emissions reduction targets be applied to them) or operating as conditionalities on climate change adaptation funds.[105] Certain industrialised countries, correspondingly, have expressed concern at the possibility for an official recognition of human rights and climate change linkages to bolster the case for extra-territorial human rights obligations or a collective and self-standing "right to a safe and secure environment," or otherwise be used as a "political or legal weapon against them."[106] These uncertain and evolving political dynamics form an important part of the context in which the international legal analysis and policy and operational implications (Parts IV-VI below) fall to be considered.

CHAPTER 2

Human Rights Impacts of Climate Change: A Survey of Illustrative Examples

Two features of the climate change problematic make it distinctive. First, the impacts are predicted to be life-changing, far beyond any environmental problem the international community has yet confronted. Global average temperature is predicted to increase by 1.8 to 6.4 degrees centigrade. This will, among other impacts, increase the severity of droughts, land degradation, and desertification, the intensity of floods and tropical cyclones, the incidence of malaria and heat-related mortality, and decrease water availability, crop yield and food security. Second, the distribution of climate impacts is uneven. Some regions are far more vulnerable than others including: the Arctic, because of the impacts of high rates of projected warming on natural systems and human communities; Africa, because of low adaptive capacity and projected climate change impacts; small islands, where there is high exposure of population and infrastructure to projected climate change impacts; and Asian and African mega deltas, due to large populations and high exposure to sea level rise, storm surges and river flooding. These two distinctive features of the climate change problematic provide the necessary context within which human rights impacts should explored.

A number of conceptual premises are worth outlining in brief at the outset of this discussion. First, invoking the notion of human rights entails both rights and duties, and in each case, for human rights to have meaning, one must identify a right-holder and a duty-bearer. Each should be anchored in legal terms according to one of the sources of public international law (traditionally identified with those specified under Article 38 of the Statute of the International Court of Justice), or some relevant provision of domestic law. Connected with this is the implicit assumption that there is something distinct about addressing climate change from a human rights perspective, and that this approach is distinguishable from an approach that simply addresses the social or human impacts of climate change. This is also because not all human or social impacts may amount to human rights impacts. Thus, it is important to emphasise at the outset that climate change may threaten or interfere with the enjoyment of a particular human right without necessarily implying that those bearing responsibilities under international law for the realisation of that right have violated their obligations under human rights law. The January 2009 OHCHR report, for example, describes the implications of climate change for a wide range of human rights, but states: "[w]hile climate change has obvious implications for the enjoyment of human rights, it is less obvious whether, and to what extent, such effects can be qualified as human rights violations in a strict legal sense."[107] Not all infringements of human rights violate human rights law. In the climate change context there may be serious challenges in disentangling the complex causal relationships between emissions from a particular country and a particular harm caused by climate change in another country, and in separating out the harm due to climate change from other possible causes. And, as noted in the OHCHR's report, "adverse effects of global warming are often projections about future impacts, whereas human rights violations are normally established after the harm has occurred."[108] With these kinds of constraints in mind, the following discussion speaks for the most part about "non-realisation" or "threats" to human rights, rather than putative legal violations in the abstract, without prejudice to more broadly textured ethical and justice claims.[109]

Another implicit element of the ensuing discussion is that human rights brings 'value added' to the discussion of approaches to the problem of climate change. Implicit in the discussion that follows are notions about the nature of that 'value added', including in legal terms. The discussion aims in part to articulate how an approach predicated on human rights can improve the understanding of climate change and make international legal and political measures to address it more effective.

This section develops the foregoing premises, by linking particular social and human impacts of climate change to specific human rights standards under international human rights treaties, thereby confirming the former as *human rights* impacts, yet without delving into difficult evidentiary and procedural questions that would be necessary to resolve specific human rights claims. The following analysis examines a sampling of human rights protected under public international law that may be (or already are being) adversely impacted by climate change. These are rights which are the subjects of obligations under treaties signed by the vast majority of countries, and which State Parties have obligations to respect, protect and fulfil.[110] The obligations principally in focus are those under the ICESCR and the UNFCCC, and the paradigmatic example will that of a State which is party to both of these instruments with binding obligations under both which must be given effect to in good faith.[111] The analysis focuses on the rights to life, food, health, housing and water, arguing that these and other rights are presently at risk from climate impacts, and the risks appear to be on the rise. It is therefore illustrative and selective, designed merely to outline the normative attributes and substantive content of the right in question, and how climate harms could lead to non-realization. It is worth noting that, while many of the rights most obviously at risk from climate impacts fall in the category of economic, social and cultural rights, human rights across the entire spectrum, including civil and political rights, are implicated. Similarly, in both doctrine and practice, all human rights have enforceable, and justiciable, dimensions.

Climate change threatens the right to life

The right to life is protected by the ICCPR, the CRC and three regional human rights treaties: the European and American Conventions and the African Charter.[112] In its General Comment on the scope and content of the right to life under Article 6 of the ICCPR, the Human Rights Committee emphasized that the "inherent right to life" cannot be interpreted in a restrictive manner, and that the protection of this right requires states to take positive measures. It would appear from the Committee's previous interpretations that a failure by state institutions to take action to prevent, mitigate or remedy life-threatening harms from climate change within that state's territory or effective control could potentially constitute a violation of the right to life.[113] The European Court of Human Rights (ECtHR) has considered cases involving the right to life in relation to environmental harms, although as will be seen in Part IV, the relevance of this jurisprudence to climate change more specifically is open to debate.[114]

Climate change has direct implications for the right to life. In its January 2009 report on climate change and human rights, the OHCHR states, on the basis of the 2007 IPCC assessment:

> A number of observed and projected effects of climate change will pose direct and indirect threats to human lives. IPCC . . . projects with high confidence an increase in people suffering from death, disease and injury from heat waves, floods, storms, fires and droughts. Equally, climate change will affect the right to life through an increase in hunger and malnutrition and related disorders impacting on child growth and development, cardio-respiratory morbidity and mortality related to ground-level ozone. Climate change will exacerbate weather-related disasters which already have devastating effects on people and their enjoyment of the right to life, particularly in the developing world. For example, an estimated 262 million people were affected by climate disasters annually from 2000 to 2004, of whom over 98 per cent live in developing countries.[115]

In keeping with this, the UN General Assembly recently adopted a resolution recognizing climate change as a possible threat to international peace and security.[116] Climate change – by redrawing the maps of water availability, food security, disease prevalence, population distribution and coastal boundaries – has the potential to exacerbate insecurity and violent conflict on a potentially large scale.[117] While the threats to life are more immediate in some countries and regions than others, a recent report by the Center for Naval Analyses in the U.S. argues that climate change acts as a threat multiplier in already fragile regions, exacerbating conditions that lead to failed states and breed terrorism and extremism, concluding that "projected climate change poses a serious threat to America's national security."[118]

Some communities, such as those living in the Arctic and in coastal regions, are particularly at risk, and are already starting to experience the adverse effects of climate change on their right to life. For example, in their December 2005 petition to the Inter-American Commission on Human Rights (IACHR), the Inuit described the effects of climate change on their right to life, saying: "[c]hanges in ice and snow jeopardize individual Inuit lives, critical food sources are threatened, and unpredictable weather makes travel more dangerous at all times of the year."[119] The jeopardy to individual lives results from the changing climate: the sea ice on which the Inuit travel and hunt freezes later, thaws earlier, and is thinner; critical food sources are threatened because warming weather makes harvestable species scarcer and more difficult to reach; a greater number of sudden, unpredictable storms and less snow from which to construct emergency shelters have already contributed to death and injuries among hunters; and the decrease in summer ice causes rougher seas and more dangerous storms, making water travel more dangerous.[120]

The Maldives' 2008 submission to the OHCHR as part of its preparation of its study on climate change and human rights described how climate change threatens its right to life. Like many other small island states, the Maldives is particularly at risk from the effects of rising sea levels as a result of warming water and melting ice sheets. Rising sea levels exacerbate inundation, storm surges, and erosion.[121] An increase of 0.5 meter would inundate 15% of Male', the most populous island in the Maldives, by 2025, and flood half of it by 2100.[122] A sea surge 0.7 meters higher than the average sea level, which would flood most of the islands in the Maldives, has been expected to occur only once a century, but may occur at least annually by 2050.[123] Because 42% of the population of the Maldives and 47% of its housing structures are located within 100 meters of the shoreline, "even partial flooding of the islands is likely to result in drowning, injury, and loss of life."[124]

Climate change threatens the right to adequate food

The ICESCR includes the right to adequate food as an element of the right to an adequate standard of living.[125] The CESCR has argued that the right to food[126] is fundamental to the inherent dignity of the human person and indispensable for the fulfilment of other human rights enshrined in the International Bill of Rights.[127] It interprets the right to adequate food as encompassing both availability of and accessibility to food and has recognised the inter-dependence between the environment and the right to food, noting that the right to adequate food requires the adoption of "appropriate economic, environmental and social policies."[128]

The threats caused by climate change to the right to food have been apparent to the CESCR for some time. According to the CESCR, "even where a State faces severe resource constraints, whether caused by a process of economic adjustment, economic recession, climatic conditions or other factors, measures should be undertaken to ensure that the right to adequate food is especially fulfilled for vulnerable population groups and individuals."[129] In his 2008 annual report to the Human Rights Council, the Special Rapporteur on the right to food voiced caution about what he perceived as disproportionate reliance upon technology-driven solutions to agricultural production in response to the challenges facing food production systems due to climate change and population growth, and outlined a number of potential negative impacts of agrofuel development (intended to substitute for fossil fuels for transport) on the right to food.[130] The Special Rapporteur has specifically encouraged sustainable agricultural practices which will improve the resilience of farming systems to climate change,[131] and has called upon the international community to encourage a diversity of resilient agricultural systems capable of coping with climate disruptions.[132]

Article 2 of the UNFCCC underscores the importance of ensuring availability of food. It requires the stabilization of GHG in the atmosphere to be achieved within a time frame sufficient to "ensure that food production is not threatened."[133] Climate impacts, and possibly climate response measures may threaten both availability and accessibility to food.[134] The IPCC documents, across a range of temperature increases, complex, localized negative impacts on small holders, subsistence farmers and fishers.[135] For lower latitudes, even for small local temperature increases, crop productivity is projected to decrease, thereby increasing the risk of hunger.[136] Increases in extreme weather events, including droughts and floods, will also negatively affect crop production,[137] thereby placing both availability and accessibility at risk. The Stern Review refers to a study that pegs the increase in the number of people at risk of hunger at 30-200 million for a 2-3 degrees celcius increase, and 250-550 million beyond 3 degrees Celsius. Around 800 million people are already at risk of hunger.[138] The UNDP estimates that an additional 600 million people will face malnutrition due to climate change, with a particularly negative effect on Sub-Saharan Africa.[139] Malnutrition was associated with 54% of child deaths in 2001.[140] Climate change is projected to exacerbate this vulnerability. The right to adequate food may also be placed at risk by policies and measures to mitigate climate change, namely, as the Special Rapporteur on the right to food has noted, the use of bio fuels as an alternative to high GHG emitting fossil fuels.[141] The use of food and feed crops for fuel increases the role of energy markets in determining the value of agricultural commodities which are direct or indirect substitutes for biofuel feed stocks.[142] Food prices, hitherto on a downward trend, could increase once more, thereby affecting accessibility.[143]

Although a State's human rights obligations are largely owed to individuals located within its own territory, jurisdiction or effective control, human rights treaty obligations may have extra-territorial dimensions in certain circumstances, for all kinds of rights. This issue is analysed in more depth in Parts IV and V. In the case of the right to food, the CESCR has recognised a number of obligations with extra-territorial effect, arising from Articles 2(1), 11, and 23 of the Covenant.[144] These include the requirement to respect the enjoyment of the right to food in other countries (e.g. refraining from food embargoes), to protect that right, to facilitate access to food, to provide the necessary aid when required, and to ensure that the right is given due attention in international aid agreements.[145] Obligations relating to international assistance and cooperation are comparatively well defined in the UNFCCC regime, as Part V(3) below sets out in more detail.

Climate change threatens the right to health

The ICESCR recognizes the right to the "highest attainable standard of physical and mental health,"[146] and the CESCR considers this right indispensable for the enjoyment of other human rights.[147] The right to health is widely protected in other international and regional instruments[148] and under national constitutions.[149] As interpreted by the CESCR and other authoritative or adjudicatory bodies, the substantive content of this right includes timely and appropriate health care, access to safe and potable water, adequate sanitation, an adequate supply of safe food, nutrition and housing, healthy occupational and environmental conditions, and access to health-related education and information.[150] These are considered the basic determinants of health which, in the assessment of the World Health Organization (WHO), climate change will place at risk.[151]

The link between environmental protection and human health has long been recognized. Most MEAs[152] acknowledge and address the impact that environmental harms can have on human health.[153] The UNFCCC in its definition of "adverse effects" of climate change" includes "significant deleterious impacts on human health and welfare,"[154] and it requires Parties to take, *inter alia*, health impacts into account in relevant social, economic and environmental policies.[155] The CRC provides that States parties shall take appropriate measures to combat disease and malnutrition "through the provision of adequate nutritious foods and clean drinking water, taking into consideration the dangers and risks of environmental pollution."[156]

Climate change is expected to have significant health impacts, including by increasing, *inter alia*, malnutrition; the number of people suffering from death, disease and injury from heat waves, floods, storms, fires and droughts; and cardio-respiratory morbidity and mortality associated with ground-level ozone.[157] The IPCC also predicts that the adverse health impacts will be greatest in low-income countries. At greater risk, in all countries, are "the urban poor, the elderly and children, traditional societies, subsistence farmers, and coastal populations."[158] Health equity is also at risk, as are the prospects for achieving the health-related Millennium Development Goals (MDGs).[159]

Relying on the IPCC assessment, the OHCHR report on climate change and human rights states:

> Climate change is projected to affect the health status of millions of people, including through increases in malnutrition, increased diseases and injury due to extreme weather events, and an increased burden of diarrhoeal, cardio-respiratory and infectious diseases. Global warming may also affect the spread of malaria and other vector borne diseases in some parts of the world. Overall, the negative health effects will disproportionately be felt in Sub-Saharan Africa, South Asia and the Middle East.[160]

Not all of the effects on the right to health will occur in the future. The Inuit have described how climate change is already affecting their ability to enjoy this right. As weather conditions change, the fish and game on which the Inuit rely disappear, adversely affecting their nutrition, new diseases move northward, the amount and quality of their drinking water decrease, and their mental health suffers because of the diminished quality of their lives.[161]

In addition to the duty to respect, protect and fulfil the right to health under the ICESCR, Article 12 requires States to cooperate, and to take joint and separate action in order to achieve the full realization of the right to health. As the Alma-Ata Declaration proclaimed, "the gross inequality in the health status of the people, particularly between developed and developing countries, as well as within countries, is politically, socially and economically unacceptable and is, therefore, of common concern to all countries."[162] In light of this, it would appear that climate impacts will only increase the onerous burdens developing countries already face in addressing health.

Climate change threatens the right to water

The right to water,[163] as an essential condition for survival, is not just a self-standing right,[164] but is recognized as inextricably linked with other human rights such as the right to an adequate standard of living, the right to the highest attainable standard of health, and the rights to adequate housing and adequate food.[165] Climate change [is projected to seriously affect the availability of water. The Stern Review records that even a 1 degree Celsius rise in temperature will threaten water supplies for 50 million people, and a 5 degrees Celsius rise in temperature will result in the disappearance of various Himalayan glaciers threatening water shortages for a quarter of China's population, and hundreds of millions of Indians.[166] The OHCHR report on climate change and human rights relies on the 2007 IPCC assessment to state: "Loss of glaciers and reductions in snow cover are projected to increase and to negatively affect water availability for more than one-sixth of the world's population supplied by melt water from mountain ranges.

Weather extremes, such as drought and flooding, will also impact on water supplies. Climate change will thus exacerbate existing stresses on water resources and compound the problem of access to safe drinking water, currently denied to an estimated 1.1 billion people globally and a major cause of morbidity and disease."[167]

As with the rights to food and health, in addition to the duties to respect, protect and fulfill this right, States have a general obligation under the Covenant to cooperate with others to achieve full realization of this right. The duty of cooperation is strengthened by the principled requirement in UNFCCC Article 3 to give the specific needs of developing countries full consideration,[168] and in UNFCCC Article 4 to "cooperate in preparing for adaptation to the impacts of climate change; develop and elaborate appropriate and integrated plans for coastal zone management, water resources and agriculture."[169]

Climate change threatens the right to adequate housing

The right to adequate housing is protected under a range of international and regional human rights instruments. Among the recognised components of the right to an adequate standard of living in Article 11 of the ICESCR, the right to adequate housing is understood by the CESCR as "the right to live somewhere in security, peace and dignity."[170] Its core substantive elements include security of tenure, protection against forced evictions, availability of services, materials, facilities and infrastructure, affordability, habitability, accessibility, location and cultural adequacy.[171]

Climate change may impact upon the right to housing in many ways, as the OHCHR report of 2009 observes, drawing from United Nations Development Programme (UNDP) and IPCC assessments: "Sea level rise and storm surges will have a direct impact on many coastal settlements. In the Arctic region and in low-lying island States such impacts have already led to the relocation of peoples and communities. Settlements in low-lying mega-deltas are also particularly at risk, as evidenced by the millions of people and homes affected by flooding in recent years."[172]

The estimates of the number of people likely to be displaced by climate change range from 50 to 250 million by the year 2050.[173] Migration – within and beyond borders – will be a last recourse for many vulnerable populations. Yet as the International Organization for Migration (IOM) has observed, the ability to migrate is a function of mobility as well as resources (both financial and social); hence "the people most vulnerable to climate change are not necessarily the ones most likely to migrate."[174] Therefore, those unable to move away from the negative effects of climate change – whether due to poverty, insecurity, disability, ill health or other factors – will find their right to adequate housing most acutely threatened.[175]

As the OHCHR report of 2009 suggests: "Human rights guarantees in the context of climate change include: (a) adequate protection of housing from weather hazards (habitability of housing); (b) access to housing away from hazardous zones; (c) access to shelter and disaster preparedness in cases of displacement caused by extreme weather events; (d) protection of communities that are relocated away from hazardous zones, including protection against forced evictions without appropriate forms of legal or other protection, including adequate consultation with affected persons."[176]

The Special Rapporteur on the right to adequate housing is in the course of preparing a thematic report on the impact of climate change on the right to adequate housing.

This was the main focus of her mission to the Maldives, the preliminary findings from which were submitted to the Human Rights Council in March 2009.[177] In her interim report the Special Rapporteur stressed the international responsibility to urgently support adaptation strategies for the impact of climate change on the Maldives, calling attention to the lessons learned from the post-tsunami reconstruction process, and called for increased research, capacity-building and innovative approaches to enable the design of adequate housing and infrastructure in the face of the imminent impacts of global warming. The Special Rapporteur also called attention to potential human rights risks in certain of the Maldivian government's adaptation strategies, namely those involving the consolidation and forced displacement of inhabitants of less populated islands to achieve economies of scale for costly investments in services and infrastructure in response to climate change.[178]

Climate change may affect the realization of a range of other human rights

In addition to the rights discussed thus far, climate change may impact the progressive realization of a range of other rights as well. Climate change has been characterised as a "profound denier of freedom of action and a source of disempowerment."[179] Climate impacts – extreme weather events, increased flood and drought risk, changing weather and crop patterns, among others – will likely hamper the realization of the rights to private and family life,[180] property,[181] means of subsistence,[182] freedom of residence[183] and movement.[184] For indigenous groups like the Inuit, climate impacts will fundamentally alter their way of life, affecting a further set of protected rights and interests,[185] in particular the right to the benefits of their culture,[186] and the right to freely dispose of natural resources.[187] There are concerns among certain groups that policies and measures to reduce emissions from deforestation, a significant contributor to climate change, may have direct relevance to indigenous peoples' rights particularly in relation to traditional rights to forest produce.[188] For these and other communities whose very existence is threatened, such as those living in small island states, climate change threatens their right to self-determination, protected by both the ICCPR and the ICESCR.[189]

Research indicates that inequalities within countries are a marker for vulnerability to climate shocks.[190] One recent quantitative assessment of the human impacts of disasters found that "countries with high levels of income inequality experience the effects of climate disasters more profoundly than more equal societies."[191] 'The effects of climate change will be felt most acutely by those segments of the population who are already in vulnerable situations due to factors such as poverty, gender, age, minority status, and disability.'[192] For example, there is a growing body of scholarship that documents the gendered impacts of climate change and climate change policy and the disproportionate impacts on women's rights.[193] The nature of that vulnerability varies widely, cautioning against generalisation. However, because women form a disproportionate share of the poor in developing countries and communities that are highly dependent on local natural resources, women will in many instances, be disproportionately vulnerable to the impacts of climate change.[194] The situation is further exacerbated by gender differences in property rights, political participation, access to information and in economic, social and cultural roles.[195] [The CEDAW Committee has issued a statement on Gender and Climate Change as a contribution to the COP 15 negotiations, drawing attention to the gender-differentiated impacts of climate change and the need for equal participation of women and men in decision-making.[196]

Another particularly vulnerable group is children. The OHCHR reports that: "[o]verall, the health burden of climate change will primarily be borne by children in the developing world."[197] In 2007, Save the Children UK reported that within the next decade up to 175 million children are likely to be affected every year by natural disasters brought about by climate change.[198] Recent research by the United Nations Children's Fund (UNICEF) identifies a wide range of circumstances – ranging from physical attributes of children to structural factors determining the distribution of economic power and social roles, such as the gendered divisions of labour – that will render climate change especially threatening to children by exacerbating existing health risks; destroying clinics, homes and schools; disrupting the natural resource base sustaining community livelihoods and nutrition and water security; provoking population displacements; and undermining support structures that protect children from harm.[199] Extreme weather events and reduced quantity and quality of water already are leading causes of malnutrition and child death and illness. Climate change will again exacerbate these stresses.

CHAPTER 3

Environmental Protection
and Human Rights Law:
Basic Concepts

Before proceeding with an analysis of the relationship between the climate change and human rights legal regimes, it is important to establish what is being compared and understand the legal fundamentals at issue. In addition, the terms "human rights," "human rights approach" and "environmental rights" are sometimes used inter-changeably, despite the important differences between them in normative and legal or institutional terms. But before examining these three concepts, it is appropriate to survey the sources of international law within which all three, to varying degrees, may be grounded, so as to provide the necessary legal context for the ensuing analysis. Moreover, given this study's emphasis on normative structure, duties and legal obligations as the distinguishing element of a human rights approach to climate change, a brief survey of the possible sources for such elements is apposite. Finally, while the study's analysis places greatest emphasis on treaties, it is contended that other, more contested, sources of law may well provide the basis for the evolution of new approaches and points of departure in this area.

Sources of International Law

The essential sources of international law are those set out in Article 38 of the Statute of the International Court of Justice (ICJ), principally treaties, custom, and general principles of law.[200] Among general norms, there are *jus cogens* norms, defined in article 53 of the 1969 Vienna Convention on the law of treaties as peremptory norms of general international law "accepted and recognized by the international community of States as a whole" as norms "from which no derogation is permitted" and which can only be modified by subsequent norms of general international law "having the same character". These categories are considered, in turn, below. While the emphasis in the present discussion is on legal frameworks open to universal membership, this should not be taken as impugning the relevance of regional and national legal regimes and accountability frameworks. Not only have the latter generated a rich and growing body of jurisprudence relevant to the human rights impacts of climate change, these are also frequently the most proximate and immediate sources of relief and redress for those whose rights may be infringed by climate change.

Climate change law, human rights law and other relevant bodies of international law such as those concerning trade and intellectual property rights, have evolved largely independently of one another. Yet these bodies of law may all have distinctive and essential roles to play in relation to particular facets of environmental or social problems, and may interact with each other in unpredictable ways.[201] This gives rise to what is known as the "fragmentation" problem.[202] However, the literature in this area indicates that, in international law, there is a strong presumption against normative conflict, with the consequence that international legal commitments relating to climate change, human rights and other relevant regimes should be interpreted, as far as possible, to give rise to compatible obligations.[203] The recommendation of the ILC would appear to indicate that human rights law could guide the interpretation of the rights and obligations under the UNFCCC and Kyoto Protocol, provided that two conditions were satisfied: (a) a situation exists whereby the norms of human rights and the norms of climate change law are both valid and applicable; and (b) there is no genuine conflict of norms.[204] These two bodies of law would then need to be considered for their mutual consistency, points of articulation and possible tensions, both at the structural level (looking at the objectives, values, normative assumptions and principles embodied by or implicit within each legal regime) as well as in their application to given factual situations.[205]

Treaties

The international climate change regime is regulated principally by the UNFCCC and its Kyoto Protocol.[206] A total of 192 countries are party to the UNFCCC and a total of 176 countries are party to the Kyoto Protocol.[207] These treaties are legally binding, with relatively determinate content even if some of the core principles remain heavily contested. Institutions have been established to facilitate the negotiation process[208] and encourage emissions reductions,[209] as well as to supervise and attempt to enforce compliance with the obligations imposed by these treaties.[210]

There are now nine "core" international human rights treaties under UN auspices, leaving aside more specialised treaty regimes under International Labour Organization (ILO), United Nations Educational, Scientific, and Cultural Organization (UNESCO) and other auspices.[211] These treaties cover rights of all kinds – civil, political, economic, social, and cultural – and some protect specific groups, such as women, children, people with disabilities and those discriminated against on the grounds of race. To a greater extent than the case of climate change, elaborate compliance mechanisms have been established under these treaties, as well as under the auspices of the United Nations Human Rights Council (UNHRC), to oversee implementation of States' international human rights commitments.[212] Generally speaking, these mechanisms are more independent in composition and character than the compliance mechanisms under the UNFCCC, and to a great extent MEAs more widely,[213] and have a potential advantage of permitting individuals, and to some extent groups, to lodge complaints about violations, rather than standing being limited to States alone.

Customary International Law

Non-treaty sources of law, including international custom, are relevant in the context of both the climate change and human rights regimes, although to a greater degree in the latter field. Under article 38(1)(b) of the Statute of the ICJ, "customary" international law can be understood as non-treaty law generated through consistent practice accompanied by a sense of legal obligation. In the climate change regime there appear to be relatively few principles which can confidently be claimed to enjoy the status of customary international law.[214] One possible exception is the "do no harm" principle,[215] and perhaps more controversially, the precautionary principle (or precautionary approach),[216] each of which will be discussed in detail in Part IV below.

By contrast, the Universal Declaration of Human Rights (UDHR)[217] constitutes a potential source of numerous customary international law rules in the human rights field. The UDHR refers to human rights of all kinds – civil and political as well as economic, social, and cultural – and states the "common understanding of the peoples of the world concerning the inalienable and inviolable rights of all members of the human family and constitutes an obligation for the members of the international community."[218] The UDHR itself is in formal terms only a "declaration" rather than a legally binding treaty. Yet there is little dispute that the UDHR is relevant evidence of customary international law, and many scholars would argue that substantial parts of the UDHR now enjoy the status of binding rules of customary international law.[219]

There is no consensus, however, as to how much of the content of the UDHR so qualifies as such. Few scholars extend the list beyond a relatively small number of freedoms such as the prohibition against slavery, genocide, arbitrary killings, prolonged arbitrary detention, systematic racial discrimination and gross violations of internationally recognized rights.[220] Some commentators have argued that the right to self-determination may also be included.[221] However, several commentators have argued that a significant range of socio-economic rights has also acquired the status of customary law.[222] It is relevant in this respect that of the 165 countries that had written constitutions in the year 2004, 116 made reference to a right to education and 73 to a right to health care.[223] The near universal adherence by UN Member States to international human rights treaties that reflect socio-economic rights (including near universal ratification of the CRC), the recent acceptance by the General Assembly of an individual complaints mechanism for the ICESCR,[224] and universal acceptance of the MDGs are relevant to, even if not dispositive of, this question.[225]

Peremptory Norms (Jus Cogens) and Obligations Erga Omnes

Jus cogens, meaning "compelling law" in Latin, are special rules of customary (or general) international law, defined in Article 53 of the Vienna Convention as peremptory norms from which no derogation is permitted.[226] While originating in the law of treaties, the concept of *jus cogens* has now been accepted as part of general international law.[227] The significance of *jus cogens* norms lies in their status as higher law that cannot be derogated from by any country,[228] irrespective of State consent.[229]

There is no clear agreement on which norms of international law qualify as *jus cogens*, beyond the widely accepted examples of the prohibition of aggression, of racial discrimination, of genocide and of slavery. The concept has not been invoked with any great degree of consistency in the practice of States and by international tribunals. It is generally understood that, in order to qualify as *jus cogens*, a given norm needs to express fundamental moral values, with acceptance and recognition by the international community of States "as a whole."[230] However, legal theorists remain divided over the extent to which peremptory norms derive their legal authority from State consent, natural law, or the demands of international public order.[231]

The threshold requirements for the emergence of *jus cogens* is certainly higher than those necessary to sustain a putative norm of customary international law, as what is required is not generality of practice but acceptance and recognition by the community of states "as a whole". Moreover, most, if not all, *jus cogens* norms are prohibitive in nature, which can make the identification of the generalised practice of States difficult to grasp, and hence the boundaries of *jus cogens* hard to identify.[232] The International Court of Justice, or its members in separate and dissenting opinions, have referred to *jus cogens* in the context of areas of law as varied as the rights of passage through a territory, human rights protection, humanitarian law, the law of the sea, self-determination, and the prohibition of the unlawful use of force. There is little doubt that treaties conflicting with the prohibition on the use or threat of force, treaties involving international crimes, and treaties contemplating the commission of acts of slave trade, piracy or genocide, would be in breach of *jus cogens*.[233] Some international tribunals have extended the concept to the execution of juveniles and to torture.[234] The fact that the UNHRC has interpreted the torture prohibition (or more accurately, the injunction against "cruel, inhuman or degrading treatment or punishment") to include a prohibition on forced evictions in some circumstances[235] might serve as an interesting signpost for the future evolution of this prohibition in response to human needs and housing rights threatened by climate change. However, there is little consensus beyond this minimum core, and certainly no evidence that this category of norm currently extends to international values principles of the climate change regime more broadly.[236]

Closely linked in historical and functional terms to peremptory norms, but conceptually and analytically distinct, is the question of obligations *erga omnes* under international law. In international law, *erga omnes* (in Latin, "towards all") describes obligations owed by States to the international community as a whole and which, by virtue of the importance of the rights involved, all States have a legal interest in protecting. International treaty regimes dealing with subject matter expressed to be of "common concern" to the international community, or "elementary considerations of humanity," may indicate the existence of a collective interest relevant to the identification of *erga omnes* obligations, although this question is controversial. International treaty regimes dealing with subject matter expressed to be of "common concern," to the international community, or "elementary considerations of humanity," may indicate the existence of a collective interest sufficient to support the emergence of *erga omnes* obligations While it has numerous preconfigurations, including the *jus cogens* concept itself,[237] the original and authoritative exposition of the *erga omnes* concept was articulated by the ICJ in the *Barcelona Traction* case in 1970:

> [A]n essential distinction should be drawn between the obligations of a State towards the international community as a whole, and those arising vis-à-vis another State in the field of diplomatic protection. By their very nature, the former are the concern of all States. In view of the importance of the rights involved, all States can be held to have a legal interest in their protection; they are obligations *erga omnes*. Such obligations derive, for example, in contemporary international law, from the outlawing of acts of aggression, and of genocide, as also from the principles and rules concerning the basic rights of the human person, including protection from slavery and racial discrimination.[238]

Clearly, *jus cogens* norms (peremptory norms) and obligations *erga omnes* have certain characteristics in common, and some commonalities in their provenance. The original examples of *erga omnes* obligations cited in the ICJ's dictum in the *Barcelona Traction* case all derived from rules of general international law belonging to *jus cogens*. Both concepts have acquired new impetus through the work of codification of the law of State responsibility undertaken by the International Law Commission (ILC).[239] Like *jus cogens* norms, obligations *erga omnes* are intended to protect the common interests of States and basic moral values. Both require significant support from the international community, and characteristic expressions attaching to the *jus cogens* concept (such as the "international community as a whole") occur also in the ICJ's dictum on obligations *erga omnes*.

Yet vital differences remain. Foremost among these, *jus cogens* refers to norms, whereas *erga omnes* refers to obligations. Peremptory rules, like other international norms, give rise not only to obligations but also to other legal relations. As Ragazzi argues, "The proof that a particular international obligation is of *erga omnes* character does not require that this obligation satisfy the tests of norms *jus cogens*. Moreover "certain legal relations resulting from a peremptory rule (such as those pertaining to the invocation of the invalidity of a treaty) do not operate *erga omnes*, but only with respect to the parties to the treaty [purporting to derogate] from the peremptory rule in question."[240] Nevertheless, in principle, obligations *erga omnes* may strengthen the protection of the fundamental values protected by *jus cogens* norms, by allowing third states to put pressure on the parties to a treaty conflicting with *jus cogens*, to dissuade them from implementing it.

At a functional level, obligations *erga omnes* play a potentially significant role in relaxing the restrictive rules of standing before international tribunals, given the interest of all States in ensuring compliance. Birnie and Boyle suggest that the significance of *erga omnes* obligations goes further still, providing a normative framework and method for the international community to hold individual States accountable before the institutions created by treaty regimes.[241] The recent work the ILC Study Group on the fragmentation of international law suggests that *jus cogens* norms and *erga omnes* obligations may be relevant in interpreting and reconciling separate specialised legal regimes under the theory of "systemic integration," under which specialised treaty regimes are assumed to form part of a coherent and integrated whole, as a function of the application of rules of treaty interpretation reflected in the Vienna Convention on the Law of Treaties and customary international law.[242] Implicit in this theory is a recognition that treaty regimes evolve in a spontaneous and largely uncoordinated fashion. According to the ILC Study Group on the fragmentation of international law, "conflicts" are prone to structural bias, both within regimes and in the interaction between regimes, reflecting the dynamic interplay between diverse constituencies and interests (financial, political, ethical, etc).[243] Indeed, the ILC Study Group recognised that, where independent inter-regime tribunals are lacking, there is a strong likelihood that conflicts will be reinterpreted to reflect structural biases.[244] Under the theory of systemic integration, the ILC Study Group argued that conflicts between existing treaties can ordinarily be resolved to satisfaction through the application of accepted rules of treaty interpretation.[245] It further argued that these interpretive rules should be applied, as far as possible, in a manner that leads to a single set of mutually compatible obligations for the States parties to each regime and, if this is not possible, then the rule which is accorded priority must at least take the subordinate rule into account in defining appropriate limits. Of relevance to the present discussion, the ILC Study Group postulated, among other things, that specialised legal regimes may not derogate from *jus cogens*, and may not deviate from general law if the obligations of general law have *erga omnes* character.[246]

As with *jus cogens*, there is no consensus on the scope and content of *erga omnes* obligations, nor on the precise criteria through which they should be identified. Since the *Barcelona Traction* case, it has been argued before the ICJ, [that in order to qualify as *erga omnes* a legal obligation should: (a) be able to expressed in absolute and unqualified terms; (b) reflect a community interest; (c) protect fundamental goods; (d) be prohibitive in nature; (e) not be owed to individual States, but to the international community at large; and (f) entail correlative rights that are "held in common," recognizing – per the ICJ's dictum in *Barcelona Traction* – that "all States can be held to have a legal interest" in their protection. But the Court has not endorsed these criteria and the law remains unsettled.

The fields of environmental law (and the UNFCCC more particularly) and human rights both potentially lend themselves to claims of common concern.[247] In principle, therefore, subject to the gravity of the particular interests concerned and the degree of international support, both fields may offer further candidates for inclusion in obligations *erga omnes* beyond the original list cited by the ICJ in *Barcelona Traction* (relating to aggression, genocide, and "basic rights of the human person, including protection from slavery and racial discrimination").[248]

Perhaps controversially, the UNHRC has argued that all internationally recognized human rights currently enjoy the status of obligations *erga omnes*, although the criteria applied by the UNHRC in reaching this determination are not entirely clear, and its position is hard to reconcile with the ICJ's original dictum in *Barcelona Traction*[249] despite the fact that the list of 'basic rights' in that dictum was not intended to be exhaustive.[250]

In the environmental field, there is some support for the view that the *erga omnes* category might extend to the following obligations: to protect and preserve the marine environment, including the territorial sea;[251] to notify other States immediately of imminent danger or damage to the marine environment (an obligation confined to coastal States);[252] to notify the international shipping community of the existence of a minefield;[253] and not to dispose of nuclear and radioactive wastes in the high seas.[254] The legal boundaries of more expansive claims, particularly to the extent that the obligations concerned are "positive" in nature, remain heavily contested. Some commentators have even suggested categorically that all environmental law obligations are *erga omnes*,[255] an optimistic proposition at best having regard to the indicative criteria for *erga omnes* obligations discussed above.[256]

General Principles of Law

According to Ian Brownlie, the general principles of international law may refer to rules of customary law, to general principles of law or to logical propositions resulting from judicial reasoning on the basis of existing international law and municipal analogies.[257] General principles of law are among the recognised sources of international law and have a lengthy history of application in disputes between States. Article 38(1)(c) of the Statute of the ICJ refers to "general principles of law recognised by civilised nations," which in effect means all nation-states.[259] It is generally understood that the general principles of international law[259] can be drawn from underlying principles and postulates of national legal systems [as well as unperfected sources of international law, for example, where a putative customary rule is not evidenced by sufficient or consistent State practice.[260] While on a formally equal footing with other sources of law referred to in Article 38(1) of the Statute of the ICJ,[261] many scholars consider general principles to be a secondary source of international law to be invoked as supplementary rules "where appropriate."[262]

According to the academic literature, one may identify at least four main functions served by general principles: (1) a source of interpretation for conventional (treaty-based) and customary international law, which has in practice been the most widely accepted and practical use of this source of law;[263] (2) a means for developing new norms of conventional and customary law; (3) a supplementary source of law; and, arguably, (4) a modifier of conventional or customary law rules.[264] The practical significance of these closely related functions, in an increasingly globalised world, may be seen in the increasing demands placed upon international law to address problems beyond the scope of existing treaty, custom or other accepted sources of law.[265] Thus, in theory, general principles may fill gaps in treaty or customary law and furnish supplementary reference norms for the purposes of adjudication and interpretation, further than those provided by natural law and other such sources.[266]

However, to at least the same degree as *jus cogens* norms and obligations *erga omnes*, there is little evident consensus on which principles derived from municipal systems or international law may qualify as "general principles" for purposes such as those enumerated above, or precisely how such determinations are to be made, or where their boundaries may lie.[267] The history of the ICJ's engagement with general principles has been as cautious as it has been lengthy, doing no service to certainty.[268] There are a number of relatively well accepted principles of judicial procedure and evidence drawn from municipal systems that have gained widespread acceptance as "general principles" applicable to the determination of international claims. Examples include the principles of *res judicata*, equity, good faith and estoppel.[269] There has also been a modest degree of explicit judicial support for the inclusion of certain human rights, notably the right to self-determination.[270] In principle, the category of "general principles" appears apt to capture a greater range of socio-economic rights than customary law, and appears to be more amenable than other non-treaty sources to the inclusion of obligations of a positive nature across human rights of all kinds. More pertinently still, it is relevant to note that the precautionary principle (while not firmly established as a customary rule) derived originally from municipal law systems, as did international norms and principles relating to environmental impact assessment.[271] The proliferation of national and regional constitutional provisions and jurisprudence concerning environmental rights may be expected to sustain many future claims for the emergence of general principles of international environmental law.[272]

Conclusions on Sources of International Law

The foregoing discussion was necessarily schematic in nature, highlighting the primary sources of international law formally recognised in Article 38(1) of the Statute of the ICJ, including sources of peremptory norms and norms giving rise to obligations *erga omnes* insofar as they may be relevant to climate change and human rights. It is not intended to detract from the normative significance and potential relevance of so-called "soft law," that is to say, legal principles emerging from non-legally binding instruments such as UN General Assembly Resolutions, Declarations, world summit outcomes and so forth.[273] Moreover, as many commentators have noted, there are limits to the extent to which positivist legal thought – emphasising State structures and the power of sanction in enforcing compliance with legal rules – in analysing and resolving international law problems.[274] It is well recognised that principles lacking the status of formally binding rules may still be "normative" in the context of practical reasoning,[275] that is, as a guide to deliberation, discourse or decision-making, whether the latter be in the legislative, judicial or administrative context,[276] or as "a legal concept exercising a kind of interstitial normativity, pushing and pulling the boundaries of true primary norms when they threaten to overlap or conflict with one another".[277] These latter sources and functions assume additional importance in the context of extra-territorial obligations concerning international cooperation and assistance, issues that are fundamental to the integrity and viability of the international climate change regime, given the limitations of the primary sources of law in these respects as will be explored in more depth in Parts IV and V.

A conclusion from the foregoing discussion, however, is that the international climate change regime has far stronger foundations in international treaty law than in non-treaty sources. By contrast, while a significant number of international human rights standards can be identified and defended through non-treaty sources, this should be seen against a sixty-year history of standard-setting and norm consolidation in the human rights field, resulting in a comprehensive and detailed *acquis* and comparatively mature and elaborate compliance mechanisms at international and regional levels. Both the climate change and human rights treaty regimes reflect binding obligations with objectively ascertainable content, and enjoy near-universal subscription.

Finally, while conclusions on this question are necessarily both qualified and speculative, *jus cogens* norms and obligations *erga omnes* may yet prove to play important roles in the human rights and environmental fields, in terms of their incrementally expanding content and – particularly for *jus cogens* rules – their comparative weight in the hierarchy of international norms.[278]

Public International Law Approaches and Beyond: Human Rights Law vs. "Human Rights Approaches"

The dominant focus of this paper is the relationship between climate change and human rights under international law, but the philosophy, language and concepts of human rights are not the sole domain of lawyers. Social scientists, development workers, civil society groups and to some extent policy-makers have been active in bringing a human rights perspective to climate change research, advocacy and campaigning, relying upon a wider range of conceptions and articulations of human rights than those embodied the international human rights framework. The purpose here is not to survey these various conceptions, but rather to clarify a few threshold definitional and conceptual issues and – further to the concluding remarks of the preceding section – draw a small number of general conclusions about the relationships between legal and "non-legal" approaches. Questions of the "value-added" of human rights in the context of climate change are dealt with subsequently.

Proponents of differing conceptions of human rights in the climate change context frequently speak of a "human rights approach" to climate change. But often the specific conceptual premises are not made clear, nor a relationship with international human rights law articulated. In general terms the expression "human rights approach" appears to draw more from human development theory and humanitarian policy and practice than, necessarily, from human rights as a legal construct. The meaning and normative and practical implications of this term varies in accordance with context and user, and the linkages with the human rights legal framework vary across a broad spectrum. This term is sometimes used inter-changeably with the term "human rights-based approaches," although the latter can arguably be seen as a broader concept capable of embracing property rights regimes – such as the emissions trading regimes under the UNFCCC – to a greater extent than the international human rights legal framework might countenance.[279]

In development practice at both policy and community level, "human rights approaches" frequently aim to give expression to generic human rights "principles" considered to be important for development practice, such as participation, accountability, equality and non-discrimination,[280] rather than the binding human rights legal standards in force in the country concerned. Such "good process" principles are commonplace in MEAs, such as the information, participation, accountability portions of the Aarhus Convention[281] and are reflected in soft law instruments such as the Rio Declaration's Principle 10.[282] But in the climate change context the term "human rights approach" has also been taken by some commentators to imply a more or less exclusive focus on litigation strategies.[283] Many others might regard this conception as unduly reductionist, quarantining human rights within legal bounds and the well-known limitations of formal redress mechanisms, and perhaps foreclosing inquiry into multi-disciplinary approaches that promote more holistic visions of human rights as an empowering vocabulary and framework for political and social change.

CHAPTER IV

The Potential Relevance of Human Rights Law to Climate Change

M̲ost human rights treaties do not refer to environmental protection.[284] The tribunals that interpret the agreements have nevertheless derived norms of environmental protection from the rights that the treaties do protect, including rights to life and health. The relevant jurisprudence is largely from regional bodies, but because of the similarity in the treaties' expressions of the rights, their interpretations may be persuasive authority for similar interpretations of human rights treaties with universal membership, such as the international human rights treaties. In the succeeding discussion, the term "environmental human rights jurisprudence" means the indirect enforcement of environmental protections through human rights claims.

General Relevance of Human Rights to the Climate Change Debate

The focus of this paper is the potential role of international law in addressing the human impacts of climate change. It is a widely held view that law plays an important role in grounding and mediating conflicting ideas and claims within a relatively objective and consensual normative framework.[285] However, while pursuing a legal analysis, it is important to bear in mind that the moral values and theories underpinning legal rights form an indispensable part of their claim to legitimacy and quest for traction in any given setting.[286] There are a number of distinctive attributes that legally-binding human rights norms and the operational principles in which they are explicitly grounded can bring to climate change mitigation and adaptation efforts, negotiations and policy-making. These may be conceived of as elements of "value-added," but in doing so the frame of inquiry should not be limited to empirical justifications, alone; the co-called "intrinsic" and "constitutive" arguments have self-standing justification, whatever the debates on the empirical evidence. The added-value of human rights in the particular context of climate change policy-making may be understood in the following ways, which may draw upon instrumental, intrinsic and constitutive rationales for human rights, recognizing also that these are not mutually exclusive and may be overlapping:[287]

- A focus upon human rights law may serve to locate policy work within the framework of internationally agreed *obligations*.[288] Acceptance of certain goods, interests or goals as rights may have the effect of establishing a hierarchy of importance among policy goals, helping to ensure that human rights are not traded off among other interests lacking that status.

■   Human rights law may help to establish a core set of minimum thresholds or basic human rights standards, which international and national mitigation and adaptation measures should take into account and respect. The international human rights framework, and jurisprudence under the ICESCR in particular, may help elaborate the substantive content of this "core minimum" set of entitlements, in a manner adapted to national conditions and resource constraints.[289]

■   The international human rights legal framework evinces an abiding concern for discrimination and a focus on vulnerability and those whose rights are most at risk. While there is no specific human rights legal instrument concerning poverty, the international human rights legal regime includes numerous treaties protecting the rights of individuals and groups who may be more vulnerable to adverse climate impacts, including women (and rural women in particular), children, indigenous peoples and ethnic minorities, scheduled castes, and persons with disabilities, among others.

■   Human rights can inform processes by placing a focus on participation as a right in itself, including ensuring that those whose rights are affected by climate change have an effective voice in setting national and international mitigation targets and policies, and that affected communities can participate in and have ownership of the design and implementation of adaptation initiatives. International human rights legal standards help establish normative foundations and essential guarantees for active, free and meaningful participation, including the rights to freedom of expression and association and self-determination.

■   Human rights may offer a normative and institutional framework for strengthened accountability of those responsible for adverse impacts of climate change, as well as national authorities and others responsible for implementing adaptation measures. This might include requirements for States to more systematically undertake and publicize social impact assessments (or human rights impact assessments) prior to and during the implementation of significant policy measures relevant in the context of mitigation and adaptation,[290] report publicly on results in implementing mitigation targets and policies, ensure effective and transparent governance of adaptation strategies and funds, and provide transparent and effective mechanism of redress for those whose rights are violated. Strengthened accountability, it is sometimes claimed, may also promote greater sustainability of the outcomes sought to be achieved in the given context.

■   The human rights framework places emphasis on more effective international cooperation. While extra-territorial obligations are comparatively less clear-cut and quantifiable under international human rights law, it may be argued that states should be encouraged to take on emissions cuts in line with their contributions to climate change harms as well as their capacity to assist, and contribute to the financing of adaptation programmes accordingly.[291]

This is of course no more than an illustrative list of attributes, drawn from the defining feature of international human rights law as a system of accountability framed around the relationship between the individual (and to some extent groups) and the state. Moreover, while the focus here is deliberately legal in orientation, the discussion does not discount the potential role of ethically-based or policy-based frameworks.

Lessons from "environmental human rights jurisprudence"[292]

Environmental human rights jurisprudence, as defined in the introduction to this Part, has drawn on each of the major categories of human rights, including civil and political rights, economic, social, and cultural rights, and peoples' rights.[293] It is noteworthy that, even though the treaties assign States different types of obligations for different categories of rights, the jurisprudence has developed very similar requirements across the board. It construes the treaties as imposing duties on States to regulate not only their own behaviour, but also that of private actors subject to their control. It sets out strict procedural duties that States must follow before causing or allowing environmental harm. And it gives States discretion in deciding on amounts of permissible environmental harm, as long as the States follow the procedural requirements and their decisions meet minimum substantive standards. These minimum standards are not always clearly defined in the abstract, but the jurisprudence of courts and tribunals has helped to flesh out the core substantive content of human rights, within and beyond the context of claims arising from environmental harms.

Duties to regulate private as well as State action

In addition to requiring states to refrain from violating human rights themselves, human rights treaties require States to take steps to protect the rights from private conduct that interferes with their enjoyment.[294] Regional tribunals and quasi-tribunals have established that this duty to protect applies to infringement of human rights caused by environmental degradation.

For example, in reviewing a complaint that the military government of Nigeria had exploited oil resources in the Ogoniland region "with no regard for the health or environment of the local communities,"[295] the African Commission on Human and Peoples' Rights found that the exploitation violated many human rights protected by the African Charter, including the right to life of the Ogoni people living in the area.[296] The Commission emphasized that Nigeria's duty was not simply to refrain from violating rights itself, but also to "protect [its] citizens . . . from damaging acts that may be perpetrated by private parties," including Shell Oil, Nigeria's partner in extracting the resources.[297]

Similarly, in a 1997 report on the situation of human rights in Ecuador, the Inter-American Commission on Human Rights said that pollution from oil exploitation and mining in the Orient region had caused grave health problems in local communities, which adversely affected the inhabitants' right to life.[298] Like the African Commission, it said that the State's human rights obligations extended beyond its own agents' contribution to the problem: the threat to life and health could "give rise to an obligation on the part of a State to take reasonable measures to prevent such risk, or the necessary measures to respond when persons have suffered injury." The State must ensure that it has measures in place to prevent life-threatening harm from pollution, including from private sources, and "respond with appropriate measures of investigation and redress" when environmental contamination infringes its residents' right to life.[299]

The most detailed environmental jurisprudence built on civil and political rights comes from the European Court of Human Rights. In cases construing the European Convention on Human Rights, the Court has established that while environmental harm may violate the right to life,[300] it need not do so to trigger State duties. Even if environmental degradation merely causes adverse effects on health and the quality of life in the home, it may interfere with the right to privacy.[301] Although the adverse effects must attain a "certain minimum level,"[302] severe endangerment of health is not necessary. It is enough for the pollution to affect "individuals' well-being and prevent them from enjoying their homes in such a way as to affect their private and family life adversely."[303] If so, the State is under an obligation to take positive steps to protect against the harm,[304] whether it caused the pollution directly or failed to protect against pollution from private actors.[305] In either case, "the applicable principles are broadly similar."[306]

Human rights bodies have also established that environmental degradation can interfere with economic, social, and cultural rights, including, in particular, the rights to the highest attainable standard of health[307] and to components of an adequate standard of living, including rights to water[308] and food.[309] As discussed in Part I above, economic, social, and cultural rights – like civil and political rights – have been construed as requiring States not only to refrain from violating the rights itself (*i.e.*, to respect the rights), but also to take positive measures, including protecting against infringements of the rights by non-State actors (*i.e.*, to protect the rights) and other appropriate measures towards the full realization of the right (*i.e.*, to fulfil the rights).

In the UN context, the CESCR has applied these duties to environmental degradation, most thoroughly in the context of its examination of the right to water. There, it said that States' duty to *respect* the right to water requires them to refrain from interfering with the enjoyment of the right, including through "unlawfully diminishing or polluting water, for example through waste from State-owned facilities,"[310] and their duty to *protect* the right requires that they adopt the necessary measures to restrain third parties from interfering with the enjoyment of the right including, again, by pollution.[311] Other positive measures required by what the Committee calls the duty to *fulfil* include the adoption of comprehensive programs to ensure that "there is sufficient and safe water for present and future generations," which may include impact assessment and the reduction and elimination of pollution.[312] In less detail, the CESCR has also indicated that States' duties to respect the right to health include refraining from "unlawfully polluting air, water and soil, e.g. through industrial waste from State-owned facilities,"[313] and that their positive duties include adopting measures against environmental health hazards by formulating and implementing "national policies aimed at reducing and eliminating pollution of air, water and soil."[314]

Procedural and Substantive Standards

International tribunals and quasi-tribunals have held that environmental harm may implicate a wide range of human rights, which in principle give rise to different types of duties. Nevertheless, in the environmental context, tribunals have derived remarkably similar duties from these various rights. Generally they require strict procedural safeguards, including prior assessment of environmental impacts, full and informed participation by those affected, and judicial recourse for States' failure to comply with their obligations.[315] They defer to States' decisions as to how to strike a balance between development and environmental protection, but the deference is not absolute. The common theme throughout the jurisprudence is that States may undertake or allow environmental degradation that interferes with the enjoyment of human rights, as long as they follow the procedural requirements and protect against environmental harm that goes too far.

For example, in construing civil and political rights (specifically, the rights to life and privacy) affected by environmental harm, the European Court of Human Rights has allowed the State a great deal of discretion to find a "fair balance" between the rights of the individual and the interests of others in the broader community, whether the harm is caused by the State directly or by a private actor.[316] In determining whether the State has found an acceptable balance, the Court has looked to domestic law as an important consideration. If the State has failed to meet domestic standards by allowing excessive levels of pollution[317] or failing to implement a domestic court's decision to close a facility,[318] then it has virtually always been found to have violated its international duties.[319] If, on the other hand, a State has complied with its own environmental law, the Court has usually upheld its actions.[320]

More generally, the European Court of Human Rights has emphasized that the decision-making process must be fair and "such as to afford due respect" to the interests protected by the Convention.[321] It has set out the specific requirements that the decision-making process must meet:

Where a State must determine complex issues of environmental and economic policy, the decision-making process must first involve appropriate investigations and studies in order to allow them to predict and evaluate in advance the effects of those activities which might damage the environment and infringe individuals' rights and to enable them to strike a fair balance between the various conflicting interests at stake. The importance of public access to the conclusions of such studies and to information which would enable members of the public to assess the danger to which they are exposed is beyond question. Lastly, the individuals concerned must also be able to appeal to the courts against any decision, act or omission where they consider that their interests or their comments have not been given sufficient weight in the decision-making process.[322]

If procedural requirements are met, "only in exceptional circumstances" will the European Court of Human Rights "revise the material conclusions of the domestic authorities."[323] The Court has made clear, however, that States' decisions must meet minimum substantive standards. In two cases, one concerning the failure of a State to prevent a mudslide that breached a dam and killed eight people, and one involving a methane explosion at a waste site, the Court said that States must establish a legal framework to effectively deter threats to the right to life and require everyone concerned to take practical measures to ensure the protection of those whose lives might be endangered.[324] In the case concerning the deadly mudslide, the Court found that Russia ignored warnings that dangerous mudslides might occur, did not institute an early-warning system that would allow people to evacuate in time, and did not allocate funds for the repair of protective dams.[325] It concluded that Russia failed to establish the legal framework necessary to deter threats to the right to life, and thereby violated its substantive obligations under the Convention.[326]

Although the Inter-American Commission on Human Rights has not developed as detailed a jurisprudence as that of the European Court of Human Rights, it has taken a broadly similar approach to States' procedural and substantive duties regarding environmental threats to the right to life. In the 1997 Ecuador report mentioned above, for example, the Inter-American Commission said, rather vaguely, that States must take "reasonable measures" to prevent the risk of harm to life and health. Like the European

Court of Human Rights, it avoided setting out concrete limits on environmental degradation, noting that States have the freedom to develop their own natural resources. Instead, it emphasized procedural safeguards, saying that protection of human rights in this context "may best be advanced through measures to support and enhance the ability of individuals to safeguard and vindicate those rights." To that end, it stressed the importance of access to information, participation in relevant decision-making processes, and judicial recourse, the same procedural rights highlighted by the European Court of Human Rights.[327]

The Inter-American Commission and the Inter-American Court of Human Rights have also recognized that, to protect the rights of minorities that rely on the natural environment, it is necessary to protect that environment.[328] In this respect, they have looked to the right to property, which they have held may be exercised collectively by an indigenous or tribal community.[329] The right to property is of particular importance to such communities because without rights to the land and resources on which they rely, "the very physical and cultural survival of such peoples is at stake. Hence the need to protect the lands and resources they have traditionally used to prevent their extinction as a people."[330] On this basis, the Inter-American Court has held that a community's right to property includes not only the right to own the land that the community has traditionally occupied, but also the right to own the natural resources it has traditionally used.[331] As in other environmental human rights cases, the Inter-American system has adopted procedural safeguards to protect this right. For example, the Inter-American Court has held that until the land traditionally occupied by a community is delimited and titled in consultation with the community, the State may not allow its "existence, value, use or enjoyment" to be affected, either by its own agents or by third parties acting with its acquiescence or tolerance.[332]

Human rights bodies examining the effect of environmental harm on economic, social and cultural rights have also developed strict procedural requirements. For example, in the 2001 *Ogoniland* decision, the African Commission concluded that Nigeria had violated the right to health of the Ogoni by allowing, and participating in, the exploitation of oil in their region. The Commission analyzed that right together with the people's right to a "general satisfactory environment" recognized by the African Charter.[333] In response to largely uncontested allegations that oil production had resulted in numerous oil spills and the disposal of toxic wastes directly into the environment, and that the resulting contamination had caused a wide range of short- and long-term health effects,[334] the Commission said that the rights to environment and health together "obligate governments to desist from directly threatening the health and environment of their citizens."[335] It held that to comply with the spirit of these rights, governments must order or at least permit "independent scientific monitoring of threatened environments," require studies of environmental and social impacts before any major industrial development, monitor projects, and provide communities information and opportunities to participate in development decisions affecting them.[336]

This emphasis on procedural measures as a way to safeguard environmental protection can be seem as similar to the approach taken by the European Court of Human Rights to environmental harm to the rights to privacy and life. It allows States to decide for themselves, within wide parameters, how to balance environmental protection with other important societal goals, such as the development of natural resources for economic growth.[337] Nevertheless, the discretion is not unbounded in this context, any more than it was in the context of the rights reviewed by the European or Inter-American Courts. The African Commission also found *substantive* violations of human rights in *Ogoniland*. In particular, it held that the destruction and contamination of food sources, both by Nigeria directly and by private parties with State authorization, had violated the Ogoni's right to food.[338]

In perhaps the most important decision on the application of the right to health to environmental harm to come out of the Council of Europe system, the European Committee of Social Rights concluded that Greece's policies toward lignite mines and power plants placed it in violation of its obligations under Article 11 of the European Social Charter, which requires States to take certain measures in furtherance of the right to health.[339] Its decision emphasizes that States do not have unlimited discretion to balance away human rights in setting their environmental policies. In addition to concluding that Greece had failed to implement procedural safeguards,[340] the Committee chastised Greece for failing to make sufficient progress toward the goal of "overcoming pollution."[341] It found, *inter alia*, that Greece had too few inspectors, that its fines were insufficient to deter violations of its air quality standards, and that it had not shown that the power plants had adopted best available techniques to reduce pollution.[342] "[E]ven taking into consideration the margin of discretion granted to national authorities in such matters," the Committee stated, "Greece has not managed to strike a reasonable balance between the interests of persons living in the lignite mining areas and the general interest."[343]

The CESCR has also specified procedural duties to protect rights from environmental harm, which are very similar to those identified by the regional bodies. The CESCR General Comment on the right to water indicates that the relevant authorities must make sure that actions that interfere with the right meet basic procedural requirements, including: "(a) opportunity for genuine consultation with those affected; (b) timely and full disclosure of information on the proposed measures; (c) reasonable notice of proposed actions; (d) legal recourse and remedies for those affected; and (e) legal assistance for obtaining legal remedies."[344] And, like the other human rights bodies, the CESCR has indicated that States also face minimum substantive standards.[345] It has stated that a State does not necessarily violate its obligations under the ICESCR by failing to prevent water pollution, if the failure was despite its best efforts, but, if the failure results in the infringement of "minimum essential levels" of the right to water, the State has violated a core obligation, although a lack of sufficient resources can almost certainly be considered an exculpatory factor, with the onus of proof being on the claimant State.[346] The CESCR's jurisprudence may be seen in the context of increasing preparedness of international, regional and national tribunals to give effect to "positive rights" claims, helping flesh out minimum substantive content of socio-economic rights, within a history and continuing general pattern of deference to legislative prerogatives.[347]

All of the rights discussed so far are human rights held by individuals. In addition, peoples may have rights recognized by human rights law. In particular, the ICCPR and the ICESCR recognize a people's right to self-determination, and state that it includes the right of all peoples to "freely dispose of their natural wealth and resources," and that "[i]n no case may a people be deprived of its own means of subsistence."[348] It could be argued that environmental degradation so massive as to deprive a people, however defined, of its means of subsistence would constitute a serious abridgement of the right to self-determination.[349]

Taking into account the consistent pattern of regional and international jurisprudence, reinforced in an increasing number of international instruments, certain commentators have suggested that administrative procedures such as those embodied in the Aarhus Convention[350] may soon lay plausible claim to the status of legally binding norms as a matter of international custom. For example, noting the process guarantees regulating policy formulation, implementation and impact assessment in Aarhus, Musungu observes that "parallel procedural requirements are spelled out in Articles III and VI of the World Trade Organizations Services Code, and in a variety of Bilateral Investment Agreements. The European Court of Human Rights has interpreted Article 6 of its Convention, a provision guaranteeing a fair and public hearing in the determination of civil rights and obligations, as implying a similar set of rights."[351] Thus, it has been argued, "although not all governments may have yet formally accepted administrative-procedure type obligations in all contexts, the obligation is coming close to customary law, and there is nothing novel in applying such principles to national governments through arrangements under the UNFCCC."[352] It is important to recognize, however, that, as it has developed, environmental human rights jurisprudence has not ventured far in prescribing specific substantive standards. General socio-economic rights jurisprudence has evolved substantially. Yet by the same token, an exclusive focus on procedural rights may present obvious limitations in the context of human rights law which protects a core of rights that society cannot decide to infringe, even if it does so through an inclusive, informed decision-making process. If a State's action (or failure to act) results in an interference with that core, then it may have violated human rights even if its action resulted from an inclusive, well-informed decision that offered full participation to all those affected.[353] Reflecting this concern, the environmental human rights jurisprudence reviewed here makes clear that it is not completely deferential to States' decisions, even if they result from a satisfactory procedure. The human rights bodies that have developed the jurisprudence have consistently stated that, while governments may balance environmental protection against other interests, that balance may not be struck in a way that violates minimum substantive standards.

Environmental Rights – A "Human Right to a Healthy Environment"

Beyond "environmental human rights jurisprudence" discussed in the preceding section, there has been considerable debate over the emergence of a self-standing "human right" to an environment of a particular quality under international law. This idea has only a relatively brief history, limited traction in international law, and comparatively limited expression in regional and national jurisprudence, and has not yet featured prominently in debates and legal claims connected with climate change. Moreover much of the normative development at the international level lies in the realm of "soft law."[354] Nevertheless, whether as a signpost to the future evolution of international law, or as part of the conceptual and normative framework within which the compatibility of established norms concerning climate change and human rights could presently be assessed, a brief treatment of this issue is warranted here.[355]

It is only in the last few decades that environmental protection has begun to be articulated in the language of human rights. Several international soft law instruments[356] as well as certain treaties recognize and protect self-standing environmental rights, whether procedural[357] or stand-alone[358] in nature. The European Charter of Fundamental Rights also recognizes the importance of environmental protection in the context of sustainable development, although this is articulated as a policy objective for the EU rather than a self-standing legal right.[359] In addition, more than a hundred national constitutions[360] recognize various formulations of environmental rights, although the extent to which these are intended to take effect as political principles as opposed to constitutional rights is both variable and debatable.[361]

As the discussion in the preceding section revealed, recent human rights jurisprudence shows a willingness of tribunals and expert bodies to acknowledge that environmental harms may be associated with violations to internationally recognized rights such as the right to life, health, respect for private and family life, among others. But for the most part this jurisprudence falls well short of signaling the emergence of a self-standing right to a healthy environment.

Yet there is a vibrant scholarship on this topic and countervailing trends at regional and national level to take into consideration. For example, it has been argued that Article 24 of the African Charter and Article 11 of the San Salvador Protocol both represent customary law,[362] building the case for the notion of an emerging right under international law more generally.[363] More tangibly still, developments in Europe may point toward an increased recognition of procedural and substantive environmental rights within Europe. It has been argued that procedural environmental rights such as the right to access to information, the right to participation, and right to access to justice, may already have reached the status of regional customary law in Europe through adoption of the Aarhus Convention and other regional legal instruments,[364] agreements, and European Commission (EC) Directives.[365] The environmental human rights jurisprudence discussed in Part IV(2) above, while not directly on point, may in due course strengthen the empirical and normative foundations and impetus towards a substantive human right to the environment in international law.[366] The complexity and quintessentially global character of climate change challenges could perhaps, eventually, build momentum towards a self-standing legal norm in this area, consistent with what appears to be a strengthening moral and philosophical case.[367]

Many have argued that the broad or vague formulations of self-standing environmental rights have presented obstacles to their reception into international law.[368] Yet some jurisprudence in this particular field suggests that these obstacles may not be insurmountable, and that as with socio-economic rights, they may be amenable to a level of definition that renders particular aspects of the right justiciable. In the *Oposa* case, for example, the Supreme Court of the Philippines issued a judgment based upon a specific finding of a violation of an autonomous environmental human right (in that case, a constitutional right to a "balanced and healthful ecology"), distinguishing itself from the usual run of environmental human rights jurisprudence in taking the interests of future generations explicitly into account.[369] In *Taskin v. Turkey*, the plaintiff relied on the right to a healthy environment in the Turkish Constitution before the European Court of Human Rights, which found this to constitute a civil right within the meaning of the ECHR.[370] And in the *Ogoniland* case, as discussed earlier, the African Commission found the government of Nigeria in violation of the right to a "satisfactory environment" under Article 24 of the African Charter, along with the right to life, health and property.[371] The

African Commission said that Article 24 "requires the State to take reasonable and other measures to prevent pollution and ecological degradation, to promote conservation, and to secure an ecologically sustainable development and use of natural resources."[372] More specifically, the Commission ruled that Article 24 obliges States to facilitate and publicize "environmental and social impact studies prior to any major industrial development" and to provide "information to those communities exposed to hazardous materials and activities and providing meaningful opportunities for individuals to be heard and to participate in the development decisions affecting their communities."[373] While the Commission's use of terms such as "reasonable" might appear vague at first glance, the "reasonableness" test has presented no obstacle to the effective adjudication of constitutional human rights in South Africa.[374] Established methods of judicial reasoning have proven capable of applying such broadly worded tests to appropriate factual contexts. The Commission's reaffirmation of environmental procedural rights is also noteworthy, perhaps contributing in some measure towards the consolidation of such rights in international law. Recent constitutional law developments in France are apposite too. The French Constitution was amended in 2005 to include a "Charter of the Environment" which affords to all citizens of France the right to live in a "balanced environment, favorable to human health."[375] The Charter has been relied upon by the French *Conseil Constitutionnel* in reviewing the constitutionality of ordinary bills, although, as of 2008, without yet finding any breach of the Charter's provisions.[376] However, the Charter was also relied upon by a local administrative court as a basis for suspending the granting of an administrative permission for a rave party to occur in a former airfield, which had subsequently been listed under domestic nature conservation law.[377] While the reported body of practice of the *Conseil Constitutionnel* and administrative courts is presently modest at best, it serves to illustrate the point that the practical application of generally worded environmental rights in the legislative and judicial processes should not be dismissed out of hand.[378]

Developments such as these will likely continue to attract a mixed reception. Beyond perceptions relating to excessive vagueness, Birnie and Boyle identify anthropocentricity and redundancy as the principal objections to the notion of an autonomous human right to a decent environment.[379] Others have averred to the particular complexity and inter-disciplinary character of environmental issues when juxtaposed with human rights;[380] difficulties in balancing putative environmental rights with existing human rights;[381] and risks of diverting attention and efforts from more achievable and, arguably, effective environmental and human rights objectives.[382] The tactical merit of litigating environmental protection in human rights forums, likewise, is not a straightforward question,[383] and UN Member States have agreed to a set of formal criteria governing standard-setting in the human rights field, which has been invoked by Member States to resist the emergence of "new" rights in other contexts in recent years.[384]

The above considerations pertain to the environmental field generally. Technical and normative complexity may prove particularly challenging in connection with climate change more particularly. For example, what degree of temperature increase should be regarded as acceptable, some temperature increase being inevitable?[385] Against which of the numerous existing standards or benchmarks can the qualitative level of protection be assessed? How should one factor in the differing impacts between people and communities, and difficult human rights trade-offs associated with States' varying development needs? To what extent should States' legal obligations relating to the human rights impacts of climate change vary according to their economic capacities and historical responsibility? How does one deal with the problem of transboundary harms and extra-territorial jurisdiction? And to what extent should communities or collectivities (characteristic of so-called "solidarity rights" or third generation rights under international law)[386] be regarded as rights-holders, and non-State actors,[387] including multinational corporations, be regarded as duty-bearers directly under a new substantive right to a climate of a certain prescribed quality?

There is presently very little direct support for a substantive human right to the environment under international treaty law, and virtually no evidence that a human right to the environment might be derived from custom or general principles of international law. On the existing state of the scholarship and evidence such a right can be characterized, at best, as an embryonic one,[388] and the more particular challenges presented by the cross-boundary nature of climate harms must also be confronted.

The Potential Application of Environmental Human Rights Law to Climate Change[389]

The preceding review indicates that States are generally responsible not only for ensuring that their own conduct does not violate human rights, but can also be responsible for protecting against interference with human rights from other sources, including private actors, and a number of human rights bodies have confirmed that this duty to protect applies to environmental degradation that harms human rights.[390] Although most of these cases involve the duty to protect against private actions that infringe a human right, States also have duties with respect to other threats beyond their control, such as natural disasters.[391]

The general approach of the environmental human rights jurisprudence surveyed in Part IV(2), supported to some degree by emerging regional custom relating to self-standing environmental rights, is to subject States to strict procedural requirements (they must assess potential environmental harm, provide information to those affected, allow them to participate in decision-making, and provide them access to judicial remedies for non-compliance) and – subject to minimum substantive standards – give States discretion within wide limits to determine how to strike the balance between environmental harm and the benefits of the activities causing it, and, thus, to decide where to set levels of environmental protection. These two standards are closely linked; qualified deference to States' environmental policy decisions only makes sense if, and to the degree that, the procedural safeguards are in place to ensure that the policy decisions reflect the informed views of all those affected by it, and that certain minimum standards are respected.

Because harm caused by climate change is a type of harm caused by environmental degradation, one might intuitively assume that the environmental human rights jurisprudence described earlier could apply to it. That jurisprudence was developed in the context of harm that does not cross borders, however, and it does not translate easily to transboundary harm such as climate change.

Furthermore, the environmental human rights jurisprudence is based on the premise that a single polity experiences both the benefits of economic development and the environmental harm that it engenders, and – subject to procedural safeguards and substantive minimum standards – has the responsibility to decide where to strike the balance between them. But climate change is not subject to a single polity; it is inherently a transboundary problem on a global scale. Moreover, human rights law primarily imposes vertical duties – that is, duties owed by a State to those within its own jurisdiction. Extending those duties diagonally, to those outside the State's jurisdiction, may seem necessary in order to apply human rights law to the global aspects of climate change, but such an extension faces serious obstacles, both legal and practical.

Even without such an extension, however, it may be argued that States might still have duties under human rights law with respect to climate change. Even if human rights law does not require States to consider the effects of climate change outside their own jurisdiction (which, as we will see is a controversial and complex issue), they may still have duties to take steps to protect those within their jurisdiction from its effects. First, there may be grounds to argue that States (particularly those with greatest responsibility for global emissions) are obligated under human rights law to try to mitigate their own emissions of GHGs, as will be considered further below.[392] Second, a clearer case may be made to argue that States are required to take steps to help their people adapt to climate change. Third, it may be argued that States have obligations to cooperate and work with other States toward a general agreement to reduce global emissions.

Thus, even if they did not have to take into account the effects of climate change on other States, human rights law may arguably be interpreted in a manner which requires States (particularly those proportionately responsible for the greatest emissions) to try to reduce their own emissions in order to protect the human rights of their own people. Of course, most States produce a fraction of one percent of global emissions of GHGs. For any one of these States to cut its emissions, even to zero, would make no appreciable contribution to the mitigation of global warming. But the question of proportionate contribution is not determinative of liability; indeed this kind of disclaimer has been put in doubt by the reasoning of the U.S. Supreme Court in *Massachusetts v. EPA*, finding that the U.S. Clean Air Act authorized the Environment Protection Authority (EPA) to regulate emissions from new motor vehicles.[393] Moreover, obligations under international human rights law are not qualified by the manner in which other States parties approach their own duties. (The climate regime, by contrast, is built more explicitly upon the principle of reciprocity). Accordingly one may argue that, if construed as a human rights obligation to take measures to protect against climate change harms, the actions and responsibilities of one State should not be conditioned on what others do, particularly in major emitting States where unilateral reductions could make a tangible even if not decisive difference to the protection and realisation of human rights locally.

In order for human rights law to require States to address the entire range of harms caused by climate change, it would have to impose duties on States with respect to those living outside their territory and, indeed, everywhere in the world. Human rights law arguably does require States to respect and to some extent, more controversially, to protect the rights of those outside their own territory or jurisdiction. But the extraterritorial application of the ICCPR, ICESCR, and other global human rights treaties is heavily contested and remains unclear.

Article 2(1) of the ICCPR requires each of its parties "to respect and to ensure to all individuals *within its territory and subject to its jurisdiction* the rights recognized in the present Covenant."[394] Some have argued that a natural reading of the word "and" in

Article 2(1)'s limitation of a State's duties to "all individuals within its territory and subject to its jurisdiction" would be that the requirements of both territory and jurisdiction must be met for the ICCPR obligations to apply.[395] However, the view adopted by the International Court of Justice, the Human Rights Committee, and most scholars, is that the language should be read disjunctively, to require each party to respect and ensure the rights of both those within its territory *and* those subject to its jurisdiction.[396]

Who falls within the extraterritorial jurisdiction of a State? In its General Comment on Article 2(1), the Human Rights Committee said that "a State party must respect and ensure the rights laid down in the Covenant to anyone *within the power or effective control of that State Party, even if not situated within the territory of the State Party.*"[397] Power or effective control can be established with respect to individuals if, for instance, they are arrested or kidnapped by a State. Control may also extend more broadly; the Human Rights Committee has suggested that a State's military control of territory beyond its own boundaries triggers its obligations under the ICCPR,[398] and the ICJ followed that view in the *Israeli Wall* case.[399]

No authoritative body has addressed whether transboundary environmental harm may bring its victims within the effective control of the State where the harm originates.[400] However, the European Court of Human Rights and the Inter-American Commission on Human Rights have examined whether other types of extraterritorial harm fall within the jurisdictional limits of the European and American Conventions, which are similar to that of the ICCPR.[401] In *Bankovic v. Belgium*, the European Court of Human Rights rejected the argument that the North Atlantic Treaty Organization (NATO) bombing of Serbia in 1999 amounted to effective control of the places bombed.[402] The court was evidently concerned that accepting the allegation would have meant that "anyone adversely affected by an act imputable to a Contracting State, wherever in the world that act may have been committed or its consequences felt, is thereby brought within the jurisdiction of that State," a reading that would have deprived the limitation of any meaning.[403] The Inter-American Commission, however, has taken a more expansive view. In 1999, it held that by shooting down an unarmed plane over international waters, agents of the Cuban government "placed the civilian pilots . . . under their authority," thereby satisfying the jurisdictional requirement of the American Convention.[404]

It is difficult to see how transboundary harm caused by climate change could meet the standard employed by the European Court of Human Rights. If dropping bombs on a city does not amount to "effective control" of its occupants, the less immediate and drastic measure of allowing pollution to move across an international border would be unlikely to constitute such control. The Inter-American Commission's test appears less strict, but it remains uncertain how it would apply to transboundary environmental harm.

Article 2(1) of the ICESCR requires each party "to take steps, individually *and through international assistance and co-operation*, especially economic and technical, to the maximum of its available resources, with a view to achieving progressively the full realization of the rights recognized in the present Covenant by all appropriate means."[405] The ICESCR thus provides a clearer basis for extraterritorial duties, although developed countries have resisted the proposition that it imposes duties on them to assist other countries meet their obligations under the Covenant.[406] A range of other treaties and international instruments support and help to give flesh to this principle, as will be discussed further in Part V below.

Almost every General Comment adopted by the CESCR, including rights to health, water, and food, it has relied on the reference to "international assistance and co-operation" to set out extraterritorial obligations.[407] A comparable approach is evident in the work of various other treaty bodies[408] and UN Special Rapporteurs, including the Rapporteurs on the right to food and right to health,[409] as well as by the OHCHR in its report on climate change and human rights.[410] Nevertheless, the ICJ suggested in its advisory opinion on the *Israeli Wall* that the Covenant's absence of a provision on the scope of its application might be due to "the fact that this Covenant guarantees rights which are essentially territorial."[411] This dictum is not only at odds with the court's finding, the ICESCR *did* apply to the government of Israel's conduct in the Occupied Palestinian Territories, but the ICJ did not elaborate or explain the further contradiction between this statement and the contrary interpretations by the expert committee charged with overseeing the ICESCR, or even note the specific reference to international assistance and cooperation in Article 2(1). On the whole, then, it seems strongly arguable that the text of the ICESCR provides a ground for extraterritorial duties, and certainly seems to *allow* States to take action, bearing in mind the fundamental human rights obligation contained in the UN Charter.

The contours of those duties remain unclear, however. One possible interpretation is that, while the primary responsibility for meeting the obligations under the ICESCR remains on the State with jurisdiction over the people concerned, States in a position to assist other States to meet those obligations are required to do so. On this basis, the CESCR has identified obligations both to provide long-term assistance and to respond to emergencies.[412] It has said that the obligation depends on the availability of resources, and that each State should contribute in accordance with its ability.[413] As applied to climate change, the implication of this interpretation is that the requirement to assist other States requires richer countries to help poorer States pay the costs of adaptation and (perhaps) mitigation.

Developed States have been reluctant to accept the proposition that the ICESCR requires them to provide any particular quantum of international financial assistance to any particular State.[414] As Philip Alston observes: "No UN body, nor any group of governments, has accepted the proposition that any given country is obligated to provide specific assistance to any other country. Moreover, the persistent rejection of such a claim by developed countries, and the failure of even the most generous of donors to locate their assistance within the context of such an obligation, would present a major obstacle to any analysis seeking to demonstrate that such an obligation has already become part of customary law."[415] The resistance may be due in part to the open-ended nature of the potential obligation and its imposition of positive, rather than negative, duties. In the three-part categorization of duties adopted by the CESCR, a duty to provide international assistance may be an extension of the duty to *fulfil*,[416] which some argue has less political support than more widely accepted duties to *respect, and with certain qualifications, to protect.*[417]

Matthew Craven suggests that one approach to the question of extraterritorial application of the ICESCR would be to recognize that while "a state is not necessarily directly responsible for conditions elsewhere in the globe, and . . . each state assumes primary responsibility for the well-being of the local populace," each State is also required "to ensure that it does not undermine the enjoyment of rights of those in foreign territory."[418] In other words, a State must not interfere with other States' ability to meet their obligations. This duty would essentially be an extraterritorial extension of the duty to *respect* human rights, perhaps the most basic human rights obligation.[419] The CESCR has regularly applied this duty of non-interference, with particular reference to the rights to health, food, and water.[420] Similarly, the duty to *protect* rights from interference by private parties could arguably be extended extraterritorially by requiring each State to prevent private actors under its jurisdiction or control from harming human rights in other States.[421] Although the duty not to interfere with other States' ability to meet their obligations under the ICESCR might be thought to be relatively straightforward, arising from general principles of good faith in the performance of international legal obligations,[422] it too has met with resistance from developed countries.[423]

Together these duties could be argued to provide some legal basis for the extension of environmental human rights jurisprudence to climate change. Pursuant to that jurisprudence, a State may comply with its obligations to respect vis-à-vis those within its own territory by satisfying procedural safeguards and making substantive decisions that do not threaten human rights. If the duties to respect rights extend extraterritorially, a State could presumably comply with them in the environmental context by extending extraterritorially the procedural safeguards developed in the environmental human rights jurisprudence. As already noted, that would require the State to undertake transboundary environmental impact assessment, provide information to everyone whose human rights might be affected by the actions under its jurisdiction, and allow them to participate in the decision-making process while respecting minimum substantive human rights standards. According to the jurisprudence, a State that followed these procedures would have wide discretion to strike the balance between environmental protection and other policies, as long as its decisions did not result in the destruction of the human rights of those outside, as well as within, its jurisdiction. To the extent that obligations to "protect" human rights also extend extra-territorially, this would require States – at a minimum – to put in place appropriate regulatory arrangements and remedial processes to safeguard against violations of human rights perpetrated abroad, including by transnational corporations headquartered in the concerned State.

One problem with arguments about extending environmental human rights law in this way, however, is that it would treat climate change as a series of individual transboundary harms, rather than as a global threat to human rights. It would require each State to assess its own contribution to extraterritorial climate change harm, and to take into account the resulting harm in making its policy decisions, but it would not require States to coordinate their responses with one another. This is an obvious shortcoming with respect to a problem whose sources and victims are all over the world.

Concluding Comments

There are numerous ways in which human rights law could inform international and national climate change mitigation and adaptation efforts. This discussion exposes the problem of the fragmentation of international law and considers the benefits of a coherent interpretation of international climate change and human rights commitments, particularly given that both the climate change and human rights treaty regimes enjoy universal membership.

The potential contributions of the international human rights regime can be seen in light of their entrenchment in a universally applicable framework of legally binding obligations owed (principally) by the State to individuals and to some extent groups. This framework may reinforce or complement international law relating to climate change by helping to set in place minimum substantive standards or thresholds applicable to climate change mitigation, adaptation and financing decisions and policies; underwriting procedural guarantees including strengthening participation, *ex ante* impact assessment, accountability and access to justice in climate change matters; and encouraging a focus on the human impacts of climate change, with priority for the most excluded groups.[424]

CHAPTER V

UNFCCC, Kyoto Protocol and Human Rights Frameworks: Complementarities and Challenges

Introduction

The following section examines the principles, norms and processes of international law as they relate to both human rights and climate change, with a principal focus on treaty law.[425] The relevance of this exercise needs to be seen in light of the fact that all of the parties to the core human rights treaties are also party to the UNFCCC, and the vast majority are also party to the Kyoto Protocol.[426] The following section focuses on the UNFCCC and Kyoto Protocol on the one hand, and international human rights treaties (the ICESCR in particular) on the other, investigating the broad objectives and key normative principles and precepts underlying each that may be relevant for future studies on the potential for mutual reinforcement.

"Do No Harm:" A Core Obligation Common to MEAs and Human Rights

One of the better established obligations under general principles of international environmental law, and an obligation with a strong claim to the status of customary international law, is the obligation not to cause significant transboundary harm, or what has become known in short-hand as the 'do no harm" principle.[427] Originating in 1941 in the *Trail Smelter* case[428] and restated in the *Nuclear Weapons* case[429] and the Stockholm and Rio Declarations,[430] many scholars view it as firmly established in customary international law,[431] connected to the requirement that States give effect to their treaty obligations "in good faith."[432] Other commentators' analyses of State practice have called into question this norm's status as a principle of customary international law, as distinct from a general principle of international law.[433]

The practical importance of the "do no harm" principle is well established in the case of transboundary pollution. Some have claimed it should also be recognized in the climate change context as well. Yet even Tuvalu, the nation facing the most imminent prospect of disappearing under rising sea levels, has so far elected for diplomatic rather than legal channels in pursuit of its claims.[434] Whatever the outstanding normative controversies, and notwithstanding the reluctance of States to submit to international adjudication of extra-territorial obligations, the "do no harm" principle frequently forms an important part of the legal context in which *ad hoc* solutions and institutional arrangements are negotiated and implemented on the international plane.[435]

There is a human rights corollary to this environmental law principle. It is argued by some that as a general principle of international law within the meaning of Article 38(1)(c) of the Statute of the ICJ, and arguably as a norm of customary international law, States owe a "duty of diligence" to ensure that their own policies, actions or possible neglect do not impede the realisation of human rights elsewhere.[436] This could arguably be viewed as an aspect of the obligation to "respect" the human rights commitments undertaken by other subjects of international law, an iteration of the "do no harm" ethic commonplace in humanitarian law and practice.[437] This obligation has long been recognized in the practice of the United Nations, for instance in the UN's acceptance of international responsibility in 1965 for damage caused in the course of the Congo operation,[438] and has come to form part of the framework within which the CESR assesses States' compliance with their obligations under the ICESCR.[439] This recognition can be seen as the logical consequence of the duty under general international law not to harm foreign nationals and to make reparations for breaches.[440] Significantly, it is also an increasingly accepted element of the legal framework within which transnational corporations and other business enterprises operate, although the extent to which non-State actors can be said to be bound directly by international human rights law remains controversial.[441]

It has been argued that a necessary implication or functional corollary of the "do no harm" obligation is the obligation to undertake environment impact assessments (EIAs). However, scholarly opinion appears to be divided on the precise content and scope of such an obligation, including how significant the prospect of environmental harm needs to be in order to trigger this obligation, as well as on its normative status under international law. Analyzing State practice and applicable international treaty regimes, Beyerlin suggests that "the EIA norm not only may be binding as a matter of treaty law but also may have grown, at least in the European context, to a (regional) customary legal rule."[442] The international human rights framework has a potentially significant role to play in terms of how EIAs, as part of broader social impact assessments, might be conceptualized and implemented, drawing from States' minimum "due diligence" obligation to avoid violating human rights, including beyond their borders.

Finally, on the "do no harm" question, it is relevant to ask: "Do no harm to *what* or *whom*?" Does this norm encompass only present or imminent harms? Alternatively, to what extent are we entitled to take into account the adverse human rights impacts that climate change may inflict upon *future* generations? The climate change and human rights regimes do not frame this question in the same way, hence it is important to analyse these regimes in order to expose the differences in approach.

Article 3 the UNFCCC urges States to take "precautionary measures to anticipate prevent or minimize the causes of climate change and mitigate its adverse effects." Some States view this as embodying a legally binding "precautionary principle" and have put this principle forward as a guiding principle in the ongoing climate change negotiations.[443] The precautionary principle is seen by some as evidence of a paradigm shift in international environmental law, from the *ad hoc* and reactive approaches that characterized early environmental regulations. There are numerous references to the precautionary principle in international law,[444] but there are divergent views on whether the precautionary principle is properly so called, how it might best be defined, what its precise content is, what obligations it creates and on whom, and whether, in its strong version, it lends itself to actualization.[445] As such its precise import and legal status remains disputed.[446]

The EU has claimed that it provides the precautionary principle in its most evolved form. The European Commission (EC) notes that the precautionary principle should be considered within a structured approach to the analysis of risk which comprises three elements: risk assessment, risk management and risk communication.[447] In the EU's view the precautionary principle is particularly relevant to the management of risk,[448] and the determination of what constitutes an "acceptable level of risk for society is an eminently political responsibility."[449]

By contrast the international human rights framework, on its face, appears not to accommodate easily the interests of future generations. The human rights legal framework appears somewhat reactive in its design, geared more towards redressing past or imminent harms than the speculative business of scientific predictions pertinent to climate change. Yet, through evolving jurisprudence and practice, preventive functions can be identified.[450] First, while the instances are few, certain international human rights bodies have interpreted particular human rights guarantees in a manner that takes account of the interests of future generations. The CESCR is an example of this, interpreting the normative content of the right to food under Article 11 of the ICESCR as including the requirement of sustainable access for present and future generations.[451]

In less direct terms, the capacity building of human rights institutions serves an preventive function. The enforcement of human rights claims (including but not limited to formal courts) may have preventive as well as reactive or corrective impacts and, through a range of feedback channels, exert enduring influence upon legislative reform and policy-making. For example, analyzing patterns and outcomes of socio-economic rights litigation in South Africa, Brazil, India, Nigeria and Indonesia, Daniel Brinks and Varun Gauri show that "legalizing demand for [socio-economic] rights might well have averted tens of thousands of deaths [in the above-named countries] and has likely enriched the lives of millions of others."[452] The obligation to "protect" human rights can be understood as having an explicitly preventive component, as protection is understood under the ICCPR and ICESCR.[453] It may be argued that good process principles such as those reflected in the Aarhus Convention and environmental human rights jurisprudence surveyed earlier (for example transparency/freedom of information, participation, non-discrimination and equality, and accountability/redress), which are embedded to varying degrees within international, regional and national human rights laws,[454] may contribute appreciably to the sustainability of climate change policy-making, with at least implicit preventive dimensions.[455]

Moreover, national experience in the codification and enforcement of "environmental rights," such as a constitutional right to a "balanced and healthy ecology" in the Philippines, along with recent jurisprudence of the Inter-American Court of Human Rights on indigenous people's rights, suggests that there may be potential for human rights-related claims to further the goal of environmental sustainability, for the benefit of future as well as present generations.[456] The legally binding nature of such rights can be contrasted to the more uncertain status of the precautionary principle and "sustainable development" principle under international law.[457]

The Principle of International Cooperation

The principle of international cooperation finds reflection in both the environmental[458] and human rights field. The climate negotiation process embodies a sophisticated attempt to achieve multilateral cooperation on a global environmental issue. The language and burden-sharing arrangement contained in the UNFCCC and Kyoto Protocol bear testimony to this. The UNFCCC underscores the notion of cooperation by noting that "the global nature of climate change calls for the widest possible cooperation by all countries."[459] It requires parties to cooperate to sustain a supportive and open international economic system which would promote sustainable economic growth.[460] Adaptation under the UNFCCC is intended to be a cooperative effort. UNFCCC Article 4(1)(e) read with Article 4(8) and (9) highlights the importance of cooperation and support, including support relating to funding, insurance and the transfer of technology to vulnerable developing countries. A series of international funds exist, including the recently operationalized Kyoto Protocol Adaptation Fund, to finance adaptation in developing countries.[461] Further, the UNFCCC obliges parties to cooperate in development and transfer of technology,[462] conservation and enhancement of GHG sinks,[463] research,[464] exchange of information,[465] and, education, training and public awareness.[466] The notion of cooperation is also central to the post-2012 negotiation which is titled "long-term cooperative action under the Convention."[467]

As indicated in Parts II and IV, above, human rights doctrine also promotes the importance of international cooperation, and legal foundations for duties are set forth in a range of international instruments. Achieving international cooperation in the promotion of human rights is among the central purposes of the international community as expressed in the UN Charter.[468] Article 55 of the Charter requires the UN to promote, *inter alia*, "universal respect for, and observance of, human rights and fundamental freedoms for all," and in Article 56, "[a]ll Members pledge themselves to take joint and separate action in co-operation with the Organization for the achievement of the purposes set forth in Article 55."[469] Subsequent treaties affirm the proposition that States' human rights duties extend beyond their borders and include cooperative action. For example, Article 2(1) of the ICESCR commits the 160 States parties to that treaty to "take steps, individually and through international assistance and cooperation … to the maximum extent of available resources," to progressively realise economic, social and cultural rights. The jurisprudence of the CESCR has sought to clarify, to some degree, the content and boundaries of the duty of international cooperation, in terms of the nature of the general obligations under Article 2(1)[470] as well as in connection with specific human rights.[471] States parties to the CRC[472] and the CRPD[473] have also committed themselves to international cooperation towards the realisation of particular rights, although quantifiable and justiciable obligations are, as ever, elusive.

There is considerable support for such obligations under non-binding international instruments as well. Article 28 of the UDHR states that: "[e]veryone is entitled to a social and international order in which the rights and freedoms set forth in this Declaration can be fully utilised."[474] Article 22 of the UDHR proclaims that economic, social and cultural rights should be realised "through national effort and international cooperation." There are many political declarations embodying formal partnership commitments of different kinds – including on subjects such as aid, trade and debt relief[475] – which might arguably be summoned as aids in interpretation of broadly textured obligations such as those found in the UN Charter or the UDHR, or alternatively as evidence of relevant State practice for the purposes of prospective customary law rules. The 1986 Declaration on the Right to Development[476] is among these, positing a right of individuals and peoples to "participate in, contribute to, and enjoy economic, social, cultural and political development, in which all human rights and fundamental freedoms can be fully realized."[477] Contained in a non-binding General Assembly Resolution rather than a formal treaty, this Declaration goes considerably further than most human rights texts in articulating a duty of international cooperation. Partly for this reason, the "right to development" has remained controversial ever since its formal emergence in the 1970s.[478]

Both the international climate and human rights treaty regimes contain explicit and commitments regarding international cooperation, bolstered by a range of non-binding instruments. The UNFCCC's commitments are more detailed, differentiated and extensive than those reflected in the major international human rights instruments, although it appears that both are honoured as much in the breach as the observance. Despite the potential for future arguments about collective duties to work together to protect human beings from the effects of climate change on their human rights it cannot presently be said that any single State or group of States is legally bound to extend any particular form or amount of international assistance to another.

Equity & "Common But Differentiated Responsibility"

Although they do not defined the term 'equity', the UNFCCC and Kyoto Protocol reflect a comparatively specific conception of equity geared to the unique features of the climate change problem, laying the ground for a scheme of differential treatment between participating countries based upon competing justice claims.[479] The three fundamental distinctions between wealthier and poorer countries reflected in the UNFCCC regime are: different historical responsibility and different relative contributions to climate change; differing likely impacts of climate change, with certain poorer countries including low-lying States being more vulnerable than many others; and different capacities to contribute to global mitigation and national adaptation efforts.[480] These distinctions are brought out explicitly in Article 3 of the UNFCCC:

> In their actions to achieve the objective of the Convention and to implement its provisions, the Parties shall be guided, *inter alia*, by the following:
>
> 1. The Parties should protect the climate system for the benefit of present and future generations of humankind, on the basis of equity and in accordance with their common but differentiated responsibilities and respective capabilities. Accordingly, the developed country Parties should take the lead in combating climate change and the adverse effects thereof.
>
> 2. The specific needs and special circumstances of developing country Parties, especially those that are particularly vulnerable to the adverse effects of climate change, and of those Parties, especially developing country Parties, that would have to bear a disproportionate or abnormal burden under the Convention, should be given full consideration.

Thus Article 3 of the UNFCCC has confirmed that differential treatment between "developing" and "developed" countries is warranted, based upon differing vulnerabilities, national capacities and historical responsibilities. The Kyoto Protocol fixes key commitments for emissions reductions only for a sub-set of "developed" countries. Differential treatment of this kind is consistent with two significant emerging principles or normative concepts in international environmental law: the "common but differentiated responsibility" principle (CBDR), originating in the Stockholm Declaration of 1972 and finding definitive expression in Principle 7 of the 1992 Rio Declaration; and what has become known as the "polluter pays" principle, stemming from international jurisprudence on transboundary environmental harm and reflected in Principle 16 of the Rio Declaration.

The following discussion first examines the idea of differential treatment between States as reflected in international environmental law (with a focus on climate change) and human rights law, and then moves to a more focused examination of the CBDR and "polluter pays" principles, leading to conclusions about how basic ideas about equity as reflected in the UNFCCC and Kyoto regimes relate to principles of international human rights law.

Accommodating Diversity: Differential Treatment[481]

Notwithstanding similarities in terms of claims to universal value, human rights and environmental approaches reflect important differences in emphasis and degree. Most new generation MEAs do not permit reservations, while human rights treaties do.[482] Further, MEAs allow for differential treatment (a price paid for universal membership), while human rights treaties, in theory, do not (reflecting the universality of human rights and incommensurability of underlying notions of human dignity). These differences in emphasis and degree between environmental and human rights treaties, in particular in the context of differential treatment, are relevant to a discussion of human rights and climate change because, if taken at face value, they may impair the ability of the international community to integrate human rights concerns into the agreed outcome of the ongoing climate negotiations.

Differential treatment refers to the use of norms that provide different, presumably more advantageous, treatment to some States. Very significant political, economic, geographic and other differences exist between States. Norms of differential treatment recognize and respond to these differences by instituting different standards for different States or groups of States. Differential treatment, broadly conceived, is deeply embedded in the fabric of new generation MEAs.[483] The UNFCCC and the Kyoto Protocol are unique in that, not only do they contain a range of differential treatment provisions relating to assistance, delayed compliance, and the like, but they are also the only agreements among the MEAs that differentiate between countries with respect to central obligations such that some have certain commitments that others do not.[484] UNFCCC Article 4(2) sets out specific commitments for a certain number of industrialized countries, alone. The Kyoto Protocol requires the industrialized States parties listed in Annex I to the UNFCCC to reduce their overall emissions of a basket of GHGs by at least 5 percent below 1990 levels in the commitment period of 2008-2012. Again, the targets and timetables contained herein, as in the UNFCCC, apply exclusively to industrialized countries. The nature and extent of differential treatment favoring "developing countries" – a category which, in contrast to the Montreal Protocol,[485] is not defined – is a central point of contestation in the ongoing negotiations on climate change.[486]

Unlike environmental treaties, human rights treaties – applicable to all persons and protecting universally agreed values on the minimum requirements for a dignified life – might in theory be expected to be hostile to ideas about differential treatment. However, human rights law contains numerous norms of differentiation.

First, the principle of universality and the fact of the universal adherence by UN Member States to international human rights treaties is off-set to some degree by a proliferation of reservations.[487] This offers States a considerable margin to tailor the relevant treaty to its own conditions, resulting in a degree of unilateral differentiation that may arguably be difficult to reconcile with the universality principle.[488] This problem is most clearly evident in the CEDAW convention,[489] where nearly 40 percent of the 180 Parties have entered reservations, many of which are general reservations transcending specific provisions, or reservations to core obligations.[490]

However, it is not just through reservations that differentiation is achieved in the human rights realm. Implicit norms of differential treatment have been incorporated into certain human rights treaties, in particular with respect to economic, social and cultural rights. For instance, as indicated above, Article 2(1) of the ICESCR[491] requires each State to take steps, "individually and through international assistance and co-operation, especially economic and technical, to the maximum of its available resources," with a view to "progressive realization" of the rights recognized in the Covenant. Article 2(1), in its terms, introduces flexibility in implementing the obligations contained in the treaty. First, it recognizes that differences in resource capacities may result in differing levels of implementation across states. And, second, by its use of the phrase "progressive realization" it recognizes the realities of the real world, and the difficulties for any country to fully realize economic, social and cultural rights.[492] In doing so, it accommodates diversity and embodies the idea of differential treatment based on differing national capacities.

However, as was seen in Part II, not all socio-economic rights obligations are necessarily resource-dependent. Recognizing this fact, Article 2(1) has in practice been interpreted to carefully circumscribe the extent of differential treatment available to States. In the CESCR's own interpretation, Article 2(1) should be read as safeguarding a "minimum core obligation to ensure the satisfaction of, at the very least, minimum essential levels of each of the rights," although it is likely that even this standard demands a degree of contextualization.[493] Furthermore, the Committee has held that "even where the available resources are demonstrably inadequate, the obligation remains for a State party to strive to ensure the widest possible enjoyment of the relevant rights under the prevailing circumstances."[494] There are, in addition, obligations to avoid arbitrary retrogression and to move as "expeditiously and effectively as possible" towards the goal of full realization of the rights identified in the ICESCR.[495] While there are specific provisions for international technical assistance for the benefit of developing countries in the recently concluded Optional Protocol to the ICESCR, States have explicitly agreed that this does not detract from States parties' own primary obligations to their own populations under the Covenant.[496] Thus, differential treatment in the ICESCR, to the extent it is countenanced, is carefully hemmed in.[497]

Differentiation of this kind is built into other treaties as well, such as the CRC and CPWD as discussed above. The Migrant Workers Convention (MWC)[498] is an unusual example of a human rights instrument predicated explicitly upon differentiation between States (in this case, "States of origin" of migrant workers, transit States, and "States of employment"), although arguably this has done little to attract adherents. In most human rights treaties (even in those such as the ICCPR where State obligations are not qualified by phrases such as "progressive realization" and "available resources"[499]) there are mechanisms to consider and accommodate, in however circumscribed a manner, differences between States at the level of implementation. For instance under the ICESCR,[500] ICCPR,[501] CEDAW[502] and the CRC[503] States are given an opportunity to indicate in their reports to the relevant treaty bodies the "factors and difficulties" affecting implementation. Among the "factors and difficulties" most often deployed are economic difficulties, political transition and instability, and traditional practices and customs.[504] The relevant committees recognize and acknowledge certain difficulties, in particular economic constraints, but urge States to do everything in their power to overcome them.[505]

Finally, as discussed earlier, the principle of differentiation is reflected in the concept of "limitations" and derogations to particular provisions of human rights treaties. Limitations condition the exercise of particular human rights in deference to wider public interests the interpretation of which is contingent to a great extent upon conditions in a given society (e.g. in the interests of public health or morals, public safety or *ordre public* – a term of art referring to fundamental considerations of public policy).[506] Derogations permit contracting States to suspend certain specified treaty obligations in times of public emergency threatening the life of the nation, subject to certain procedural and substantive requirements including necessity and proportionality.[507]

In sum, differential treatment exists across the board in human rights treaties. Even the Vienna Declaration and Programme of Action which underscores the universality of human rights notes that the "significance of national and regional particularities and various historical, cultural and religious backgrounds must be borne in mind."[508] Since human rights treaties embrace differentiation and explicitly recognize the different implementation challenges faced by industrialized and low-income countries, there can be no fundamental incompatibility assumed between these and the burden-sharing arrangements between developing and industrialized countries under the climate change regime.

Common but Differentiated Responsibilities

As discussed above, differential treatment has a relatively long tradition in MEAs, and a key principle governing the code of conduct of States parties to the UNFCCC is the CBDR principle.[509] The CBDR principle brings together several strands of thought. First, it establishes unequivocally the common responsibility of States for the protection of the global environment. Next, it builds upon the acknowledgement by industrial countries that they bear the primary responsibility for creating the global environmental problem by taking into account the contributions of States to environmental degradation in determining their levels of responsibility under the regime. In doing so, it recognizes broad distinctions between States, whether on the basis of economic development or consumption levels.

However, the core content of the CBDR principle as well as the nature of the obligation it entails remain contested.[510] From the literature one can discern at least two contrasting views on the content of the CBDR principle: 1) that the principle "is based on the differences that exist with regard to the level of economic development;"[511] or alternatively, 2) that it is based on "differing contributions to global environmental degradation and not in different levels of development."[512] There is also disagreement as to the nature of the obligation entailed by the CBDR principle. While some argue that it is obligatory others contend that it is only discretionary. Subject to the future course of debates on the source, content and legal status of the CBDR principle, it is clear that the

UNFCCC and Kyoto Protocol, in their terms, require consideration of differential treatment between countries in the application of treaty obligations.

The "Polluter Pays" Principle

The polluter pays principle complements the CBDR principle. This principle does not find explicit reference in existing climate treaties, but is part of the CBDR principle, insofar as the CBDR principle countenances differentiation on grounds of differing contributions to environmental harm. It is also part of the conceptual apparatus of the Kyoto Protocol in that only industrialized countries, responsible historically for two thirds of GHG emissions, have mitigation targets.

The polluter pays principle requires that the "polluter should, in principle, bear the cost of pollution."[513] Although based on intuitively sound legal ground and a logical extension of the customary international law principle that States have an obligation to "ensure that activities within their jurisdiction and control respect the environment of other states or of areas beyond national control,"[514] this principle does not enjoy universal support. The guarded language used in the construction of the polluter pays principle bears testimony to the caution with which states approach international responsibilities. The principle is formulated in recommendatory rather than mandatory terms,[515] and contains little discernible substantive content. Moreover, the application of the principle, to the extent that it must be implemented "without distorting international trade and investment," is subject to highly restrictive conditions.[516]

Nevertheless, some countries have suggested that the polluter pays principle constitutes one of the core principles guiding the construction of a post-2012 climate change regime.[517] The international human rights framework might be construed as supporting this position, to the extent that this framework demands a focus on the accountability of States and other entities for identifiable harms caused by their emissions, subject to the various qualifications regarding causation and attribution discussed earlier.[518]

Conclusions on Complementarities and Tensions

The goals and objectives of MEAs and human rights treaties are obviously not identical: the former are generally framed around transboundary harms and a more explicit and embracing conception of the global good, with a comparatively pressing appeal – on empirical, ethical and legal grounds – to theories of international responsibility and collective action. Although the international human rights treaty regime is a compact between States, the chief preoccupation of international human rights law generally is to establish a framework of claims and duties between individuals (and to some extent groups) and the State.

Notwithstanding differences in overall goals and approaches, the foregoing analysis also reveals the extent to which each treaty framework grapples with similar challenges, and how from structural and normative perspectives they can be seen as reflecting certain analogous principles and precepts. The literature and analyses reviewed here reveals the potential for mutual reinforcement between principles underpinning both regimes, with the human rights framework drawing attention to the human face of climate change and bolstering accountability at the supra-national level, in particular, while also lending support for strengthened accountability for human rights impacts of transboundary environmental harms, with a particular focus on the "do no harm" principle under customary international law. Human rights legal obligations and principles – as elaborated through national, regional and international compliance mechanisms – may also strengthen information, voice and participation in climate change policy.

CHAPTER VI.

Potential Operational Implications and Areas for Further Research

Notwithstanding the urgency of the climate change problem, and despite the very clear human rights risks, only very recently has governmental support begun to galvanise around the human rights dimensions of this issue, and the potential role that human rights law, principles and institutions could play in the climate change response. Explicit human rights arguments are yet to gain traction to any appreciable extent within the climate change negotiations under the UNFCCC framework.[519] On the one hand, a total of eighty-eight UN member states from various regions supported the Human Rights Council's consensus resolution 10/4 (2009), which encourages greater involvement by human rights expert bodies in the UNFCCC process.[520] With one notable exception – a proposal to include human rights protection as a new criterion or guiding principle for adaptation measures[521] – the relatively few human rights proposals ventured so far in the climate negotiations have been modest, re-characterising adverse climate change impacts in human rights terms, apparently linked to broader global justice concerns and demands for strengthened commitments and support from industrialised countries.[522]

In previous rounds of climate negotiations, Argentina had raised human rights in the context of "enhanced action on adaptation" arguing that further research on the impacts of climate change on human rights realization "will be useful in ensuring that climate response takes place within a strong sustainable development framework."[523] But the relationship between human rights and sustainable human development was not articulated. Chile had proposed that a shared vision on climate change be based, *inter alia*, on a human rights perspective,[524] but, again, without suggesting specific entry points, strategies or approaches. However, if proper consideration is to be given to the interplay and coherence between the human rights and climate regimes, the normative premises must be clearly articulated together with a more tangible sense of practical implications for climate change policy-making, as well as priorities for further research.[525] This final part of the paper is intended to make a contribution towards the latter objectives, building upon the main findings on the normative inter-relationships discussed in the preceding parts.

A Frame for Policy Choices

Research and practical experience elsewhere suggests that the most important potential contributions of the international human rights framework in practical terms may be to help frame, rather than necessarily resolve, difficult policy choices and trade-offs.

Some argue that the human rights framework can help to do this by strengthening arguments and incentives for the establishment of a minimum floor of social entitlements, and helping to ensure that, whatever policy choices are concluded respect good process principles of the kind discussed above.[526] Others have argued that the human rights framework may bring a distinctive contribution to the value basis for decision-making, informing hard economic choices relating to the short-run and long-run distributional consequences of climate change, questions that the discipline of economics, alone, may not be fully equipped to deal with.[527]

Within these general parameters, there are three levels at which it might be useful to look at the more specific contributions of the human rights legal framework to climate change decision-making:

A Normative Focus on Human Welfare

A defining feature of a human rights approach is its normative focus on human welfare (i.e. "the dignity and worth of the human person.")[528] The primary objective of the climate change regime is the "stabilization of greenhouse gas concentrations in the atmosphere at a level that would prevent dangerous anthropogenic interference with the climate system."[529] A joint concern for and focus upon the human being can be seen on a superficial level as an overlapping concern of both legal regimes.[530] The human rights framework can serve an important function in helping to draw attention to the human face of climate change harms and anthropogenic causes.

Procedural rights standards – improving decision-making processes

But what is it that constitutes "dangerous" anthropogenic interference with the climate system? And how is it to be determined? The IPCC notes that this is a value judgment[531] determined through socio-political processes, taking into account considerations such as development, equity, and sustainability, as well as uncertainties and risk."[532] Wolfgang Sachs argues that it involves two valuations: "what kind of danger is acceptable, and what kind of danger is acceptable for whom?"[533] In the negotiations for a post-2012 climate agreement, the EU, among others,[534] has suggested that the future regime should aim to limit temperature increase to 2 degrees Celsius (some increase being inevitable), the most ambitious limit on the table. Drawing from the analysis above,[535] the human rights legal framework offers criteria for the *process* of negotiations, as well as decision-making on climate change policy issues more generally. While certain process guarantees enjoy firmer footing in international law than others, as we have seen, active and informed participation – including by the most disadvantaged or vulnerable groups – can not only provide critical inputs to decision-making processes but also enhance the legitimacy and sustainability of outcomes. *Ex ante* human rights impact assessments, as part of environmental assessments, can help decision-makers and negotiators to identify in a more reliable, systematic and timely fashion the likely winners and losers of any proposed policy measure, as an operational expression of the "do no harm" principle. Whatever the eventual outcomes of a particular negotiation or policy-making process, the human rights legal framework urges that minimally effective and accessible redress mechanisms be in place to ensure that those whose human rights were overlooked or traded-off against other interests are adequately compensated.

Finally, the scheme of socio-economic rights obligations reflected in the ICESCR and CRC could add important qualitative dimensions to decision-making in the climate change context. The above treaty obligations place an onus on States parties to move progressively forward in realising socio-economic rights, avoid arbitrary retrogression in the realisation of rights, undertake maximum efforts to realise rights within all available resources with priority given to the most excluded or vulnerable, ensure a core minimum level of rights for all, and – where best efforts are not sufficient – request international assistance. These process criteria obviously provide no more than a framework for complex policy decisions and trade-offs on climate change matters. They have obvious application in connection with planning decisions at the national or local levels on adaptation measures. However they could also arguably play an important role as criteria for prioritising among competing national claims for international assistance, cooperation and technology transfer for climate change mitigation and adaptation.

Substantive human rights standards – a focus on outcomes

Notwithstanding the important role played by procedural rights, a focus on individual human rights appears to offer little guidance in situations where rights seemingly conflict, as they often do. The critical role of procedural rights in framing, ordering and resolving such conflicts was already noted; however, relatively few procedural rights are firmly entrenched in international human rights law. Conflicts between rights appear particularly pronounced in many developing countries, where human development progress and efforts to provide energy for all are likely to lead to rapid increases in GHGs. Such increases could result directly or indirectly in the loss of small islands and low lying areas. The claims of some to development (and energy to fuel development), which might be indispensible for the progressive realisation of socio-economic rights in a given country, may directly conflict with the rights of others to their culture, livelihoods and territorial integrity. On what principled basis can one reconcile such claims?

Political philosopher Caney argues that, since in such a paradigmatic case both sets of rights relate to vital interests (of sufficient importance to impose obligations on others), it should be possible to satisfy both.[536] There are many fossil-fuel intensive climate endangering activities in other (primarily industrialized) parts of the world that relate to "relatively trivial interests" which, it is argued, should be cut back[537] in order to create space for increased GHG emissions for individuals without access to electricity, as well as to protect the territorial integrity and human rights of people in especially vulnerable situations.

The idea of "human rights thresholds" finds support in the analysis of human rights law and jurisprudence in Parts II and IV, in particular the idea of a "minimum core content" of socio-economic rights that should be respected at all times, and which should be prioritised in international assistance and cooperation. A minimum core bundle of rights that is to some degree amenable to quantification and, arguably, non-derogable, appears to correlate intuitively with Shue's concept of "survival emissions," or non-trivial emissions, providing a tailored national benchmark for the minimum level of GHG emissions needed to achieve the levels of economic growth commensurate with the resource requirements for the sustained realisation of that bundle of rights.

Of course, there are a number of important assumptions underpinning the above proposition. First, quantitative assessment of human rights obligations is subject to significant administrative and methodological constraints. Moreover, that economic growth flowing from any given level of GHG emissions in any given country will translate to human rights improvements for the poorest and those most vulnerable to climate change cannot be assumed. An objective inequality measure would be among the measures needed for the latter purpose. At a more basic level still, there is considerable disagreement in the scholarly literature on the CESCR's idea of a "minimum core,"[538] a state of affairs not helped by the Committee's apparently inconsistent application of this concept since the latter's formal inception in 1990.[539] National courts – even those more actively disposed towards positive socio-economic rights claims – have not so far appeared especially quick to embrace it.[540] Nevertheless, pending further conceptualisation and practical application of this concept at international and national levels, the idea of a minimum core content of socio-economic rights may yet prove capable of providing objective content and legal reinforcement to a "human rights threshold" concept anchored in States' own treaty obligations.

Strengthening legal accountability

Courts are beginning to focus on climate litigation. In the *Nigerian Gas Flaring Case*[541] the High Court of Nigeria held that the practice of gas flaring by Nigeria in the Niger Delta, violated guaranteed constitutional rights to life and dignity.[542] Litigation under tort and administrative law has had impacts at the national level: the U.S. Supreme Court declared that carbon dioxide is an air pollutant under that country's Clean Air Act with the consequence that automobile emissions should be regulated;[543] a ruling in Australia that GHG emissions from the burning of coal must be taken into account in a planning decision to approve a new coal mine;[544] and a ruling in Germany requiring public disclosure of the climate change impacts of German export credits.[545] In 2008, a federal lawsuit in the U.S. that sought to force two export credit agencies (the U.S. Import-Export Bank, and the U.S. Overseas Private Investment Corporation) to address the global warming implications of their overseas financing activities was settled, establishing important legal precedents related to global warming,[546] and as of 2009 judgement was awaited on a suit brought against oil companies by Inuit peoples in Alaska under the tort of public nuisance for harms due to climate change.[547]

Finally, while the focus of the present discussion is on legal accountability mechanisms, fuller exploration of administrative mechanisms is also needed, beginning with EIAs (informed by human rights concerns). As indicated earlier, EIAs find support under general principles of international law, regional custom in Europe, as well as, arguably, emerging global administrative law,[548] and can be viewed as an operational extension or application of the "do no harm" rule in general international law. Practically, it may be that one way of integrating human rights considerations into responses to climate change would be to integrate them within EIAs.[549] There are numerous practical experiences of human rights impact assessments from which to draw, removing the need to re-invent the wheel from a technical or methodological standpoint, a prominent example of which is the IFC Guide To Human Rights Impact Assessment[550] The UNFCCC has developed a "Compendium of Methods and Tools to Evaluate Impacts of, and Vulnerability and Adaptation to, Climate Change,"[551] which include IPCC Technical Guidelines for Assessing Climate Change Impacts and Adaptations[552] as well as the United Nations Environment Programme (UNEP) Handbook on Methods for Climate Change Impact Assessment and Adaptation Strategies.[553]

While there is no template for a human rights impact assessment, the principal elements that emerge from the literature and practice include: (a) incorporating internationally recognized human rights as the explicit subject of the assessment;[554] (b) identify indicators for the assessment that are consistent with relevant international human rights standards; (c) focusing upon people who are most excluded and marginalized along with responsible actors (not necessarily limited to organs of the State), drawing conclusions in terms of impact on the enjoyment of human rights and fulfilment of obligations; (d) striving to ensure that the assessment, as far as possible, contributes to building the capacities of relevant national stakeholders (defined in human rights jargon as "rights holders" and "duty bearers"); (e) ensuring that the process of carrying out the assessment respects "good process" principles such as those outlined earlier, both as a general matter of policy, and more particularly to the extent that those principles enjoy solid foundations in international human rights law binding upon the country(ies) concerned; and (f) seeking to involve human rights mechanisms and actors as far as possible, for example national human rights institutions, subject to their mandated functions and capacities.[555]

Quantitative assessments of human rights performance

Some suggest that human rights principles and tools of analysis could serve a valuable function in deepening the ideas of differential treatment and "equity" embodied in the UNFCCC, and helping to prioritise between poorer countries' claims for international support, and at least indirectly, galvanize support for international cooperation and strengthened aid commitments. All States parties to either the ICESCR or CRC undertake to take steps individually and through international assistance and cooperation to the maximum of their available resources on socio-economic rights, with a particular focus on minimum survival needs and the most excluded individuals and groups, as a prerequisite to valid claims for international assistance. Under these instruments, any retrogression must be strongly justified.

There is an emerging body of research and practice in the field of quantitative assessments of human rights, going directly to the question of whether governments are dedicating sufficient resources and policy effort towards the realization of their obligations under the ICESCR. The expanding field of rights-based budget analysis may offer promising avenues for further development and exploitation to these ends.[556] There are a numerous other monitoring tools and approaches being developed and tested as well, for application at national as well as sub-national levels. For example, the Center for Economic and Social Rights produces fact sheets revealing cross-country comparisons of budget expenditure on various rights to support advocacy as well as periodic reviews by the CESCR of national reports under the ICESCR.[557] The University of East Anglia and the Overseas Development Institute are pursuing similar purposes through a more elaborate and data-intensive approach using econometric analysis, costing exercises and modeling of affordability constraints.[558] A more simplified approach relying upon cross-country comparisons is the "Index of Economic and Social Rights Fulfilment" initiative of Lawson-Remer, Fukuda-Parr and Randolph, a composite index purporting to reveal comparative insights about the adequacy of government efforts in fulfilling a defined bundle of socio-economic rights.[559] This expanding field of inter-disciplinary research may offer potential to help those most at risk from climate change to ensure that their own governments, at the least, are doing their utmost to realize basic socio-economic rights obligations embedded within national adaptation responses, while contributing an important qualitative dimension to ideas about "equity" in international burden-sharing. These methods may also help more effectively monitor donor transparency and performance, subject to the further evolution of "positive" extra-territorial human rights obligations under international law.

Engaging the private sector

Progress on climate change depends to a great extent upon an active private sector, including business leaders, investors, commercial banks, insurance companies, and trading corporations. The private sector's role is critical in connection with all four pillars of the 2007 Bali Action Plan: mitigation, adaptation, financing and technology transfer. As discussed earlier, a variety of adaptation funding channels are available under the UNFCCC, however they have a complex architecture, high transaction costs, and available resources are limited compared with the scale of demands: hundreds of millions of dollars, compared with the billions required for adaptation.[560] While official aid flows remain critical for many lower income countries,[561] Foreign Direct Investment (FDI, or intra-firm trade) and private capital flows to developing countries had, until the onset of the 2008 global financial crisis, been playing an increasingly important role.[562] Fossil fuel, agribusiness, forestry and manufacturing industries have drawn sustained criticism for adverse environmental and social impacts from rising global GHG emissions, and for prioritising investment in fossil fuels over renewable energy sources. But at the same time, the role of industry is central to prospects for the development and dissemination of clean new technologies for both mitigation and adaptation purposes, for the effective and equitable operation of emissions trading regimes, and for supporting national transformations to climate-sensitive and climate-resilient economies.

Many private actors are now showing an explicit interest in human rights.[563] There are any number of voluntary codes and corporate social responsibility initiatives of indirect if not direct relevance to human rights and the environment, from the UN Secretary-General's "Global Compact" initiative[564] to the Equator Principles, a set of nine principles and associated benchmarks for the financial industry to manage social and environmental issues in project financing.[565] Many if not most major banks, financial institutions and transnational corporations have adhered to these or other voluntary codes and some have developed human rights policies[566] and climate-friendly policies, projects or partnership initiatives.[567] The IFC, together with the International Business Leaders Forum, has developed a sophisticated "human rights impact assessment" tool to ensure that private investors are not complicit in human rights violations occurring through IFC-supported projects.[568] It seems a striking paradox that an innovative methodological development of this sort, constructed explicitly around the framework of international human rights law, should have emerged from the IFC and business leaders, rather than States parties to the treaty sources of that law.

Voluntarism and corporate social responsibility aside, to what extent might private sector actors have responsibilities for human rights? There is an abundant literature on this topic, which is currently the subject of inquiry by the Special Representative of the UN Secretary General (SRSG) on Business and Human Rights, John Ruggie.[569] It is difficult to summarise the history and literature in this area,[570] however the SRSG has proposed a simple tripartite policy framework for transnational corporations (TNCs) and business entities with regard to human rights that has attracted widespread endorsement of States as well as business leaders. Without questioning the primacy of States as principal duty-bearers under international law, the SRSG has stated that TNCs and other such actors have responsibilities to "respect" international human rights law within the sphere of their activities (while hedging to a degree on the legal as distinct from moral basis for this responsibility), and that states have duties to "protect" human rights by putting in place an appropriate regulatory regime addressing the human rights implications of TNCs' activities, as well as "remedy" any violations.[571] This framework was unanimously approved by the United Nations Human Rights Council in 2008, and has begun to be discussed and applied at the national level in a number of countries, and the focus of SRSG during the remainder of his mandate is to translate the framework into practical guiding principles. On 22 November 2010, the SRSG posted the draft, "Guiding Principles for the Implementation of the UN 'Protect, Respect and Remedy' Framework" on his online consultation forum.[572] The SRSG has not given significant treatment to the possible connections between human rights and climate change specifically, however further clarity on business human rights responsibilities will help articulate convincing normative and operational relationships between these two fields in the longer term.

The foregoing suggests priorities for a graduated programme for further research in the short to longer-term timeframes to explore the nexus between climate change and human rights through the lens of private sector responses.[573] In the view of the significant practical momentum and political consensus surrounding the SRSG's work at present, a potentially desirable approach in the short-term might be to – in effect – build theory from practice, by supporting, replicating and evaluating national initiatives to apply the SRSG's tripartite framework of TNCs and business enterprises' human rights duties (as embodied in the SRSG's forthcoming guiding principles) in the myriad contexts where it may be relevant.[574] Further support might also be given to the application and progressive refinement of the IFC's human rights impact assessment tool, in a manner that seeks to integrate partner countries' responsibilities under environmental, trade, intellectual property and investment regimes. A focus on "due diligence" obligations associated with the responsibility to "respect" potentially offers a pragmatic window into the political space where consensus is strongest, as well as a potentially vibrant field of existing practice where methodology development (including the field of human rights, social and environmental impact assessment) is already advanced. Alternatively, or in addition, there could be mileage in focusing upon practical mechanisms of accountability relevant to the access to "remedy" for victims of human rights violations, of a judicial or administrative kind, including mechanisms established by TNCs and business entities themselves,[575] which similarly offers a considerable body of existing experience from which to draw.

Technology Access and Transfer

Notwithstanding the challenges discussed in Parts IV and V about extending the regulatory reach of international law to the sphere of extra-territorial responsibilities, it seems likely that many low income countries which are most vulnerable to adverse climate change impacts, and the most vulnerable groups within those countries, may have great difficulties adapting to foreseeable risks without access to technology in a wide range of areas that they do not presently possess, and which they might not be expected to generate internally within a meaningful timeframe.[576] The role of technology will be more critical still in the mitigation context,[577] although as with adaptation a great many existing technologies could be deployed in many contexts at comparatively little cost, and in many cases with quick positive returns.[578]

Under Article 4 of the UNFCCC State parties, taking into account their common but differentiated responsibilities and their specific priorities, objectives and circumstances have undertaken, among other things, to" "[c] Promote and cooperate in the development, application and diffusion, including transfer of technologies, practices and processes that control, reduce or prevent anthropogenic emissions of greenhouse gases ... in all relevant sectors..." The Bali Action Plan, moreover, calls for a range of cooperative actions including: "enhanced national/international action on mitigation of climate change, including the consideration of mitigation actions by developing countries supported and enabled by technology, financing and capacity-building and cooperative sectoral approaches and sector-specific actions, in order to enhance implementation of Article 4, paragraph 1(c) of the UNFCCC;" and "enhanced action on the provision of financial resources and investment to support action on mitigation and adaptation and technology cooperation, including the consideration of innovative means of funding to assist developing country Parties that are particularly vulnerable to the adverse impacts of climate change in meeting the cost of adaptation."[579] However, these provisions have allegedly proved difficult to implement in practice, due to lack of agreement on their meaning and the complexity in identifying technology-related needs and priorities.[580]

In the process leading up to the Copenhagen Conference, technology matters were being addressed in two main Subsidiary bodies under the UNFCCC: the Subsidiary Body for Scientific and Technological Advice (SBSTA), including its Expert Group on Technology Transfer (EGTT), and the Subsidiary Body for Implementation (SBI).[581] While Article 4 of the UNFCCC, the Bali Plan of Action, and the mandates of the above subsidiary bodies contemplate technology in a broad sense, the issue of transfer of technology and related intellectual property issues have dominated the discussions among States as well as among other actors. While the focus on technology transfer is important, some commentators have suggested that the current approach and debate is too narrow particularly insofar as specific sectoral technology needs are concerned.[582] Taking the health sector as an example, there may be barriers related to innovation in the health technology sector particularly with respect to incentive and financing mechanisms; barriers related to the structure of the health technology markets and, in particular, the pricing and technology transfer models; and political or ideological barriers associated with the lack of an evidence-based monitoring framework.[583] It has been argued that a "framework based on the right to health can help ensure that the solutions contemplated under the Bali Action Plan are not too narrow and that all the three levels of barriers are adequately addressed to enable access to relevant health technologies for reducing climate change-related health vulnerabilities especially in developing countries."[584]

It is difficult to generalize further about the possible contributions of human rights to such a complex field as technology policy. The International Council on Human Rights Policy has carried out an extensive research project on these questions, with a final report published in early 2010.[585] In general terms, however, the comparative advantages and contributions of human rights could be seen in light of the factors discussed in Part II. In relation to technology policy, human rights could assist with the process of analysis, identifying obstacles to the development and transfer of needed technologies, as well as the definition of responses and the determination of legal obligations in regard to technology-related needs and policies, plausibly contributing to "more equitable, more comprehensive and more effective policies" for technology transfer.[586] As a framework of entitlements and obligations with the State as principal duty-bearer, approaches to technology policy that are grounded in international human rights law may indicate avenues for public action in correcting market failures in order to provide incentives and information needed to ensure the transfer of accessible and adequate technologies to poorer regions and least developed countries.[587]

A New International Instrument on Climate-Induced Displacement?[588]

If we really care for the texture of international law and its intellectual integrity, we should do something solid about the practical problems that are encouraging its distortion, and not simply spend our time lamenting it.[589]

On current predictions, as many as 200 million people may be displaced as a consequence of climate change by the year 2050, that is to say, approximately one person in every fourteen world-wide.[590] Entire nations, such as the Maldives and Tuvalu, are likely, if current GHG emission trends continue, to be lost to sea level rise, rendering their inhabitants stateless. Tuvalu is negotiating agreements with Australia and New Zealand to move its 12,000 strong population,[591] and the Maldives has started saving to buy land to resettle its 400,000 strong population to India or Sri Lanka.[592] Australia's previous government (reportedly) refused Tuvalu's request twice, while New Zealand agreed to accept 75 immigrants every year.[593] Restrictive definitions in international refugee law, a regime already overburdened due to institutional and resource constraints, will preclude claims arising therein.[594] Discrimination issues are also endemic in forced displacement and refugee law, with the most vulnerable individuals and populations often being least able to migrate, and facing serious protection concerns when they do.[595] As discussed in Part III, to the extent that forced displacement is or may be attributable to anthropogenic climate change (particularly fossil-fuel intensive activities of industrialised countries geared to comparatively trivial uses), this appears to open up a large lacuna in the existing normative and institutional edifice of international law.

Given the very possible scale of the human tides to come, and in light of the current state of the existing international refugee regime, some commentators have called for a new international agreement on what are sometimes called "climate refugees," or on the human rights of those displaced by climate change. The proposals vary in the scale of ambition. A minimalist approach might be the revision of the 1951 Convention on the Status of Refugees to include climate (or environmental) refugees and to offer legal protections similar to those for refugees fleeing political persecution.[596] Others have argued for a new convention modelled on human rights principles providing temporary protections for environmental displacement and addressing root causes,[597] while others have argued for regional efforts under the umbrella of the UNFCCC.[598]

More ambitiously, Docherty and Giannini have argued for a new climate change refugee legal instrument that draws on multiple areas of the law, including human rights, humanitarian, and international environmental law, to address situations where gradual or sudden disruption "consistent with climate change," where human activity has "more likely than not" contributed to the disruption, leads to temporary or permanent trans-boundary forced migration.[599] This proposal would be supported by the establishment of a global fund,[600] a separate coordinating agency, legal enforcement procedures, and a body of scientific experts charged with making independent determinations on the types of environmental disruptions encompassed by the proposed definition of climate change refugee, States parties' proportionate contributions to the proposed global fund in line with the "common but differentiated responsibility" criterion, as well as conduct general studies about the problem of climate change as it relates to refugee flows.[601] Hodgkinson et. al. propose a similar scheme but de-link it from the 1951 Refugee Convention framework, arguing that much climate-related displacement is likely to take place within national borders and that those most acutely vulnerable will often not be in a position to migrate internationally.[602]

However, proposals linked to the revision of the 1951 Convention must confront the fact of internal resistance to such proposals within UNHCR.[603] In any case, as the proposal of Hodginson et. al. has recognised, the traditional approach in refugee law of individualised decision-making in accordance with case-by-case application of technical legal criteria appears uniquely ill-suited to the scale and nature of climate-induced displacement.[604] As one commentator has put it, in the current climate of hostility towards asylum-seekers, the "unpleasant politics of definitions" is best dealt with by doing "our utmost to defend the 1951 Convention, while at the same time calling for improved international legal regimes and institutions to protect other kinds of forced migrants."[605] However, there are also serious obstacles facing proposals for an entirely new regime. Some of these are conceptual or legal in nature, such as defining "climate induced displacement" or "climate refugee, "given the multiple causes of displacement and slow-onset of climate-induced displacement in particular.[606]

It is worth recalling that on current predictions most people displaced by climate change are likely to remain within their own nation, rather than cross borders.[607] This underscores the importance of ensuring the more widespread enforcement of existing national human rights protections, including the 1998 Guiding Principles on Internal Displacement,[608] which – while not legally binding in and of themselves – constitute a synthesis and reformulation of norms of binding international human rights and humanitarian law of relevance to those displaced within their countries by internal conflict, natural disasters and other situations of forced displacement (including, conceivably, factors related to climate change). Pending further research and consensus-building towards specific new norms or institutions, the 1998 Guiding Principles might be seen as "not just a starting point in their own right, but also a model for the process of aggregating and adapting the norms and principles from a wide range of international instruments to protect the rights of the 'environmentally displaced.' "[609]

CHAPTER VII.

List of References

Books

A DICTIONARY OF HUMAN RIGHTS (David Robertson ed., 2007).

ADJUDICATING CLIMATE CONTROL: SUB-NATIONAL, NATIONAL AND SUPRA-NATIONAL APPROACHES (Hari M. Osofsky & William C. G. Burns eds., 2008).

AGARWAL, ANIL & SUNITA NARAIN, GLOBAL WARMING IN AN UNEQUAL WORLD: A CASE OF ENVIRONMENTAL COLONIALISM (1991).

AKEHURST, MICHAEL, A MODERN INTRODUCTION TO INTERNATIONAL LAW (5th ed. 1984).

ANANTHAPADMANABHAN, G. ET. AL., HIDING BEHIND THE POOR (2007).

ANDERSON, MARY, DO NO HARM: HOW AID CAN SUPPORT PEACE – OR WAR (1999).

BAER, PAUL ET. AL., THE GREENHOUSE DEVELOPMENT RIGHTS FRAMEWORK: THE RIGHT TO DEVELOPMENT IN A CLIMATE CONSTRAINED WORLD (2nd rev. ed., 2008).

BAER, PAUL ET. AL., THE RIGHT TO DEVELOPMENT IN A CLIMATE CONSTRAINED WORLD (2008).

BALS, CHRISTOPH ET. AL., CLIMATE CHANGE, FOOD SECURITY AND THE RIGHT TO ADEQUATE FOOD (2008).

BARRO, ROBERT, DETERMINANTS OF ECONOMIC GROWTH: A CROSS-COUNTRY EMPIRICAL STUDY (1997).

BIRNIE, PATRICIA W. & A. E. BOYLE, INTERNATIONAL LAW AND THE ENVIRONMENT (2nd ed., 2002).

BODANSKY, DANIEL, THE ART AND CRAFT OF INTERNATIONAL ENVIRONMENTAL LAW (2009).

BREMS, EVA, HUMAN RIGHTS: UNIVERSALITY AND DIVERSITY (2001).

BROWNLIE, IAN, PRINCIPLES OF PUBLIC INTERNATIONAL LAW (1998).

BROWNLIE, IAN, THE HUMAN RIGHT TO DEVELOPMENT (1989).

CARLSTON, S., LAW AND ORGANIZATION IN WORLD SOCIETY (1962).

CHAYES, ABRAM & ANTONIA CHAYES, THE NEW SOVEREIGNTY: COMPLIANCE WITH INTERNATIONAL REGULATORY AGREEMENTS (1995).

Cheng, Bin, General Principles of Law as Applied by International Courts and Tribunals (1953).

Clapham, Andrew, Human Rights Obligations of Non-State Actors (2006).

CNA CORPORATION, NATIONAL SECURITY AND THE THREAT OF CLIMATE CHANGE (2007).

CORE OBLIGATIONS: BUILDING A FRAMEWORK FOR ECONOMIC, SOCIAL AND CULTURAL RIGHTS (Audrey Chapman & Sage Russell eds., 2002).

CRAIG, PAUL & GRAINNE DE BÚRCA, E.U. LAW: TEXT, CASES, Materials (4th ed. 2007).

Craven, Mathew R., The International Covenant on Economic, Social and Cultural Rights: A Perspective on its Development (1995).

de Sadeleer, Nicholas, Environmental Principles: From Political Slogans to Legal Rules (2002).

Deng, Frances Mading et. al., Sovereignty as Responsibility: Conflict Management in Africa (1996).

Doelle, Meinhard, From Hot Air to Action? Climate Change, Compliance and the Future of International Environmental Law (2005).

Dworkin, Ronald, Taking Rights Seriously (1999).

Economic, Social and Cultural Rights in Action (Mashood A. Baderin & Robert McCorquodale eds., 2007).

Elson, Diane, Budgeting for Women's Rights: Monitoring Government Budgets for Compliance with CEDAW (2006).

Foti, J. et. al., Voice and Choice: Opening the Door to Environmental Democracy (2008).

Gauri, Varun & Dan Brinks, Courting Social Justice: Judicial Enforcement of Social and Economic Rights in the Developing World (2008).

Gillespie, Alexander, International Environmental Law, Policy and Ethics (1997).

Global Commons Institute, Contraction and Convergence: A Global Solution for a Global Problem, (1994–2008).

Hannum, Hurst, Autonomy, Sovereignty, and Self-Determination: The Accommodation of Conflicting Rights (1996).

Hayward, Tim, Constitutional Environmental Rights (2005).

Human Rights and the Environment: Conflicts and Norms in a Globalizing World (Lyuba Zarsky ed., 2002).

Human Rights Approaches to Environmental Protection (Alan Boyle & Michael Anderson eds., 1996).

Human Rights, Sustainable Development and the Environment (Antônio Augusto Cancado Trindade ed., 1992).

Humphreys, Stephen, The Human Rights Dimensions of Climate Change: A Rough Guide (2008).

Hunter, David et. al., International Environmental Law and Policy (1998).

Joseph, Sarah et. al., The International Covenant on Civil and Political Rights: Cases, Materials, and Commentary (2000).

Kiss, Alexandre & Dinah Shelton, International Environmental Law (1991).

Lauterpacht, H., The Development of International Law by the International Court (rev. ed. 1958).

Linking Human Rights and the Environment (Romina Picolotti & Jorge D. Taillant eds., 2003).

Lomborg, Bjorn, The Skeptical Environmentalist (2001).

Mwandosya, Mark J., Survival Emissions: A Perspective From The South On Global Climate Negotiations (1999).

Naylor, Rosamond L. et. al., The Ripple Effect: Biofuels, Food Security and the Environment (2007).

Non-State Actors and Human Rights (Philip Alston ed., 2005).

Nowak, Manfred, U.N. Covenant on Civil and Political Rights: CCPR Commentary (2005).

OXFORD HANDBOOK ON INTERNATIONAL RELATIONS (Christian Reus-Smit & Duncan Snidal, eds, 2008).

POGGE, THOMAS, WORLD POVERTY AND HUMAN RIGHTS (2002).

QUINN, GERARD & LEO FLYNN, THE U.N. CHARTER ON FUNDAMENTAL RIGHTS (2005).

RAGGAZZI, MAURIZIO, THE CONCEPT OF INTERNATIONAL OBLIGATIONS ERGA OMNES (1997).

RAJAMANI, LAVANYA, DIFFERENTIAL TREATMENT IN INTERNATIONAL ENVIRONMENTAL LAW (2006).

RESERVATIONS TO HUMAN RIGHTS TREATIES AND THE VIENNA CONVENTION REGIME (Ineta Ziemele ed., 2004).

RHYNE, CHARLES, INTERNATIONAL LAW: THE SUBSTANCE, PROCESS, PROCEDURES AND INSTITUTIONS FOR WORLD PEACE WITH JUSTICE (1971).

ROBERTS, TIMMONS & BRADLEY C. PARKS, A CLIMATE OF INJUSTICE: GLOBAL INEQUALITY, NORTH-SOUTH POLITICS AND CLIMATE POLICY (2007).

ROSENNE, SHABTAI, PRACTICE AND METHODS OF INTERNATIONAL LAW (1984).

ROTHSCHILD, DONALD, ET. AL., SOVEREIGNTY AS RESPONSIBILITY: CONFLICT MANAGEMENT IN AFRICA (1996).

SALMAN, SALMAN & SIOBHÁN MCINERNEY-LANKFORD, THE HUMAN RIGHT TO WATER, LEGAL AND POLICY DIMENSIONS (2004).

SANDS, PHILIPPE, PRINCIPLES OF INTERNATIONAL ENVIRONMENTAL LAW (2nd ed., vol. 1, 2003).

SAVE THE CHILDREN UK, THE LEGACY OF DISASTERS: THE IMPACT OF CLIMATE CHANGE ON CHILDREN (2007).

SEIDERMAN, IAN, HIERARCHY IN INTERNATIONAL LAW: THE HUMAN RIGHTS DIMENSION (2001).

Sepúlveda, Magdalena, The Nature of the Obligation under the Covenant on Economic, Social and Cultural Rights (2003).

SHUE, HENRY, BASIC RIGHTS (1996).

SKOGLY, SIGRUN, BEYOND NATIONAL BORDERS: STATES' HUMAN RIGHTS OBLIGATIONS IN INTERNATIONAL COOPERATION (2006).

SMITH, JOSEPH & DAVID SHEARMAN, CLIMATE CHANGE LITIGATION: ANALYSING THE LAW, SCIENTIFIC EVIDENCE & IMPACTS ON THE ENVIRONMENT, HEALTH & PROPERTY (2006).

Stern, Nicholas, Climate Change and the Creation of a New Era of Progress and Prosperity (2009).

STIFTUNG, FRIEDRICH EBERT & CENTER FOR INTERNATIONAL ENVIRONMENTAL LAW, HUMAN RIGHTS AND CLIMATE CHANGE: PRACTICAL STEPS FOR IMPLEMENTATION (2009).

TAMS, CHRISTIAN J., ENFORCING OBLIGATIONS ERGA OMNES IN INTERNATIONAL LAW (2005).

THE INTERNATIONAL LAW COMMISSION'S ARTICLES ON STATE RESPONSIBILITY: INTRODUCTION, TEXT AND COMMENTARIES (James Crawford ed., 2002).

TRANSNATIONAL CORPORATIONS AND HUMAN RIGHTS (Olivier de Schutter ed., 2006).

TROUWBORST, ARIE, EVOLUTION AND STATUS OF THE PRECAUTIONARY PRINCIPLE IN INTERNATIONAL LAW (2002).

VERHEYEN, RODA, CLIMATE CHANGE DAMAGE AND INTERNATIONAL LAW: PREVENTION DUTIES AND STATE RESPONSIBILITY (2005).

WALKER, SIMON, HUMAN RIGHTS IMPACT ASSESSMENT OF TRADE AGREEMENTS: ADDING VALUE? (forthcomming 2009).

WEISS, EDITH BROWN ET. AL., INTERNATIONAL ENVIRONMENTAL LAW AND POLICY (1998).

WORLD HEALTH ORGANIZATION & OFFICE OF THE HIGH COMMISSIONER ON HUMAN RIGHTS, HEALTH, HUMAN RIGHTS AND POVERTY REDUCTION STRATEGIES (2009).
WORLD HEALTH ORGANIZATION, PROTECTING HEALTH FROM CLIMATE CHANGE (2008).

Articles, Chapters in Edited Collections, Reports and Papers

3D & Associates, *Menace sur le droit à l'alimentation de l'enfant : la protection intellectuelle des semences (Burkina Faso)*, Report submitted to the Committee on the Rights of the Child (Oct. 2009).

Abate, Randall S., *Climate Change, the United States and the Impacts of Arctic Melting: A Case Study in the Need for Enforceable International Environmental Human Rights*, 26 STAN. ENVTL. L.J. 3 (2007).

Adam, David, *Indigenous Rights Row threatens Rainforest Protection Plan*, THE GUARDIAN (Dec. 9, 2008).

Adam, David, *Stern Attacks Politicians for Climate "Devastation,"* THE GUARDIAN (Mar. 13, 2009).

Alston, Philip & Gerard Quinn, *The Nature and Scope of States Parties' Obligations under the International Covenant on Economic, Social and Cultural Rights*, 9 HUM. RTS. Q. 156 (1987).

Alston, Philip, *A Third Generation of Solidarity Rights: Progressive Development or Obfuscation of International Human Rights Law*, 29 NETH. INT'L L. REV. 307 (1982).

Alston, Philip, *Conjuring Up New Human Rights: A Proposal for Quality Control*, 78 AM. J. INT'L L. 607 (1984).

Alston, Philip, *People's Rights: Their Rise and Fall*, in PEOPLE'S RIGHTS (Alston ed., 2001).

Alston, Philip, *Ships Passing in the Night: The Current State of the Human Rights and Development Debate as Seen Through the Lens of the Millennium Development Goals*, 27 HUM. RTS. Q. 755 (2005).

Aminzadeh, Sara C., *A Moral Imperative: The Human Rights Implications of Climate Change*, 30(2) HASTINGS INT'L & COMP. L. REV. 231 (2007).

Anderson, Edward & Andy McKay, *Human Rights, the MDG Income Poverty Target and Economic Growth*, Background paper for U.N./OHCHR Africa and Asia Regional MDGs and Human Rights Dialogues for Action (forthcoming 2009).

Anderson, Edward & Marta Foresti, *Assessing Compliance: the Challenge for Economic and Social Rights*, OXFORD J. HUM. RTS. PRAC. (Sept. 11, 2009).

Anderson, Michael R., *Human Rights Approaches to Environmental Protection: An Overview*, in HUMAN RIGHTS APPROACHES TO ENVIRONMENTAL PROTECTION (Alan Boyle & Michael Anderson eds., 1996).

Arsajani, Mahnoush H. & W. Michael Reisman, *The Quest for an International Liability Regime for the Protection of the Global Commons*, in INTERNATIONAL LAW THEORY AND PRACTICE, ESSAYS IN HONOUR OF ERIC SUY (K. Wellens ed.,1998).

Atapattu, Sumundu, *The Public Health Impact of Global Environmental Problems and the Role of International Law*, 30 AM. J. L. & MED. 283 (2004).

Atapattu, Sumundu, *The Right to a Healthy Life or the Right to Die Polluted? The Emergence of a Human Right to a Healthy Environment under International Law*, 17 TUL. ENVTL. L.J. 65 (2002).

Australian Human Rights Commission, *The Australian Mining and Resource Sector and Human Rights: 2009 Good Practice, Good Business, Fact Sheet No. 3* (2009).

Balakrishnan, Radhika, Diane Elson & Raj Patel, *Rethinking Macro Economic Strategies from a Human Rights Perspective (Why MES with Human Rights II)*, Carnegie Policy Innovations (Feb. 2009).

Barsh, Russel Lawrence, *The Right To Development as a Human Right: Results of the Global Consultation*, 13 HUM. RTS Q. 322 (1991).

Bassiouni, M. Cherif, *A Functional Approach to General Principles of International Law*, 11 MICH. J. INT'L L. 768 (1989-90).

Baxi, Upendra, *Voices of Suffering and the Future of Human Rights*, 8 TRANSNT'L & CONTEMP. PROBS. 125 (1998).

Betten, Lammy, *The EU Charter on Fundamental Rights: A Trojan Horse or a Mouse?*, 17 INT'L J. COMP. LAB. L. & INDUS. REL. 151 (2001).

Beyerlin, Ulrich, *Different Types of Norms in International Environmental Law: Policies, Principles and Rules*, in OXFORD HANDBOOK OF INTERNATIONAL ENVIRONMENTAL LAW (Daniel Bodansky et. al., eds., 2007).

Biermann, Frank, *Reforming Global Environmental Governance: From UNEP towards a World Environment Organization*, in GLOBAL ENVIRONMENTAL GOVERNANCE: PERSPECTIVES ON THE CURRENT DEBATE (Lydia Swart & Estelle Perry, eds., 2007).

Bodansky, Daniel et. al., *International Environmental Law: Mapping the Field*, in OXFORD HANDBOOK OF INTERNATIONAL ENVIRONMENTAL LAW (Daniel Bodansky et. al., eds., 2007).

Bodansky, Daniel, *Customary (and Not So Customary) International Environmental Law*, 3 IND. J. GLOBAL LEGAL STUD. 105 (1995).

Bodansky, Daniel, *Deconstructing the Precautionary Principle*, in BRINGING NEW LAW TO OCEAN WATERS (D.D. Caron & H.N. Schieber eds., 2004).

Bourguignon, François, *The Growth Elasticity of Poverty Reduction: Explaining Heterogeneity across Countries and Time Periods*, in INEQUALITY AND GROWTH: THEORY AND POLICY IMPLICATIONS (T.S. Eicher and S.J. Turnovsky eds., 2003).

Boyle, Alan, *Human Rights or Environmental Rights? A Reassessment*, 18 FORDHAM ENVTL. L. REV. 471 (2007).

Boyle, Alan, *Principle of Cooperation: the Environment*, in UNITED NATIONS AND THE PRINCIPLES OF INTERNATIONAL LAW (Vaughan Lowe & Colin Warbrick eds., 1994).

Boyle, Alan, *The Role of International Human Rights Law in the Protection of the Environment*, in HUMAN RIGHTS APPROACHES TO ENVIRONMENTAL PROTECTION (Alan Boyle & Michael Anderson eds., 1996).

Bradsher, Keith, *UN programme to fight global warming is target of criticism*, NEW YORK TIMES (May 8, 2007).

Bratspies, Rebecca, *Rethinking Decisionmaking in International Environmental Law: A Process-Oriented Inquiry into Sustainable Development*, 32 YALE J. INT'L L. 363 (2007).

Brinks, Daniel M. & Varun Gauri, *A New Policy Landscape: Legalizing Social and Economic Rights in the Developing World*, in COURTING SOCIAL JUSTICE: JUDICIAL ENFORCEMENT OF SOCIAL AND ECONOMIC RIGHTS IN THE DEVELOPING WORLD (Varun Gauri & Daniel Brinks 2008).

Brookings, *The Guiding Principles on Internal Displacement* (2009), http://www.brookings.edu/projects/idp/gp_page.aspx.

Brown, Oli & Elec Crawford, *Rising Temperatures, Rising Tensions: Climate Change and the Risk of Violent Conflict in the Middle East*, International Institute for Sustainable Development (2009).

Brown, Oli, *Migration and Climate Change*, International Organization for Migration, Migration Research Series No. 31 (2008).

Brownlie, Ian, *The Rights of Peoples in Modern International Law*, in THE RIGHTS OF PEOPLES (James Crawford ed., 1988).

Bueno de Mesquita, Judith & Paul Hunt, *The Human Rights Responsibility of International Assistance and Cooperation in Health*, in UNIVERSAL HUMAN RIGHTS AND EXTRATERRITORIAL OBLIGATIONS (Mark Gibney & Sigrun Skogly eds., 2009).

Buergenthal, Thomas, *The World Bank and Human Rights*, in THE WORLD BANK AND INTERNATIONAL FINANCIAL INSTITUTIONS AND THE DEVELOPMENT OF INTERNATIONAL LAW (Edith Brown Weiss et. al., eds., 1999).

Buergenthal, Thomas, *To Respect and to Ensure: State Obligations and Permissible Derogations*, in THE INTERNATIONAL BILL OF RIGHTS (Louis Henkin ed., 1981).

Burleson, Elizabeth, *Energy Policy, Intellectual Property, and Technology Transfer to Address Climate Change*, 18 TRANSN'L L. CONTEMP. PROBS. 69 (2009).

Burns, William C. G., *Potential Causes of Action for Climate Change Impacts Under the United Nations Fish Stocks Agreement*, 7(2) J. SUSTAINABLE DEV. L. & POL'Y 34 (2007).

Burns, William C. G., *Potential Causes of Action for Climate Change Damages in International Fora: The Law of the Sea Convention*, 1(2) J. SUSTAINABLE DEV. L. & POL'Y 27 (2006).

Cameron, Edward, *The Human Dimension of Global Climate Change*, 15 HASTINGS W.-NW J. ENVTL. L. & POL'Y 1 (2009).

Caney, Simon, *Climate Change and Injustice: A Human Rights Perspective*, J. GLOBAL ETHICS (forthcoming 2008-9).

Caney, Simon, *Climate Technology Transfer: A Derivation of Rights- and Duty-Bearers from Fundamental Human Rights*, Background Paper, International Council on Human Rights Policy (July 9-10, 2009).

Caney, Simon, *Cosmopolitan Justice, Responsibility and Global Climate Change*, 18 LEIDEN J. INT'L L. 747 (2005).

Caney, Simon, *Global Justice, Rights and Climate Change*, 19 CAN. J. L. & JURISPRUDENCE 255 (2006).

Caney, Simon, *Human Rights, Climate Change and Discounting*, 17(4) ENVTL POL. 536 (2008).

Carrillo-Salcedo, Juan-Antonio, *Book Reviews and Notes: The Concept of International Obligations Erga Omnes. By Maurizio Ragazzi*, 92 AM. J. INT'L L. 791 (1998).

Cassese, Antonio, *The Self-Determination of Peoples*, in THE INTERNATIONAL BILL OF RIGHTS – THE COVENANT ON CIVIL AND POLITICAL RIGHTS (Louis Henkin ed., 1981).

Center for International Environmental Law, *Technology Transfer in the UNFCCC and Other International Legal Regimes: The Challenge of Systemic Integration*, Background Paper, International Council on Human Rights Policy Review Meeting (July 2009).

Center for Naval Analyses Corporation, *National Security and the Threat of Climate Change* (2007).

Charlesworth, Andrew, *Clean Development Mechanism rejections skyrocket: UN regulators respond to "incompetence" claim by clamping down on approvals*, BUSINESSGREEN (Apr. 14, 2008).

Charlesworth, Hilary & Christine Chinkin, *The Gender of Jus Cogens*, 15 Hum. Rts. Q. 63 (1993).

Charney, Jonathan I., *Universal International Law*, 87 Am. J. Int'l L. 529 (1993).

Chellaney, Brahma, *Climate Change and Security in Southern Asia: Understanding the National Security Implications*, 152(2) Royal United Services Inst. J. 63 (Apr. 2007).

Christian Aid, *Growing Pairs: The Possibilities and Problems of Biofuels* (2009).

Christian Aid, *Human Tide: The Real Migration Crisis* (May 2007).

Churchill, Robin, *Environmental Rights in Existing Human Rights Treaties*, in Human Rights Approaches to Environmental Protection (Alan Boyle & Michael Anderson eds., 1996).

Climate Institute, *Breaking Through on Technology: Perspectives for Australia* (June 2009).

Cook, Kate, *Environmental Rights as Human Rights*, 2 Eur. Hum. Rts. L. Rev. 196 (2002).

Cordes-Holland, Owen, *The Sinking Of The Strait: The Implications of Climate Change for Torres Strait Islanders' Human Rights Protected by the International Covenant on Civil and Political Rights*, Australian National University Honors Thesis (Oct. 2007).

Craven, Matthew, *The Violence of Dispossession: Extra-Territoriality and Economic, Social, and Cultural Rights*, in Economic, Social and Cultural Rights in Action (Mashood A. Baderin & Robert McCorquodale eds., 2007).

Criddle, Evan & Evan Fox-Decent, *A Fiduciary Theory of Jus Cogens*, 34 Yale J. Int'l L. 331 (2009).

Crouch, Brad, *Tiny Tuvalu in Save Us Plea Over Rising Seas*, Sunday Mail (Oct. 5, 2008).

d'Aspremont, Jean, *Softness in International Law: A Self-Serving Quest for New Legal Materials*, 19(5) Eur. J. Int'l L. 1075 (2008).

Darrow, Mac & Louise Arbour, *The Pillar of Glass: Human Rights in the Development Operations of the United Nations*, Am. J. Int'l L. (forthcoming 2009).

Davis, Megan, *Indigenous Struggles in Standard-Setting: The United Nations Declaration on the Rights of Indigenous Peoples*, 9(2) Melb. J. Int'l L. (2008).

de Boco, Gauthier, *Human Rights Impact Asssessments*, 27(2) Neth. Q. Hum. Rts. 139 (2009).

de Búrca, Grainne, *The Drafting of the European Union Charter of Fundamental Rights*, 26 Eur. L. Rev. 126 (2001).

de Schutter, Oliver, *Extraterritorial Jurisdiction as a tool for improving the Human Rights Accountability of Transnational Corporations*, Background Paper: Seminar of Legal Experts (Nov. 3-4, 2006).

de Visscher, Paul, *De l'Immunite de juridiction de l'Organisation des Nations Unies et du caractere discretionnaire de la competence de protection diplomatique*, 25 Revue Critique de Jurisprudence Belge 449 (1971).

Dennis, Michael J., *Application of Human Rights Treaties Extraterritorially in Times of Armed Conflict and Military Occupation*, 99 Am. J. Int'l L. 119 (2005).

Di Leva, Charles E. & Sachiko Morita, *Maritime Rights of Coastal States and Climate Change: Should States Adapt to Submerged Boundaries?*, Law and Dev. Working Paper Series No. 5 Legal Vice Presidency, World Bank (2008).

Docherty, Bonnie & Tyler Giannini, *Confronting a Rising Tide: A Proposal for a Convention on Climate Change Refugees*, 33-2 Harv. Envtl. L. Rev. 349 (2009).

Driesen, David, *Sustainable Development and Market Liberalism's Shotgun Wedding: Emissions Trading Under the Kyoto Protocol*, 83 Ind. L.J. 21 (2008).

du Bois, Francois, *Social Justice and the Judicial Enforcement of Environmental Rights and Duties*, in Human Rights Approaches to Environmental Protection (Alan Boyle & Michael Anderson eds., 1996).

Dupuy, Pierre-Marie, *The Danger of Fragmentation or Unification of the International Legal System and the International Court of Justice*, 31 N.Y.U. J. Int'l L. & Pol. 791 (1999).

Dupuy, René-Jean, *Humanity and the Environment*, 2 Colo. J. Int'l Envtl. L. & Pol'y 202 (1991).

Ebeku, Kaniye S.A., *Constitutional Right to a Healthy Environment and Human Rights Approaches to Environmental Protection in Nigeria: Gbemre v. Shell Revisited*, 16(3) Rev. Eur. Cmty. & Int'l Envtl. L. 312 (Dec. 2007).

Eide, Asbjörn, *Economic, Social and Cultural Rights as Human Rights*, in Economic, Social and Cultural Rights: A Textbook (Asbjörn Eide, Catarina Krause & Allen Rosas eds., 2001).

Falstrom, Dana Zartner, *Stemming the Flow of Environmental Displacement: Creating a Convention to Protect Persons and Preserve the Environment*, 6 Colo. J. Int'l Envtl. L. & Pol'y 1 (2001).

Farber, Daniel A., *Apportioning Climate Change Costs*, 26 UCLA J. Envtl. L. & Pol'y 21 (Dec. 2007).

Farber, Daniel A., *Basic Compensation for Victims of Climate Change*, 155 U. Pa. L. Rev. 1605 (2007).

Farber, Daniel A., *The Case for Climate Compensation: Justice for Climate Change Victims in a Complex World*, 2008 Utah L. Rev. 377 (2008).

Faure, Michael & Andre Nollekaemper, *International Liability as an Instrument to Prevent and Compensate for Climate Change*, 26 Stan. Envtl. L.J. 123 (2007).

Felner, Eitan, *A New Frontier in Economic and Social Rights Advocacy? Turning Quantitative Data into a Tool for Human Rights Accountability*, 9 Sur: Int'l J. Hum. Rts. 109 (Dec. 2008).

Fitzmaurice, Malgosia, *International Protection of the Environnent*, 293 Recueil des Cours 165 (2001).

Freestone, David, *The Precautionary Principle*, in International Law and Global Climate Change (Robin Churchill & David Freestone eds., 1991).

Friends of the Earth, *A Dangerous Distraction: Why Offsetting Is Failing the Climate and People: The Evidence* (2009).

Gaja, Giorgio, *Jus Cogens Beyond the Vienna Convention*, 172 Hague Recueil 1981-III (1981).

Gauri, Varun, *Social Rights and Economics: Claims to Health Care and Education in Developing Countries*, 32(3) World Development 465 (2004).

Gender and Climate Change Network, *Women for Climate Justice Position Paper* (Dec. 2007).

George, Jane, *ICC Climate Change Petition Rejected*, Nunatsiaq News (2006).

Glahn, Benjamin, *"Climate Refugees?" Addressing the International Legal Gaps*, 63(3) Int'l Bar News 17 (June 2009).

Goodwin-Gill, Guy, *Ordre Public Considered and Developed*, 94 LQR 354 (1978).

Guillaume, Gilbert, *The Future of International Judicial Institutions*, 44 Int'l Comp. L. Q. 848 (1995).

Halvorssen, Anita M., *Common, but Differentiated Commitments in the Future Climate Change Regime — Amending the Kyoto Protocol to Include Annex C and the Annex C Mitigation Fund*, 18 Colo. J. Int'l Envtl. L. & Pol'y 247 (2007).

Handl, Gunther, *Controlling Implementation of and Compliance with International Environmental Commitments: The Rocky Road from Rio*, 5 Colo. J. Int'l Envtl. L. & Pol'y 305 (1994).

Handl, Gunther, *Human Rights and Protection of the Environment: A Mildly Revisionist View*, in Human Rights, Sustainable Development and the Environment (Antônio Augusto Cancado Trindade ed., 1992).

Handl, Gunther, *The Legal Mandate of Multilateral Development Banks as Agents for Change Toward Sustainable Development*, 92 Am. J. Int'l L. 642 (1998).

Hannum, Hurst, *Human Rights*, in The United Nations and International Law (Christopher Joyner ed., 1997).

Hannum, Hurst, *The Status of the Universal Declaration of Human Rights in National and International Law*, 25 Ga. J. Int'l & Comp. L. 287 (1995-6).

Harrington, Joanna, *Climate Change, Human Rights and the Right to be Cold*, 18 Fordham Envtl. L. Rev. 513 (2007).

Hayes, David & Joel Veauvais, *Carbon Sequestration*, in Global Climate Change and U.S. Law (Michael Gerard, ed., 2007).

Herrmann, Richard, *Linking Theory to Evidence in International Relations*, in Handbook of International Relations (Walter Carlsnaes et. al., eds., 2002).

Higgins, Rosalyn, *Derogations Under Human Rights Treaties*, 48 Brit. Y.B. Int'l L. 281 (1978).

Hodgkinson, David et. al., *Towards a Convention for Persons Displaced by Climate Change: Key Issues and Preliminary Responses*, The New Critic, issue 8 (Sept. 2008).

Holwick, Scott, *Transnational Corporate Behavior and Its Disparate and Unjust Effects on the Indigenous Cultures and the Environment of Developing Nations: Jota v. Texaco, a Case Study*, 11 Colo. J. Int'l Envtl. L. & Pol'y 183 (2000).

Howse, Robert & Ruti G. Teitel, *Beyond the Divide: The Covenant on Economic, Social and Cultural Rights and the World Trade Organisation*, in Dialogue on Globalization, Occasional Paper No. 30 (Apr. 2007).

Hsu, Shi-Ling, *A Realistic Evaluation of Climate Change Litigation Through the Lens of a Hypothetical Lawsuit*, 79 U. Colo. L. Rev. 701 (2008).

Human Rights and Equal Opportunity Commission of Australia, *Background Paper: Human Rights and Climate Change* (2008).

Hunter, David, *The Implications of Climate Change Litigation for International Environmental Law Making*, in Adjudicating Climate Control: Sub-National, National And Supra-National Approaches (Hari M. Osofsky & William C. G. Burns eds., 2008).

Institut de Droit International, *Obligations Erga Omnes in International Law*, First and Second Report of the Special Rapporteur Giorgi Gaja, 71 Y.B. Inst. of Int'l L. (2005).

Institute for Development Studies, *Voices from the South: the Impact of the Financial Crisis on Developing Countries* (Nov. 2008).

International Council on Human Rights Policy, *Duties sans Frontieres: Human Rights and Global Social Justice* (2003).

International Council on Human Rights Policy, *Human Rights and Climate Change Technology Policy: The Roles of Technology in Ensuring Basic Human Rights in a Climate Constrained World* – draft report (2011) available at http://www.ichrp.org/en/projects/138.

International Council on Human Rights Policy / Center for International Environmental Law (CIEL), *Technology Transfer in the UNFCCC and Other International Legal Regimes: The Challenge of Systemic Integration* working paper (2010) available at http://www.ichrp.org/en/projects/138

Johnson, Douglas, *Global Climate Change: National Security Implications*, Strategic Studies Institute Colloquium Brief (May 2007).

Kamchibekova, Damira, *State Responsibility for Extraterritorial Human Rights Violations*, 13 BUFFALO H.R. L. REV. 87 (2007).

Kaufmann, Daniel, *Human Rights and Governance: The Empirical Challenge*, in HUMAN RIGHTS AND DEVELOPMENT: TOWARDS MUTUAL REINFORCEMENT (Mary Robinson & Philip Alston eds., 2005).

Kellersmann, Bettina, *Die Gemeinsame, Aber Differenzierte Verantwortlichkeit Von Industriestaaten Und Entwicklungsländern Für Den Schutz Der Globalen Umwelt* (2000).

Kingsbury, Benedict et. al., *The Emergence of Global Administrative Law*, 68 L. & CONTEMP. PROB. 15 (2005).

Kinley, David & Junko Tadaki, *From Talk to Walk: The Emergence of Human Rights Responsibilities for Corporations Under International Law*, 44 VA. J. INT'L L. 931 (2004).

Kiss, Alexandre Charles, *Permissible Limitations on Rights*, in THE INTERNATIONAL BILL OF RIGHTS: THE COVENANT ON CIVIL AND POLITICAL RIGHTS (Louis Henken ed., 1981).

Klein, Pierre, *La responsabilité des organizations financiers et les droits de la personne*, REVUE BELGE DE DROIT INTERNATIONAL 97 (1999).

Knox, John H., *Climate Change and Human Rights Law*, 50 VA. J. INT'L L. __ (forthcoming 2009).

Knox, John H., *Climate Change as a Global Threat to Human Rights*, United Nations Consultation on the Relationship between Climate Change and Human Rights (Oct. 22, 2008).

Knox, John H., *Diagonal Environmental Rights*, in EXTRATERRITORIAL OBLIGATIONS IN HUMAN RIGHTS LAW (Mark Gibney & Sigrun Skogly eds., forthcoming 2009).

Knox, John H., *Horizontal Human Rights Law*, 102 AM. J. INT'L L. 1 (2008).

Knox, John H., *Linking Human Rights and Climate Change at the United Nations*, 33 HARV. ENVTL. L. REV. 477 (2009).

Koivurova, Timo, *International Legal Avenues to Address the Plight of Victims of Climate Change: Problems and Prospects*, 22 ENVTL. L. & LITIG. 267 (2007).

Koskenniemi, Martii, *Breach of Treaty or Non-Compliance? Reflections on the Enforcement of the Montreal Protocol*, 3 Y.B. INT'L ENVTL. L. 123 (1992).

Koskenniemi, Martii, *The Preamble of the Universal Declaration on Human Rights*, in THE UNIVERSAL DECLARATION OF HUMAN RIGHTS (G. Alfredsson & A. Eide eds., 1999).

Kotzé, Louis J., *The Judiciary, the Environmental Right and the Quest for Sustainability in South Africa: A Critical Reflection*, 16(3) REV. EUR. CMTY. & INT'L ENVTL. L. 298 (Dec. 2007).

Kravchenko, Svitlana, *Right to Carbon or Right to Life: Human Rights Approaches to Climate Change*, 9 VT. J. OF ENVTL. L. 513 (2008).

Kravchenko, Svitlana, *The Aarhus Convention and Innovations in Compliance with Multilateral Environmental Agreements*, 18 COLO. J. INT'L ENVTL. L. & POL'Y 1 (2007).

Lammers, J. G., *General Principles of Law Recognised by Civilised Nations*, in ESSAYS IN THE DEVELOPMENT OF THE INTERNATIONAL LEGAL ORDER (F. Kalshoven, P.J. Kuyper & J. G. Lammers eds., 1980).

Langford, Malcolm, *The Justiciability of Social Rights: From Practice to Theory*, in SOCIAL RIGHTS JURISPRUDENCE: EMERGING TRENDS IN INTERNATIONAL AND COMPARATIVE LAW (Malcolm Langford ed., 2009).

Langford, Malcom and Jeff King, *Committee on Economic, Social and Cultural Rights: Past, Present, Future*, in SOCIAL RIGHTS JURISPRUDENCE: EMERGING TRENDS IN INTERNATIONAL AND COMPARATIVE LAW (Malcolm Langford ed., 2009).

Lawson-Remer, Terra et. al., *An Index of Economic and Social Rights Fulfillment: Concept and Methodology*, Working Paper (June 15, 2009).

Lee, John, *The Underlying Legal Theory to Support a Well-Defined Human Right to a Healthy Environment as a Principle of Customary International Law*, 25 COLUM. J. ENVTL. L. 283 (2000).

Liebenberg, Sandra, *Adjudicating Social Rights Under a Transformative Constitution*, in SOCIAL RIGHTS JURISPRUDENCE: EMERGING TRENDS IN INTERNATIONAL AND COMPARATIVE LAW (Malcolm Langford ed., 2009).

Limon, Marc, *Human Rights and Climate Change: Constructing a Case for Political Action*, 33 HARV. ENVTL. L. REV. 439 (2009).

Linderfalk, Ulf, *The Effects of* Jus Cogens *Norms: Whoever Opened the Pandora's Box, Did You Ever Think About the Consequences*, 18(5) EUR. J. INT'L L. 853 (2007).

Lowe, Vaughan, *Sustainable Development and Unsustainable Arguments*, in INTERNATIONAL LAW AND SUSTAINABLE DEVELOPMENT: PAST ACHIEVEMENTS AND FUTURE CHALLENGES (Alan Boyle & David Freestone eds., 1999).

Mabey, Nick, *Delivering Climate Security: International Security Responses to a Climate Changed World*, Royal United Services Institute, Whitehall Papers No. 69 (Apr. 23, 2008).

Magraw, Daniel Barstow, *Legal Treatment of Developing Countries: Differential, Contextual and Absolute Norms*, 69(1) COLO. J. INT'L ENVTL. L. & POL'Y 69 (1990).

Malone, Linda A. & Scott Pasternack, *Exercising Environmental Human Rights and Remedies in the United Nations System*, 27 WM. & MARY ENVTL. L. & POL'Y REV. 365 (2002).

Marong, Alhaji, *From Rio to Johannesburg: Reflections on the Role of International Legal Norms in Sustainable Development*, 16 GEO. INT'L ENVTL. L. REV. 21 (2003).

Marrani, David, *The Second Anniversary of the Constitutionalisation of the French Charter for the Environment: Constitutional and Environmental Implications*, 10 ENVTL. L. REV. 9 (2008).

Max, Arthur, *U.N. Climate Chief Confident of Global Warming Pact*, WASH. POST (June 12, 2009).

McAdam, Jane & Ben Saul, *Weathering Insecurity: Climate-Induced Displacement and International Law*, in HUMAN SECURITY AND NON-CITIZENS: LAW, POLICY AND INTERNATIONAL AFFAIRS (Alica Edwards & Carla Ferstman eds., 2009).

McCallion, Kenneth F., *Lex and the Lorax: Enforcing Environmental Norms under International Law: International Environmental Justice: Rights and Remedies*, 26 HASTINGS INT'L & COMP. L. REV. 427 (2003).

McGoldrick, Dominic, *Extraterritorial Application of the International Covenant on Civil and Political Rights*, in EXTRATERRITORIAL APPLICATION OF HUMAN RIGHTS TREATIES (Fons Coomans & Menno T. Kamminga eds., 2004).

McGoldrick, Dominic, *Sustainable Development and Human Rights: An Integrated Conception*, 45 INT'L & COMP. L.Q. 796 (1996).

McInerney-Lankford, Siobhán, *Climate Change and Human Rights: An Introduction to Legal Issues*, 33-2 HARV. ENVTL. L. REV. 431 (2009).

McInerney-Lankford, Siobhán, *Human Rights and Development: Some Institutional Perspectives*, 25(3) NETH. Q. HUM. RTS. 459 (2007).

McIntyre, Owen & Thomas Mosedale, *The Precautionary Principle as a Norm of Customary International Law*, 9 J. ENVTL. L. 221 (1997).

McKay, Andy & Polly Vizard, *Rights and Economic Growth: Inevitable Conflict or Common Ground?* (Mar. 2005).

McKibben, Bill, *Can Obama Change the Climate?* 56(10) N.Y. REV. BOOKS 39 (June 11 – July 1, 2009).

McLachlan, Campbell, *The Principle of Systemic Integration and Article 31(3)(c) of the Vienna Convention*, 54(2) I.C.L.Q. 279 (2005).

Meron, Theodor, *Extraterritoriality of Human Rights Treaties*, 89 AM. J. INT'L L. 78 (1995).

Merrills, J.G., *Environmental Rights*, in THE OXFORD HANDBOOK OF INTERNATIONAL ENVIRONMENTAL LAW (Daniel Bodansky et. al., eds., 2007).

Middaugh, Marguerite E., *Linking Global Warming to Inuit Human Rights*, 8 SAN DIEGO INT'L L.J. 179 (2006).

Miller, Alan, *International Trade and Development*, in GLOBAL CLIMATE CHANGE AND U.S. LAW (Michael B. Gerard, ed., 2007).

Mitchell, Ronald B., *International Environment*, in HANDBOOK ON INTERNATIONAL RELATIONS (Walter Carlsnaes et. al., eds., 2002).

Moberg, Kara, *Extending Refugee Definitions to Cover Environmentally Displaced Persons Displaces Necessary Protection*, 94 IOWA L. REV. 1107 (2009).

Musungu, Sisule F., *Health: Human Rights, Climate Vulnerability and Access to Technology*, Background Paper (draft), International Council on Human Rights Policy (July 2009).

Myers, Norman, *Environmental Refugees: An Emergent Security Issue*, 13th Economic Forum, Prague (May 23-7, 2005).

Narula, Smita, *The Right to Food: Holding Global Actors Accountable under International Law*, 44 COLUM. J. TRANSNAT'L L. 691 (2006).

Oliva, Maria Julia, *Promoting Technologies for Adaptation: A Role for the Right to Food?*, International Council on Human Rights Policy, Review Meeting (July 2009).

Orellana, Marcos A., *Criminal Punishment for Environmental Damage: Individual and State Responsibility at a Crossroad*, 17 GEO. INT'L ENV. L. REV. 673 (2005).

Orford, Anne, *Globalization and the Right to Development*, in Peoples' Rights (Philip Alston, ed., 2001).

Osofsky, Hari M., *Climate Change Litigation as Pluralist Legal Dialogue*, 26 STAN. ENVTL. L.J. 181 (2007).

Osofsky, Hari M., *Climate Change, Environmental Justice and Human Rights: A Response to Professor Posner*, Annual Meeting of the Law and Society Association (July 24, 2007).

Osofsky, Hari M., *Learning from Environmental Justice: A New Model for International Environmental Rights*, 24 STAN. ENVTL. L.J. 71 (2005).

Osofsky, Hari M., *The Geography of Climate Change Litigation: Implications for Transnational Regulatory Governance*, 83 WASH. U. L.Q. 1789 (2005).

Osofsky, Hari M., *The Inuit Petition as a Bridge? Beyond the Dialectics of Climate Change and Indigenous Peoples' Rights*, 31(2), AM. INDIAN L. REV. 675 (2007).

Overseas Development Institute, *Achieving Economic and Social Rights: The Challenge of Assessing Compliance*, ODI Briefing Paper No. 46 (Dec. 2008).

Overseas Development Institute, *Children in Times of Economic Crisis: Past Lessons, Future Policies*, Background Note (Mar. 2009).

Oxfam, *Climate Wrongs and Human Rights: Putting People at the Heart of Climate-Change Policy*, Oxfam Briefing Paper (Sept. 2008).

Parsons, Claudia, *Small Islands Win U.N. Vote on Climate Change Security*, REUTERS (June 3, 2009).

Pauwelyn, Joost, *Bridging Fragmentation and Unity: International Law as a Universe of Inter-Connected Islands*, 25 MICH. J. INT'L L. 903 (2004).

Pavoni, Riccardo, *Biosafety and Intellectual Property Rights: The Jurisprudence of the European Patent Office as a Paradigm of an International Public Policy Issue*, in Environment, Human Rights and International Trade (Francesco Francioni, ed., 2001).

Pécoud, Antoine & Paul de Guchteneire, *Migration, Human Rights and the United Nations: an Investigation into the Law Ratification Record of the U.N. Migrant Workers Convention* (Oct. 2004).

Pedersen, Ole W., *European Environmental Human Rights and Environmental Rights: A Long Time Coming?*, 21 GEO. INT'L ENVTL. L. REV. 73 (2008).

Peterson, Luke & Kevin Gray, *International Human Rights in Bilateral Treaty and Investment Treaty Arbitration*, International Institute for Sustainable Development Research Paper (2003).

Peterson, Luke, *Human Rights and Bilateral Investment Treaties: Mapping the role of human rights within investor-state arbitration*, Rights and Democracy (2009).

Picone, P., *Obblighi reciproci ed obblighi erga omnes delgli Stati nel campo della protezione internazionale dell'ambiente marino dall'inquinamento*, in DIRITTO INTERNAZIONALE E PROTEZIONE E PROTEZIONE DELL'AMBIENTE MARINO (V. Starace, ed., 1983).

Pogge, Thomas, *Human Flourishing and Universal Justice*, in HUMAN FLOURISHING (E. F. Paul et. al. eds., 1999).

Pogge, Thomas, *Recognized and Violated by International Law: the Human Rights of the Global Poor*, 18 LEIDEN J. INT'L L. 717 (2005).

Popovic, Neil A.F., *In Pursuit of Environmental Human Rights: Commentary on the Draft Declaration of Principles on Human Rights and Environment*, 27 COLUM. HUM. RTS. L. REV. 487 (1996).

Porter, Bruce, *The Crisis of ESC Rights and Strategies for Addressing It*, in ROAD TO A REMEDY: CURRENT ISSUES IN LITIGATION OF ECONOMIC, SOCIAL AND CULTURAL RIGHTS (John Squires et. al. eds., 2005).

Posner, Eric A. & Alan O. Sykes, *An Economic Analysis of State and Individual Responsibility Under International Law*, U. Chi. L. School, John M. Olin Law and Economics Working Paper No. 279 (2006).

Posner, Eric A. and Cass R. Sunstein, *Climate Change Justice*, 96 Geo. L.J. 1565 (2007).

Posner, Eric A., *Climate Change and International Human Rights Litigation: A Critical Appraisal*, 155 U. PA. L. REV 1925 (2007).

Prott, Lyndel V., *Cultural Rights as Peoples' Rights in International Law*, in THE RIGHTS OF PEOPLES (James Crawford ed., 1988).

Purdy, Ray, *Governance Reform of the Clean Development Mechanism After Poznań*, 3(1) CARBON & CLIMATE L. REV. 5 (2009).

Rajamani, Lavanya, *Differential Treatment in the International Climate Regime*, 2005 Y.B. Int'l
    Envtl. L. 81 (2007).

Rajamani, Lavanya, *Differentiation in the Post-2012 Climate Regime*, 4(4) Pol'y Q. 48 (2008).

Rajamani, Lavanya, *From Berlin to Bali and Beyond: Killing Kyoto Softly*, 57(3) Int'l & Comp.
    L. Q. 909 (2008).

Rajamani, Lavanya, *The Right to Environmental Protection in India: Many a Slip between the
    Cup and the Lip?*, 16(3) Rev. Eur. Cmty. & Int'l Envtl. L. 274 (Dec. 2007).

Ratha, Dilip et. al., *Beyond Aid: New Sources and Innovative Mechanisms for Financing Devel-
    opment in Sub-Saharan Africa*, in Innovative Financing for Development (Suhas
    Ketar & Dilip Ratha, eds., 2009).

Raustiala, Kal & Anne-Marie Slaughter, *International Law, International Relations and Com-
    pliance*, in Handbook on International Relations (Walter Carlsnaes et. al., eds.,
    2002).

Ravallion, Martin, *A Poverty-Inequality Trade off?*, 3 J. Econ. Inequality 169 (2005).

Ravallion, Martin, *Growth, Inequality and Poverty: Looking Beyond Averages*, 29 World Dev.
    1803 (2001).

Redgwell, Catherine, *Life, the Universe and Everything: A Critique of Anthropocentric Rights*,
    in Human Rights Approaches to Environmental Protection (Alan Boyle & Mi-
    chael Anderson eds., 1996).

Redgwell, Catherine, *The Law of Reservation in Respect of Multilateral Conventions*, in Hu-
    man Rights Norms as General Norms and a State's Right to Opt Out (Gardner
    et. al., eds., 1997).

Reed, RoseMary, *Rising Seas and Disappearing Islands: Can Island Inhabitants Seek Redress
    Under the Alien Tort Claims Act?*, 11 Pac. Rim L. & Pol'y J. 399 (2002).

Restatement (Third) of the Foreign Relations Law of the United States (1987).

Revkin, Andrew C., *Maldives Considers Buying Dry Land if Sea Level Rises*, N.Y. Times
    (Nov. 10, 2008).

Robinson, Mary, *"Forward" to International Council on Human Rights Policy*, in Hum-
    phreys, Stephen, The Human Rights Dimensions of Climate Change: A Rough
    Guide (2008).

Rodriguez-Rivera, Luis E., *Is the Human Right to Environment Recognized Under Interna-
    tional Law? It Depends on the Source*, 12 Colo. J. Int'l Envtl. L. & Pol'y 1 (2001).

Sachs, Wolfgang, *Climate Change and Human Rights*, World Econ. & Dev. Special Report
    (2007).

Salmon, Jean J. A., *De Quelques Problemes poses aux tribunaux belges par les actions de citoy-
    ens belges contre l'O.N.U. en raison de faits survenus sur le territoire de la Republique
    Democratique du Congo*, 81 J. Trib. 713 (1966).

Sands, Philippe, *Human Rights, Environment and the Lopez Ostra Case: Context and Conse-
    quences*, 6 Eur. Hum. Rts. L. Rev. 597 (1996).

Sands, Philippe, *The Environment, Community and International Law*, 30 Harv. Int'l L.J.
    393 (1989).

Sartor, Olivier, *Climate off-set Arithmetic Doesn't Add Up*, ABC News (May 25, 2009).

Saul, Ben & Jane McAdam, *An Insecure Climate for Human Security? Climate-Induced Dis-
    placement and International Law*, Legal Studies Research Paper 08/131 (Oct. 2008).

Schachter, Oscar, *International Law in Theory and Practice: General Course in Public Interna-
    tional Law*, 178 Receuil des Cours 21 (1982).

Schachter, Oscar, *The Emergence of International Environmental Law*, 44 J. Int'l Aff. 457 (1991).

Scheinin, Martin, *Extraterritorial Effect of the International Covenant on Civil and Political Rights*, in Extraterritorial Application of Human Rights Treaties (Fons Coomans & Menno T. Kamminga eds., 2004).

Schmitz, Hans-Peter & Kathryn Sikkink, *International Human Rights*, in Handbook on International Relations (Walter Carlsnaes et. al., eds., 2002).

Scott, Craig & Philip Alston, *Adjudicating Constitutional Priorities in a Transnational Context: A Comment on Soobramoney's Legacy and Grootboom's Promise*, 16 S. Afr. J. Hum. Rts. 206 (2000).

Seymour, Dan & Jonathan Pincus, *Human Rights and Economics: The Conceptual Basis for their Complementarity*, 26(4) Dev. Pol'y Rev. 387 (2008).

Seymour, Frances, *Forests, Climate Change and Human Rights: Managing the Risks and Trade-offs*, in Human Rights and Climate Change (Stephen Humphreys, ed., forthcoming 2009).

Shabalala, Dilandyebo & Marcos Orellana, *Technology Transfer in the UNFCCC and other International Legal Regimes: The Challenge of Systemic Integration*, International Council on Human Rights Policy Review Meeting (July 2009).

Shelton, Dinah, *Background Paper 2: Human Rights and the Environment: Jurisprudence of Human Rights Bodies*, UNEP-OHCHR Expert Seminar on Human Rights and the Environment (2002).

Shelton, Dinah, *Environmental Rights*, in People's Rights (Philip Alston ed., 2001).

Shelton, Dinah, *Human Rights and the Environment: Jurisprudence of Human Rights Bodies*, UNEP-OHCHR Expert Seminar on Human Rights and the Environment (2002).

Shelton, Dinah, *Human Rights, Environmental Rights and the Right to Environment*, 28 Stan. J. Int'l L. 103 (1991).

Shelton, Dinah, *The Environmental Jurisprudence of International Human Rights Tribunals*, in Linking Human Rights and the Environment (Romina Picolotti & Jorge D. Taillant eds., 2003).

Sherman, John, *Embedding a Rights Compatible Grievance Process for External Stakeholders with Business Culture*, Corporate Social Responsibility Initiative Report No. 36 (Aug. 2009).

Shue, Henry, *Subsistence Emissions and Luxury Emissions*, 15 (1) Law & Pol'y 39 (1993).

Shue, Henry, *The Unavoidability of Justice*, in The International Politics of the Environment (Andrew Hurrell & Benedict Kingsbury eds., 1992).

Simma, Bruno & Philip Alston, *The Sources of Human Rights Law: Custom, Jus Cogens and General Principles*, 12 Aust. Y.B. Int'l L. 82 (1992).

Sinden, Amy, *Climate Change and Human Rights*, 27 J. Land Resources & Envtl L. 255 (2007).

Sohn, Louis, *The New International Law: Protection of the Rights of Individuals Rather than States*, 32 Am. U. L. Rev. 1 (1982).

Söllner, Sven, *The Breakthrough of the Right to Food*, 11 Max Planck Yearbook of UN Law 391 (2007).

Spelliscy, Shane, *The Proliferation of International Tribunals: A Chink in the Armor*, 40 Colum. J. Transnat'l L. 143 (2002).

Stern, Nicholas, *Stern Review on the Economics of Climate Change* (Oct. 30, 2006).

Strauss, Andrew, *The Legal Option: Suing the United States in International Forums for Global Warming Emissions*, 33 ENVTL. L. REP. 10185 (2003).

Sunstein, Cass, *Beyond the Precautionary Principle*, University of Chicago Legal Theory and Public Law Working Paper No. 38 (2003).

Toebes, Brigit, *The Right to Health*, in ECONOMIC, SOCIAL AND CULTURAL RIGHTS: A TEXTBOOK (Asbjörn Eide, Catarina Krause & Allen Rosas eds., 2001).

Toope, Stephen J., *Confronting Indeterminacy: Challenges to International Legal Theory*, 19 C.C.I.L. PROCS. 209 (1990).

Tully, Stephen, *Like Oil and Water: A Sceptical Appraisal of Climate Change and Human Rights*, 15 AUST. INT'L L. J. 213 (2008).

United Kingdom Department for International Development, *Implementing the UK's Conditionality Policy*, DFID Practice Paper (May 2009).

Vandenhole, Wouter, *EU and Development: Extraterritorial Obligations under the International Covenant on Economic, Social and Cultural Rights*, in CASTING THE NET WIDER: HUMAN RIGHTS, DEVELOPMENT AND NEW DUTY-BEARERS (Margot E. Salomon et al., eds., 2007).

Voigt, Christina, *State Responsibility for Climate Change Damages*, 77 (1-2) NORDIC J. OF INT'L L. 1 (2008).

Wagner, Martin & Donald M. Goldberg, *An Inuit Petition to the Inter-American Commission on Human Rights for Dangerous Impacts of Climate Change*, Presented at the 10th Conference of the Parties to the Framework Convention on Climate Change (Dec. 15, 2004).

Walker, Andrew, *Will Shell payout change the Nigeria Delta?*, BBC NEWS (June 9, 2009).

Warren, R. et. al, *Understanding the Regional Impacts of Climate Change*, Research Report Prepared for the Stern Review on the Economics of Climate Change, Research Working Paper No. 90, Tyndall Centre for Climate Change (Sept. 2006).

Watt-Cloutier, Sheila, *Climate Change and Human Rights*, in HUMAN RIGHTS DIALOGUE: "ENVIRONMENTAL RIGHTS" (Apr. 22, 2004).

Weil, Prosper, *Towards Relative Normativity in International Law*, 77 AM. J. INT'L L. 413 (1983).

Weisburd, A. Mark, *The Emptiness of the Concept of Jus Cogens, As Illustrated by the War in Bosnia-Herzegovina*, 17 MICH. J. INT'L L. 1 (1995-96).

Wiener, Jonathan, *Precaution* , in OXFORD HANDBOOK OF INTERNATIONAL ENVIRONMENTAL LAW (Daniel Bodansky et. al., eds., 2007).

Williams, Angela, *Turning the Tide: Recognizing Climate Change Refugees in International Law*, 30 L & POL'Y 502 (2008).

Wirth, David A., *The Rio Declaration on Environment and Development: Two Steps Forward and One Back, or Vice Versa?*, 29 GA. L. REV. 599 (1995).

Woodcock, Andrew, *Jacques Maritain, Natural Law and the Universal Declaration of Human Rights*, 8 J. HISTORY OF INT'L L. 245 (2006).

World Commission on the Social Dimension of Globalization, *A Fair Globalization: Creating Opportunities for All*, ILO, Geneva (Feb. 2004).

Yamin, A.E. & O. Parra-Vera, *How do Courts set Health Policy? The Case of the Colombian Constitution Court*, 6(2) PLoS Medicine (2009).

Yoshida, O., *Soft Enforcement of Treaties: The Montreal Protocol's Noncompliance Procedure and the Functions of Internal International Institutions*, 10 Colo. J. Int'l Envtl. L. & Pol'y 95 (1999).

Young, Katherine, *The Minimum Core of Economic and Social Rights: A Concept in Search of Content*, 33 Yale J. Int'l L. 113 (2008).

Cases

Advisory Opinion on Western Sahara, 1975 I.C.J. 12 (Oct. 16, 1975).

Alejandre v. Cuba, Case86/99, Inter-Am. C.H.R. OEA/Ser.L/V/II.106, doc. 3 (1999).

Arrondelle v. United Kingdom, 5 Eur. Ct. H.R. 118 (1983).

Australian Conservation Fund v. Minister for Planning, [2004] VCAT 2029 (Oct. 29, 2004).

Banković et. al. v. Belgium, 12 Eur. Ct. H.R. 333 (2001).

Barcelona Traction (Belgium v. Spain), 1970 I.C.J. 4 (Feb. 1970).

Bosnia and Herzegovina v. Serbia and Montenegro (Case Concerning the Application of the Convention on the Prevention and Punishment of the Crime of Genocide), 1993 I.C.J. 3 (Apr. 1993).

Brigido Simon v. Commission on Human Rights, G.R. No. 100150, 229 SCRA 17 (Jan. 5, 1994) (Phil.).

Budayeva v. Russia, Application No. 15339/02 (Eur. Ct. H.R. Mar. 20, 2008).

Bund für Umwelt und Naturschutz Deutschland e.V. & Germanwatch e.V. v. the Federal Republic of Germany, VG 10 A 215.04, 10th Chamber of the Administrative Court (Jan. 10, 2006).

Commission Nationale de Droits de l'Homme et des Libertés v. Chad, Comm. No. 74/92, 2000 Afr. H.R.L. Rep. 66 (1995).

Consumer Education and Research Centre v. Union of India, 1995, 3 S.C.C. 42 (India).

Continental Shelf Case (Tunisia v. Libyan Arab Jamahiriya), 1982 I.C.J. 18 (Feb. 23, 1982).

Decision Regarding Communication 155/96 (Social and Economic Rights Action Center/ Center for Economic and Social Rights v. Nigeria), 96 AJIL 937 (2002).

East Timor (Portugal v. Australia), 1995 I.C.J. 139 (June 1995).

Fadeyeva v. Russia, 45 Eur. Ct. H.R. 10 (2005).

FEANTSA v. France, 47 Eur. Ct. H.R. 15 (2007).

Gabcíkovo-Nagymaros (Hungary v. Slovakia), 1997 I.C.J. 7 (Sept. 1997).

Giacomelli v. Italy, 45 Eur. Ct. H.R. 38 (2006).

Guerra and Others v. Italy, 26 Eur. Ct. H.R. 357 (1998).

Hatton and Others v. United Kingdom, 34 Eur. Ct. H.R. 1 (2002).

India People's Union for Civil Liberties v. Union of India, 1997, A.I.R. 1997 S.C. 568 (India).

Indigenous Cmty. Yakye Axa v. Para., Inter.-Am. Ct. H.R. (ser. C) No. 146 (June 17, 2005).

Indigenous Community of Awas Tingni v. Nicaragua, Inter-Am. Ct. H.R. (Ser. C) No. 79 (Aug. 31, 2001).

Jonah Gbemre v. Shell Petroleum Development Co. (Nigeria) Ltd. et. al., Unreported Suit No. FHC/B/CS/53/05 (Nov. 14, 2005) (Benin).

Kreuz v. Poland, 12 Eur. Ct. H.R. 371 (2001).

Lopez Ostra v. Spain, 20 Eur. Ct. H.R. 277 (1994).

López v. Uruguay, (Communication No. 52/1979), Human Rights Committee, U.N. Doc. CCPR/C/OP/1 (1981 & 1985).

Lubicon Lake Bank v. Canada, U.N. DOC. SUPP. NO. 40 (A/45/40) (1990).

Marangopoulos Foundation for Human Rights v. Greece, Eur. Comm. of Social Rights, Complaint No. 30/2005, Decision on the Merits (Dec. 6, 2005).

Marcel Claude Reyes v. Chile, Inter-Am. Ct. H.R. (ser. C) No. 151 (2006).

Mariele Cecilia Viceconte v. Ministry of Health and Social Welfare, Poder Judicial de la Nación, Causa no 31.777/96 (June 2, 1998) (Argentina).

Massachusetts v. EPA, 549 U.S. 497 (2007).

Maya Indigenous Cmty. of the Toledo Dist. v. Belize, Case 12.053, Inter-Am.C.H.R., Report No. 40/04, OEA/Ser.L/V/II.122 doc. 5 rev. (2004).

Moreno Gómez v. Spain, App. No. 4143/02, Eur. Ct. H.R. (2004).

MOX Plant Case (Ireland v. U.K.), Order No. 3, 42 I.L.M. 1187 (2003).

Native Village of Kivalina v. ExxonMobil Corp. (N.D. Cal. Feb. 26, 2008).

North Sea Continental Shelf (W. Ger. v. Den.; W. Ger. v. Neth.), 1969 I.C.J. 3 (Feb. 20, 1969).

Nuclear Tests (Australia. v. France), 1974 I.C.J. 253 (Dec. 20, 1974).

Ogoniland Case (Social and Economic Rights Action Center v. Nigeria), Communication 155/96 (African Commission on Human & Peoples' Rights, Oct. 2001).

Oneryildiz v. Turkey, 2004-XII Eur. Ct. H.R. 79 (2004).

Oposa et. al. v. Factoran, G. R. No. 101083, 224 S.C.R.A. 792 (S.C., July 30, 1993) (Phil.), reprinted in 33 I.L.M. 173 (1994).

Paschim Banga Khet Mazdoor Samiti v. State of West Bengal, (1996) AIR SC 2426 (India).

Plotnikov v. Russian Federation, Communication No. 784/1997, U.N. Doc. CCPR/C/65/D/784/1997 (May 5, 1999).

Prosecutor v. Furundzija, Case No. ICTR IT-95-17/1-T, Judgement, (Dec. 10, 1998).

Sara et. al. v. Finland, Comm. No. 431/1990, Hum. Rts. Comm., U.N. Doc. CCPR/C/50/D/431/1990 (1994).

Saramaka People v. Surin, 2007 Inter-Am. Ct. H.R. (ser. C) No. 172 (Nov. 28, 2007).

Social Economic Rights Action Center for Economic & Social Rights v. Nigeria, African Commission on Human & Peoples' Rights, Comm. No. 155/96 (2001).

South West Africa Cases (Ethiopia v. South Africa; Liberia v. South Africa), 1966 I.C.J. 6 (July 18, 1966).

Southern Bluefin Tuna (Austl. & N.Z. v. Japan), Jurisdiction and Admissibility (LOS Convention Annex VII Arb. Trib. Aug. 4, 2000), 39 I.L.M. 1359 (2000).

Tanase and others v. Romania, Eur. Ct. H.R., Application no. 62954 (May 26, 2009).

Taskin v. Turkey, 2004-X Eur. Ct. H.R. 1149 (Nov. 10, 2004).

Trail Smelter Case (United States v. Canada), 3 R.I.A.A. 1905 (1938 & 1941).

Velásquez Rodríguez v. Honduras, Inter-Am. Ct. H.R. (ser. C) No. 4 (July 29, 1988).

Z and Others v. United Kingdom, 34 Eur. Ct. H.R. 3 (2002).

International Agreements

Additional Protocol to the American Convention on Human Rights in the area of Economic, Social, and Cultural Rights (Protocol of San Salvador), Nov. 17, 1988, 28 I.L.M. 156.

Additional Protocol to the European Social Charter Providing for a System of Collective Complaints, Sept. 11, 1995, 34 I.L.M. 1453.

African Charter on Human and People's Rights, June 27, 1981, 21 I.L.M. 58.

American Convention on Human Rights, Nov. 22, 1969, 9 I.L.M. 673.

American Declaration on the Rights and Duties of Man, Apr. 1948, OAS Resolution XXX, OEA/Ser.L.V/II.82 doc.6 rev.1.

Basel Convention on the Control of Transboundary Movements of Hazardous Wastes and their Disposal, Mar. 22, 1979, 28 I.L.M. 656.

Cartagena Protocol on Biosafety to the Convention on Biological Diversity, Jan. 29, 2000, 39 I.L.M. 1027.

Charter of the United Nations, June 26, 1945, 59 Stat. 1031, T.S. 993, 3 Bevans 1153.

Convention against Torture and Other Cruel, Inhuman or Degrading Treatment or Punishment, Dec. 10, 1984, 24 I.L.M. 535.

Convention Concerning Indigenous and Tribal Peoples, June 27, 1989, 28 I.L.M. 1382.

Convention on Access to Information, Public Participation in Decision-Making and Access to Justice in Environmental Matters (Aarhus Convention), June 25, 1998, 38 I.L.M. 517.

Convention on Biological Diversity, June 5, 1992, 31 I.L.M. 818.

Convention on Cluster Munitions, Dec. 3, 2008.

Convention on Long-Range Transboundary Air Pollution, Nov. 13, 1979, 18 I.L.M. 1442.

Convention on the Elimination of All Forms of Discrimination against Women (CEDAW), Dec. 18, 1979, 19 I.L.M. 33.

Convention on the Prevention and Punishment of the Crime of Genocide, Dec. 9, 1948, 78 U.N.T.S. 277.

Convention on the Prohibition of the Development, Production, and Stockpiling of Bacteriological (Biological) and Toxin Weapons and on their Destruction, Apr. 10, 1972, 26 U.S.T. 583, 1015 U.N.T.S. 163.

Convention on the Rights of Persons with Disabilities, Dec. 13, 2006, U.N. Doc. A/RES/63/192.

Convention on the Rights of the Child, Nov. 20, 1989, 28 I.L.M. 1448.

Draft Articles on the Prevention of Transboundary Harm from Hazardous Activities, Nov. 30, 2001, 53rd Sess., Int'l L. Comm'n, Supp. No. 10, ch. V.E.1, art. III, IV, U.N. Doc. A/56/10.

European Convention for the Protection of Human Rights and Fundamental Freedoms (European Convention on Human Rights), Nov. 4, 1950, 213 U.N.T.S. 222.

European Social Charter, Oct. 18, 529 U.N.T.S. 89.

European Union Charter of Fundamental Rights, Dec. 7, 2000, OJ 2000 C 364.

Geneva Convention Relative to the Protection of Civilian Persons in Time of War, Aug. 12, 1949, 19 I.L.M. 1524.

Geneva Convention Relative to the Treatment of Prisoners of War, Aug. 12, 1949, 19 I.L.M. 1524.

Hague Declaration on the Environment, Mar. 11, 1989, 28 I.L.M. 1308.

International Convention on the Elimination of All Forms of Racial Discrimination, Dec. 25, 1965, 5 I.L.M. 352.

International Convention on the Protection of the Rights of All Migrant Workers and Members of Their Families, Dec. 18, 1990, 30 I.L.M. 1521.

International Covenant on Civil and Political Rights, Dec. 16, 1966, 6 I.L.M. 368.

International Covenant on Economic, Social and Cultural Rights, Dec. 16, 1966, 6 I.L.M. 360.

International Convention on the Protection of the Rights of All Migrant Workers and
    Members of Their Families, U.N. Doc. A/RES/45/158 (Dec. 18, 1990).
Kyoto Protocol to the United Nations Framework Convention on Climate Change, Dec.
    11, 1997, 37 I.L.M. 22.
Monterrey Consensus, Mar. 22, 2002, 3 U.N. Doc. A/CONF.198/3.
Optional Protocol to the International Covenant on Economic, Social and Cultural Rights
    Permitting Individual Complaints, U.N. Doc A/RES/63/117 (Dec. 10, 2008).
Protocol on Explosive Remnants of War (Protocol V) to the Convention on Prohibi-
    tions or Restrictions on the Use of Certain Conventional Weapons which may be
    Deemed to be Excessively Injurious or to have Indiscriminate Effects, Nov. 27,
    2003, U.N. Doc. CCW/MSP/2003/2.
Rotterdam Convention on the Prior Informed Consent Procedure for Certain Hazardous
    Chemicals and Pesticides in International Trade, Sept. 10, 1998, 38 I.L.M. 1.
United Nations Convention on the Law of the Non-Navigable Uses of International Wa-
    tercourses, May 21, 1997, 36 I.L.M. 700.
United Nations Convention on the Law of the Sea, Dec. 10, 1982, 33 I.L.M. 1309.
United Nations Framework Convention on Climate Change, May 9, 1992, 31 I.L.M. 849.
Vienna Convention on the Law of Treaties May 23, 1969, 8 I.L.M. 679.
Vienna Declaration and Programme of Action, June 14-25, 1993, 32 I.L.M. 1661.

International Documents and Resultions

Arctic Council, *Arctic Climate Impact Assessment Report* (Carolyn Symon et. al. eds., 2005).
Stephen Castles, *Environmental Change and Forced Migration: Making Sense of the Debate*,
    UNHCR New Issues in Refugee Research, Paper No.70 (Oct. 2002).
Copenhagen Declaration on Social Development, U.N. Doc A/CONF.166/9 (1995).
Council of Europe Committee of Ministers, *Resolution on Complaint No. 30/2005 by the
    Marangopoulos Foundation for Human Rights (MFHR) against Greece*, Res. CM/Re-
    sChS(2008)1 (Jan. 16, 2008).
de Schutter, Olivier, *Report of the Special Rapporteur on the Right to Food: Building Resil-
    ience: a Human Rights Framework on World Food and Nutrition Security*, U.N. Doc A/
    HRC/9/23 (Sept. 8, 2008).
Danish Institute for Human Rights, *Human Rights and Climate Change: Exploring the nex-
    us, the human rights implications and regulatory frameworks* (2009)
Report: DIHR Workshop on Human Rights and Climate Change, Copenhagen, 29-30
Edwards, Alice, *Summary of a background paper entitled: Displacement, statelessness and
    questions of gender equality and the Convention on the Elimination of All Forms of Dis-
    crimination against Women*, prepared for a joint seminar between UNHCR and
    CEDAW, UN Doc. CEDAW/C/2009/II/WP.3 (July 16-7, 2009).
European Commission, Communication from the Commission on the Precautionary
    Principle, COM (2000)1 (Feb. 2, 2000).
European Communities, *Measures Affecting the Approval and Marketing of Biotech Products
    – Dispute Settlement*, WT/DS291, WT/DS292, WT/DS293 (Sept. 29, 2006).
European Parliamentary Assembly Recommendation on the Environment and Human
    Rights, Rec. 1614 (June 27, 2003).
European Union, *An EU Strategy for Biofuels*, COM (2006) 34 final (Mar. 18, 2006).

European Union, Communication from the Commission to the Council, the European Parliament, the European Economic and Social Committee, and the Committee of the Regions, Limiting Global Climate Change to 2° Celsius: The way ahead for 2020 and beyond, COM/2007/0002 final (Oct. 1, 2007).

European Union, Parliamentary Assembly of the Council of Europe, Recommendation 1614 on Environment and Human Rights (June 27, 2003).

Exchange of Letters Constituting an Agreement Between the United Nations and Belgium Relating to the Settlement of Claims Filed Against the United Nations in the Congo by Belgian Nationals, 1965 U.N. Jurid. Y.B. 39 (Feb. 20, 1965).

Food and Agriculture Organization, *Voluntary Guidelines to Support the progressive realization of the right to adequate food in the context of national food security* (Nov. 2004).

Global Canopy Programme, *Forests Now Declaration* (2007).

Guissé, El Hadji, *Report of the Special Rapporteur of the Sub-Commission on the Right to Drinking Water Supply and Sanitation on the relationship between the enjoyment of economic, social and cultural rights and the promotion of the realization of the right to drinking water supply and sanitation* U.N. Doc E/CN.4/Sub.2/2002/10 (2002).

Hunt, Paul, *Report of the Special Rapporteur on the Right of Everyone to the Highest Attainable Standard of Physical and Mental Health*, U.N. Doc. E/CN.4/2003/58 (2003).

Inter-American Commission on Human Rights, *Report 62/02, Case 12.285, Michael Domingues*, (Oct. 15, 2001).

Inter-American Commission on Human Rights, *Third Report on the Situation of Human Rights in Paraguay*, OEA/Ser/L/VII.110, doc. 52 (2001).

Intergovernmental Panel on Climate Change, *Climate Change 2007: Third Assessment Report* (2001).

Intergovernmental Panel on Climate Change, *Climate Change 2007: Fourth Assessment Report* (Susan Solomon et. al., eds., 2007).

International Court of Justice, Advisory Opinion on the Legal Consequences of the Construction of a Wall in the Occupied Palestinian Territory, 2004 ICJ Rep. 136 (July 9, 2004).

International Court of Justice, The Legality of the Threat or Use of Nuclear Weapons, Advisory Opinion, 1996 ICJ Rep. 241 (July 8, 1996).

International Finance Corporation, *Guide to Human Rights Impact Assessment and Management: Road-Testing Draft* (June 2007).

International Law Association, International Committee on Legal Aspects of Sustainable Development, *Report Of The Sixty-Sixth Conference* (1995).

International Law Commission, *Conclusions of the Work of the Study Group on the Fragmentation of International Law: Difficulties Arising from the Diversification and Expansion of International Law, Report of the International Law Commission to the General Assembly*, 61 U.N. GAOR Supp. (No. 10) U.N. Doc. A/61/10 (2006).

International Law Commission, *Fragmentation of International Law: Difficulties Arising from Diversification and Expansion of International Law: Report of the Study group of the International Law Commission*, U.N. Doc. A/CN.4/L.682 (Apr. 13, 2006).

International Organization for Migration, *Migration and Climate Change* (2008).

Kothari, Miloon, *Report of the Special Rapporteur on Adequate Housing as a Component of the Right to an Adequate Standard of Living*, U.N. Doc. E.CN.4/2002/59 (Jan. 2002).

Ksentini, Fatma Zohra, *Report of the Special Rapporteur on Human Rights and the Environment*, E.CN.4/Sub.2/1994/9 (July 1994).

Malé Declaration on the Human Dimension of Global Climate Change (Nov. 14, 2007).

Montreal Protocol on Substances That Deplete the Ozone Layer, 26 I.L.M. 1550 (Sept. 16, 1987).

Need to Ensure a Healthy Environment for the Well-being of Individuals, G.A. Res. 45/94, U.N. Doc. A/RES/45/94 (Dec. 14, 1990).

Organization for Economic Co-operation and Development, Development Assistance Committee, *Action-Oriented Policy Paper on Human Rights and Development* (2007).

Organization for Economic Co-operation and Development, Environment and Economics: Guiding Principles Concerning International Economic Aspects of Environmental Policies, C(72)128 (May 26, 1972).

Organization of American States, Human Rights and Climate Change in the Americas, Res. 2429, AG/RES. 2429 (XXXVIII-O/08) (June 3, 2008).

Organization of American States, Human Rights and Climate Change in the Americas, Resolution 2429, AG/RES. 2429 (XXXVIII-O/08) (June 3, 2008).

Organization of American States, Inter-American Commission on Human Rights, *Petition Seeking Relief from Violations Resulting from Global Warming Caused by Acts and Omissions of the United States* (2005).

Organization of American States, Inter-American Court of Human Rights, *Report on the Situation of Human Rights in Ecuador*, OEA/Ser.L./V/II.96, Doc. 10, Rev. 1 (Apr. 24, 1997).

Organization of American States, Proposed American Declaration on the Rights of Indigenous Peoples (Mar. 1997).

Proclamation of Teheran, Final Act of the International Conference on Human Rights, U.N. Doc. A/Conf. 32/41 at 3 (1968).

Rio Declaration on Environment and Development, U.N. Doc. A/CONF.151/26 (Vol. 1) (Aug. 12, 1992).

Rolnik, Raquel, *Report of the Special Rapporteur on Adequate Housing as a Component of the Right to an Adequate Standard of Living, and on the Right to Non-Discrimination in this Context*, U.N. Doc. A/HRC/10/7/Add.4 (Mar. 3, 2009).

Statute of the International Court of Justice, 39 AJIL Supp. 215 (1945).

Stockholm Declaration on the Human Environment of the United Nations Conference on the Human Environment, June 16, 1972, 11 I.L.M. 1416 (1972).

Tearfund, *Adaptation and the Post 2012 Framework* (Nov. 2007).

United National Environment Programme, *Handbook on Methods for Climate Change Impact Assessment and Adaptation Strategies* (Feenstra et. al., 1998).

United Nations Children's Fund, *Climate Change and Children: A Human Security Challenge* (Nov. 2008).

United Nations Children's Fund, *Our Climate, Our Children, Our Responsibility* (2008).

United Nations Climate Change Conference, Dec. 3-15, 2007, *Report of the Conference of the Parties on its Thirteenth Session*, U.N. Doc FCCC/CP/2007/6/Add.1 (Mar. 15, 2008).

United Nations Collaborative Programme on Reducing Emissions for Deforestation and Forest Degradation in Developing Countries (UN-REDD) Framework Document (June 20, 2008).

United Nations Commission on Human Rights, *Report of the Representative of the Secretary General, Mr. Frances Deng, submitted pursuant to Commission on Human Rights Resolution 1997/39*, U.N. Doc. E/CN.4/1998/53/Add.1 (Feb. 11, 1998).

United Nations Commission on Human Rights Res. 1993/77 on Forced Evictions (Mar. 10, 1993).

United Nations Commission on Human Rights Res. 1998/72 on the Right to Development (Apr. 22, 1998).

United Nations Commission on Human Rights Res. 2004/28 on the Prohibition of Forced Evictions (Apr. 16, 2004).

United Nations Conference on Environment and Development, June 3-14, 1992, *Report Annex I: Rio Declaration on Environment and Development*, U.N. Doc A/CONF.151/26/Rev.1 (Aug. 12, 1992).

United Nations Conference on Trade and Development, *Keeping Aid Afloat: No Stone Unturned, Policy Brief No. 7* (Mar. 2009).

United Nations Declaration on the Right to Development, G.A. Res. 41/128, A/RES/41/128 (Dec. 4, 1986).

United Nations Declaration on the Rights of Indigenous Peoples, G.A. Res. 61/295, A/RES/61/295 (Oct. 2, 2007).

United Nations Department of Economic and Social Affairs, *Report on the World Social Situation* (2009).

United Nations Development Programme, *Human Development Report 2000: Human Rights and Human Development* (2000).

United Nations Development Programme, *Human Development Report 2005: International Cooperation at a Crossroad: Aid, Trade and Security in an Unequal World* (2005).

United Nations Development Programme, *Human Development Report 2006: Beyond Scarcity: Power, Poverty and the Global Water Crisis* (2006).

United Nations Development Programme, *Human Development Report 2007/2008: Fighting Climate Change: Human Solidarity in a Divided World* (2007).

United Nations Development Programme, *Human Development Report 2009: Overcoming Barriers: Human Mobility and Development* (forthcoming 2009).

United Nations Economic and Social Council, Commission on Human Rights, Working Group to Consider Options Regarding the Elaboration of an Optional Protocol to the International Covenant on Economic, Social, and Cultural Rights, *Report on Economic, Social and Cultural Rights*, U.N. Doc. E/CN.4/2005/52 (Feb. 10, 2005).

United Nations Economic and Social Council, Permanent Forum on Indigenous Issues, *Report on the Second Session*, U.N. Doc E/2003/43, E/C.19/2003/22 (2003).

United Nations Economic and Social Council, Permanent Forum on Indigenous Issues, *Report on the Seventh Session*, U.N. Doc E/2008/43, E/C.19/2008/13 (2008).

United Nations Environment Programme, *From Conflict to Peace-Building: The Role of Natural Resources and the Environment* (Feb. 2009).

United Nations Environment Programme, *Global Green New Deal, Policy Brief* (Mar. 2009).

United Nations Fourth World Conference on Women, *Platform for Action*, U.N. Doc A/CONF.177/20 (Sept. 1995).

United Nations Framework Convention on Climate Change, Ad Hoc Working Group on Long-Term Cooperative Action, *Ideas and Proposals on the elements contained in paragraph 1 of the Bali Action Plan, Submissions of Parties, Addendum* (Part II), UNFCCC/AWGLCA/2008/MISC.5/Add.2 (Dec. 10, 2008).

United Nations Framework Convention on Climate Change, Ad Hoc Working Group on Long-Term Cooperative Action under the Convention, *Submission by the Czech Republic on Behalf of the European Community and its Member States* (Apr. 28 2009).

United Nations Framework Convention on Climate Change, Ad Hoc Working Group on Long-Term Cooperative Action under the Convention, *Submission of Argentina*, UNFCCC/AWGLCA/2008/MISC.5 (Oct. 27, 2008).

United Nations Framework Convention on Climate Change, Ad Hoc Working Group on Long-Term Cooperative Action under the Convention, *Submission of the Maldives on behalf of the Least Developed Countries*, UNFCCC/AWGLCA/2008/MISC.1 (Mar. 3, 2008).

United Nations Framework Convention on Climate Change, Ad Hoc Working Group on Long-Term Cooperative Action under the Convention, *Submission of Australia*, UNFCCC/AWGLCA/2008/MISC.1/Add.2 (Mar. 20, 2008).

United Nations Framework Convention on Climate Change, *Annual Compilation and Accounting Report for Annex B Parties under the Kyoto Protocol*, U.N. Doc FCCC/KP/CMP/2008/9/Rev.1 (Nov. 27, 2008).

United Nations Framework Convention on Climate Change, *Annual report of the Executive Board of the clean development mechanism to the Conference of the Parties serving as the meeting of the Parties to the Kyoto Protocol*, U.N. Doc. FCCC/KP/CMP/2008/4 (Nov. 14, 2008).

United Nations Framework Convention on Climate Change, *Bali Action Plan*, Decision 1/CP.13 (Dec. 2007).

United Nations Framework Convention on Climate Change, *Compendium of methods and tools to evaluate impacts of, and vulnerability and adaptation to, climate change* (2005).

United Nations Framework Convention on Climate Change, *Investment and Financial Flows to Address Climate Change*, UNFCCC/TP/2008/7 (Nov. 26, 2008).

United Nations Framework Convention on Climate Change, *Nairobi Work Programme on Impacts, Vulnerability and Adaptation to Climate Change* (Apr. 2007).

United Nations Framework Convention on Climate Change, *Report of the Conference of the Parties on its Seventh Session, Addendum*, UNFCCC/CP/2001/13/Add.1 (Jan. 21, 2002).

United Nations Framework Convention on Climate Change, *Report of the Conference of the Parties on its Eleventh Session, Addendum*, FCCC/CP/2005/5/Add.1 (Mar. 30, 2006).

United Nations Framework Convention on Climate Change, Report of the Subsidiary Body for Implementation on its twentieth session, UNFCCC/SBI/2004/10 (Aug. 31, 2004).

United Nations General Assembly Resolution, Conference on Environment and Development, G.A. Res. 44/228, U.N. Doc. A/RES/44/228 (Dec. 22, 1989).

United Nations General Assembly Resolution, Declaration on Principles of International Law concerning Friendly Relations and Co-operation among States in accordance with the Charter of the United Nations, G.A. Res. 2625 (XXV), U.N. Doc. A/8082 (Oct. 24, 1970).

United Nations General Assembly Resolution, Declaration on the Right to Development, G.A. Res. 41/128, U.N. Doc. A/RES/41/128 (Dec. 4, 1986).

United Nations General Assembly Resolution, High Commissioner for the Promotion and Protection of all Human Rights G.A. Res. 48/141, U.N. Doc. A/RES/48/141 (Dec. 20, 1993).

United Nations General Assembly Resolution, Need to Ensure a Healthy Environment for the Well-being of Individuals, G.A. Res. 45/94, U.N. Doc. A/RES/45/94 (Dec. 14, 1990).

United Nations General Assembly Resolution, Problems of the Human Environment, G.A. Res. 2398 (XXIII), U.N. Doc. A/ Res/2398/23 (Dec. 3, 1968).

United Nations General Assembly Resolution, Setting International Standards in the Field of Human Rights, G.A. Res. 41/120, U.N. Doc. A/RES/41/120 (Dec. 4, 1986).

United Nations General Assembly Resolution, The Right to Development, G.A. Res. 59/185, U.N. Doc. A/RES/59/185 (Dec. 20, 2005).

United Nations High Commissioner for Human Rights, *Executive Committee Conclusion No. 105 (LVI), Conclusions on Women and Girls at Risk* (Oct. 6, 2006).

United Nations High Commissioner for Human Rights, *Special Representative of the Secretary-General on human rights and transnational corporations and other business enterprises* (June 18, 2008).

United Nations High Commissioner for Human Rights, *State Responsibilities to Regulate and Adjudicate Corporate Activities under the United Nations' core Human Rights Treaties*, Individual Report on the ICCPR (June 2007).

United Nations High Commissioner for Human Rights, *State Responsibilities to Regulate and Adjudicate Corporate Activities under the United Nations' core Human Rights Treaties*, Individual Report on the ICESCR (June 2007).

United Nations Human Rights Committee, *Concluding Observations for Canada*, U.N. Doc. CERD/C/CAN/CO/18 (May 2007).

United Nations Human Rights Committee, *Concluding Observations for the United States*, U.N. Doc. CERD/C/USA/CO/6 (Feb. 2008).

United Nations Human Rights Committee, *Concluding Observations for the United States*, U.N. Doc. CCPR/C/USA/CO/3/Rev.1 (Dec. 18, 2006).

United Nations Human Rights Committee, *Concluding Observations of the Human Rights Committee: Israel*, U.N. Doc. CCPR/CO/78/ISR (Aug. 21, 2003).

United Nations Human Rights Committee, General Comment No. 12, The Right of Self-Determination of Peoples (1984).

United Nations Human Rights Committee, General Comment No. 15: The Position of Aliens under the Covenant (1986).

United Nations Human Rights Committee, General Comment No. 23, The Rights of Minorities (1994).

United Nations Human Rights Committee, General Comment No. 24, Issues relating to reservations made upon ratification or accession to the Covenant or the Optional Protocols thereto, or in relation to declarations under article 41 of the Covenant (1994).

United Nations Human Rights Committee, General Comment No. 28, Equality of Rights Between Men and Women (Article 3), U.N. Doc. CCPR/C/21/Rev.1/Add.10 (Mar. 29, 2000).

United Nations Human Rights Committee, General Comment No. 31, Nature of the General Legal Obligation on States Parties to the Covenant, U.N. Doc. CCPR/C/21/Rev.1/Add.13 (2004).

United Nations Human Rights Council, *Draft Report of the Human Rights Council on its Tenth Session*, U.N. Doc A/HRC/10/L.11 (Mar. 31, 2009).

United Nations Human Rights Council, Human Rights and Climate Change Resolution 7/23 (Mar. 28, 2008).

United Nations Human Rights Council, *Promotion and Protection of all Human Rights, Civil, Political, Economic, Social, and Cultural Rights, Including the Right to Development,* U.N. Doc. A/HRC/8/5 (Apr. 7, 2008).

United Nations Human Rights Council, *Promotion and Protection of all Human Rights, Civil, Political, Economic, Social, and Cultural Rights, Including the Right to Development,* U.N. Doc. A/HRC/11/13 (Apr. 22, 2009).

United Nations Human Rights Council, *Report of the Special Representative of the Secretary-General on the issue of human rights and transnational corporations and other business enterprises,* U.N. Doc. A/HRC/11/13 (Apr. 22, 2009).

United Nations Intergovernmental Panel on Climate Change, *Climate Change 2007: Synthesis Report* (Nov. 12-17, 2007).

United Nations International Conference on Population and Development, Sept. 5-13, 1994, Program of Action Report, 5-13 September 1994, U.N. Doc DPI/1618/POP (March 1995).

United Nations Millennium Declaration, G.A. Res. 55/2, U.N. Doc. A/RES/55/2 (Sept. 6-8, 2000).

United Nations Office of the High Commissioner for Human Rights, *Report on the Relationship Between Climate Change and Human Rights,* U.N. Doc. A/HRC/10/61 (Jan. 15, 2009).

United Nations Office of the High Commissioner for Human Rights, *Claiming the MDGs: A Human Rights Approach* (2008).

United Nations Office of the High Commissioner for Human Rights, *Frequently Asked Question on a Human Rights-Based Approach to Development Cooperation* (2006).

United Nations Office of the High Commissioner for Human Rights, *Frequently Asked Question on Economic, Social and Cultural Rights, Fact Sheet No. 33* (2008).

United Nations Office of the High Commissioner for Human Rights, *Principles and Guidelines on a Human Rights Approach to Poverty Reduction Strategies* (2006).

United Nations Office of the High Commissioner for Human Rights, Report of the high-level task force on the implementation of the right to development on its fifth session, U.N. Doc A/HRC.12/WG.2/TF.2 (June 17, 2009).

United Nations Office of the High Commissioner for Human Rights, Human Rights and Climate Change, Resolution 7/23 (Mar. 28, 2008).

United Nations Permanent Forum on Indigenous Issues, *Report on the second session,* Economic and Social Council, E/2003/43, E/C.19/2003/22 (May 12-23, 2003).

United Nations Permanent Forum on Indigenous Issues, *Report on the seventh session,* Economic and Social Council, E/2008/43, e/c.19/2008/13 (Apr. 21-May 2, 2008).

United Nations Water Conference, Mar. 14-25, 1977, *Mar Del Plata Action Plan* (Mar. 1977).

United Nations, Agreement for the Implementation of the Provisions of the United Nations Convention on the Law of the Sea of 10 December 1982 Relating to the Conservation and Management of Straddling Fish Stocks and Highly Migratory Fish Stocks, 34 I.L.M. 1542 (1995).

United Nations, Committee on Economic Social and Cultural Rights, General Comment No. 3: The Nature of State Parties Obligations, E/C.3/1991/3 (1990).

United Nations, Committee on Economic Social and Cultural Rights, General Comment No. 4: The Right to Adequate Housing, E/C.4/1992/23 (1991).

United Nations, Committee on Economic Social and Cultural Rights, General Comment No. 6: The Economic, Social and Cultural Rights of Older Persons, E/C.6/1996/22 (1995).

United Nations, Committee on Economic Social and Cultural Rights, General Comment No. 7: The Right to Adequate Housing: Forced Evictions (art. 11(1)), E/1998, 22 (1997).

United Nations, Committee on Economic Social and Cultural Rights, General Comment No. 8: The Relationship between Economic Sanctions and Respect for Economic, Social and Cultural Rights, E/C.12/1997/8 (1997).

United Nations, Committee on Economic Social and Cultural Rights, General Comment No. 12: The Right to Adequate Food, E/C.12/1999/5 (1999).

United Nations, Committee on Economic Social and Cultural Rights, General Comment No. 14: The Right to the Highest Attainable Standard of Health, E/C.12/2000/4 (2000).

United Nations, Committee on Economic Social and Cultural Rights, General Comment No. 15: The Right to Water, E/C.12/2002/11 (2003).

United Nations, Committee on Economic Social and Cultural Rights, General Comment No. 17, The Right of Everyone to Benefit from the Protection of the Moral and Material Interests Resulting From Any Scientific, Literary or Artistic Production of Which He or She is the Author, E/C.12/GC/17 (2006).

United Nations, Committee on Economic Social and Cultural Rights, General Comment No. 19, The Right to Social Security, U.N. Doc. E/C/12/CG/19 (Feb. 2008).

United Nations Global Compact, *Overview of the UN Global Compact*, June 30, 2009, http://www.unglobalcompact.org/AboutTheGC/index.html.

United Nations, *Report of the High Commissioner for Human Rights on the implementation of economic, social and cultural rights*, U.N. Doc. E/2009/90 (June 8, 2009).

United Nations, World Summit on Sustainable Development, Aug. 26 – Sept. 4, 2002, *Report*, U.N. Doc. A/56/19 (Jan. 8, 2003).

Universal Declaration on Human Rights, G.A. Res. 217A, U.N. GAOR, 3d Sess., 1st plen. mtg., U.N. Doc A/810 (Dec. 12, 1948).

World Bank, *Global Monitoring Report: A Development Emergency* (2009).

World Bank, *Growth and Poverty Reduction: Case Studies from West Africa* (Quentin Wodon, ed., 2007).

World Bank, *Realising Human Rights through Social Guarantees: An Analysis of New Approaches to Social Policy in Latin America and South Africa* (Feb. 2008).

World Bank, *Swimming Against the Tide: How Developing Countries are Coping with the Global Crisis*, (Mar. 2009).

World Bank, *The Global Economic Crisis: Assessing Poverty with a Vulnerability Lens* (Apr. 2009).

World Bank, *World Development Indicators* (2008).

World Bank, *World Development Report 2006: Equity and Development* (2006).

World Health Assembly, Resolution on Climate Change and Health, WHA61.19 (May 24, 2008).

Zielger, Jean, *Report of the Special Rapporteur on the Right to Food in Accordance with Commission on Human Rights Resolution 2002/25*, U.N. Doc E/CN.4/2003/54 (2003).

Statements, Notes, Interviews, Presentations, and Press Releases

Agrawala, Shardul, *A Development Cooperation Perspective on Mainstreaming Climate Change, OECD Environment Directorate*, Presentation to the Asia Pacific Gateway on Climate Change and Development (Apr. 23, 2008).

de Schutter, Olivier, United Nations Special Rapporteur on the Right to Food, *Contribution to the UN Commission on Sustainable Development at its 17th Session* (Apr. 5, 2009).

den Elzen, Michel, *Emission Reduction Trade-Offs for Meeting Concentration Targets*, Bonn Climate Change Talks, Presentation at the IPCC In-Session Workshop, FCCC SB-STA 28 (June 6, 2008).

Interview with Mohamed-Salah Dembri, Ambassador of Algeria, Chair of the Open-ended Working Group of the U.N. Human Rights Commission on the Right to Development, Right to Development – A Test of International Solidarity, 14 South Bulletin 4 -5 (June 15, 2001).

Letter from the U.N. Secretary General to Heads of State in the Context of Treaty Event: Focus 2002, Sustainable Development (Apr. 30, 2002).

McAdam, Jane, *Climate Change "Refugees" and International Law*, South Wales Bar Association address (Oct. 24, 2007).

News Release, Human Rights Watch, *U.S.: Treaty signing signals policy shift* (July 24, 2009).

Note, Secretariat of the U.N. Framework Convention on Climate Change, *Promoting Effective Participation in the Convention Process*, UNFCCC/SBI/2004/5 (Apr. 16, 2004).

Press Release, Centre for Human Rights and Environment, OAS Approves Human Rights and Climate Change Resolution (June 4, 2008).

Press Release, Economic, Social and Cultural Rights: Legally Entitlements Rather than Charity, Say U.N. Experts, United Nations (Dec. 10, 2008).

Press Release, Inter-American Commission on Human Rights, IACHR Announces Webcast of Public Hearings of the 127th Regular Period of Sessions, No 8/07 (Feb. 26, 2007).

Statement, Ambassador George Moose, U.S. Delegation, Explanation on Vote L.15, Right to Development, 57th Session of the U.N. Commission on Human Rights (Apr. 18, 2001).

Statement, Forest People's Program, *Statement by the International Forum of Indigenous Peoples on Climate Change (IFIPCC)*at the 13th session of Conference of the Parties to the UNFCCC SBSTA 27, agenda item 5/REDD (2007).

Statement, Olivier de Schutter, Special Rapporteur on the Right to Food, Interactive Thematic Dialogue of the U.N. General Assembly on the Global Food Crisis and the Right to Food (Apr. 6, 2009).

Statement, Representatives of Arctic Indigenous Peoples Organizations on the Occasion of the 11th Conference of Parties to the Framework Convention on Climate Change (Dec. 6, 2005).

Constitutions

La Constitution, Charte de l'environnement de 2004 (Fr.).

Constitution of South Africa

Key Impacts as a Function of Increasing Global Average Temperature Change

WATER	Increased water availability in moist tropics and high latitudes[1]				
	Decreasing water availability and increasing drought in mid-latitudes and semi-arid low latitudes [2]				
	0.4 to 1.7 billion[3]	1.0 to 2.0 billion[3]	1.1 to 3.2 billion[3]	Additional people with increased water stress	

Increasing amphibian extinction [4]
About 20 to 30% species at increasingly high risk of extinction [4]
Major extinctions around the globe [4]

ECOSYSTEMS
Increased coral bleaching[5]   Most corals bleached[6]   Widespread coral mortality[6]

Increasing species range shifts and wildfire risk[7]
Terrestrial biosphere tends toward a net carbon source, as: [8]
~15%
~40% of ecosystems affected

FOOD
Crop productivity
Low latitudes
Decreases for some cereals[9]
All cereals decrease[9]

Increases for some cereals[9]
Decreases in some regions[9]
Mid to high latitudes

COAST
Increased damage from floods and storms[10]

About 30% loss of coastal wetlands[11]

Additional people at risk of coastal flooding each year   0 to 3 million[12]   2 to 15 million[12]

HEALTH
Increasing burden from malnutrition, diarrhoeal, cardio-respiratory and infectious diseases[13]

Increased morbidity and mortality from heatwaves, floods and droughts[14]

Changed distribution of some disease vectors[15]   Substantial burden on health services[16]

SINGULAR EVENTS
Local retreat of ice in Greenland and West Antarctic[17]
Long term commitment to several metres of sea-level rise due to ice sheet loss[17]
Leading to reconfiguration of coastlines world wide and inundation of low-lying areas[18]

Ecosystem changes due to weakening of the meridional overturning circulation[19]

0   1   2   3   4   5°C

Global mean annual temperature change relative to 1980-1999 (°C)

APPENDIX B:

States parties to: ICESCR, ICCPR, CERD, CEDAW, CRC, FCCC, and Kyoto Protocol

Country	ICESCR	ICCPR	CERD	CEDAW	CRC	FCCC	Kyoto Protocol
Afghanistan	√	√	√	√	√	√	
Albania	√	√	√	√	√	√	√
Algeria	√	√	√	√	√	√	√
Andorra		√	√	√	√		
Angola	√	√		√	√	√	√
Antigua and Barbuda			√	√	√	√	√
Argentina	√	√	√	√	√	√	√
Armenia	√	√	√	√	√	√	√
Australia	√	√	√	√	√	√	√
Austria	√	√	√	√	√	√	√
Azerbaijan	√	√	√	√	√	√	√
Bahamas			√	√	√	√	√
Bahrain	√	√	√	√	√	√	√
Bangladesh	√	√	√	√	√	√	√
Barbados	√	√	√	√	√	√	√
Belarus	√	√	√	√	√	√	√
Belgium	√	√	√	√	√	√	√
Belize		√	√	√	√	√	√
Benin	√	√	√	√	√	√	√
Bhutan				√	√	√	√
Bolivia (Plurinational State of)	√	√	√	√	√	√	√
Bosnia and Herzegovina	√	√	√	√	√	√	√
Botswana		√	√	√	√	√	
Brazil	√	√	√	√	√	√	
Brunei Darussalam				√	√	√	
Bulgaria	√	√	√	√	√	√	√
Burkina Faso	√	√	√	√	√	√	√
Burundi	√	√	√	√	√	√	√
Cambodia	√	√	√	√	√	√	√
Cameroon	√	√	√	√	√	√	√
Canada	√	√	√	√	√	√	√
Cape Verde	√	√	√	√	√	√	√
Central African Republic	√	√	√	√	√	√	
Chad	√	√	√	√	√	√	
Chile	√	√	√	√	√	√	√
China	√		√	√	√	√	√
Colombia	√	√	√	√	√	√	√
Comoros			√	√	√	√	
Congo	√	√	√	√	√	√	√
Cook Islands				√	√	√	√
Costa Rica	√	√	√	√	√	√	√
Côte d'Ivoire	√	√	√	√	√	√	√
Croatia	√	√	√	√	√	√	√

Country							
Cuba			√	√	√	√	√
Cyprus	√	√	√	√	√	√	√
Czech Republic	√	√	√	√	√	√	√
Democratic People's Republic of Korea	√	√		√	√	√	√
Democratic Republic of the Congo	√	√	√	√	√	√	√
Denmark	√	√	√	√	√	√	√
Djibouti	√	√		√	√	√	√
Dominica	√	√		√	√	√	√
Dominican Republic	√	√	√	√	√	√	√
Ecuador	√	√	√	√	√	√	√
Egypt	√	√	√	√	√	√	√
El Salvador	√	√	√	√	√	√	√
Equatorial Guinea	√	√	√	√	√	√	√
Eritrea	√	√	√	√	√	√	√
Estonia	√	√	√	√	√	√	√
Ethiopia	√	√	√	√	√	√	√
Fiji			√	√	√	√	√
Finland	√	√	√	√	√	√	√
France	√	√	√	√	√	√	√
Gabon	√	√	√	√	√	√	√
The Gambia	√	√	√	√	√	√	√
Georgia	√	√	√	√	√	√	√
Germany	√	√	√	√	√	√	√
Ghana	√	√	√	√	√	√	√
Greece	√	√	√	√	√	√	√
Grenada	√	√		√	√	√	√
Guatemala	√	√	√	√	√	√	√
Guinea	√	√	√	√	√	√	√
Guinea-Bissau	√			√	√	√	√
Guyana	√	√	√	√	√	√	√
Haiti		√	√	√	√	√	√
Holy See			√		√		
Honduras	√	√	√	√	√	√	√
Hungary	√	√	√	√	√	√	√
Iceland	√	√	√	√	√	√	√
India	√	√	√	√	√	√	√
Indonesia	√	√	√	√	√	√	√
Iran (Islamic Republic of)	√	√	√		√	√	√
Iraq	√	√	√	√	√		
Ireland	√	√	√	√	√	√	√
Israel	√	√	√	√	√	√	√
Italy	√	√	√	√	√	√	√
Jamaica	√	√	√	√	√	√	√
Japan	√	√	√	√	√	√	√
Jordan	√	√	√	√	√	√	√
Kazakhstan	√	√	√	√	√		
Kenya	√	√	√	√	√		
Kiribati				√	√	√	√
Kuwait	√	√	√	√	√	√	√
Kyrgyzstan	√	√	√	√	√	√	√

Lao People's Democratic Republic	√		√	√	√	√	√
Latvia	√	√	√	√	√	√	√
Lebanon	√	√	√	√	√	√	√
Lesotho	√	√	√	√	√	√	√
Liberia	√	√	√	√	√	√	√
Libyan Arab Jamahiriya	√	√	√	√	√	√	√
Liechtenstein	√	√	√	√	√	√	√
Lithuania	√	√	√	√	√	√	√
Luxembourg	√	√	√	√	√	√	√
Madagascar	√	√	√	√	√	√	√
Malawi	√	√	√	√	√	√	√
Malaysia				√	√	√	√
Maldives	√	√	√	√	√	√	√
Mali	√	√	√	√	√	√	√
Malta	√	√	√	√	√	√	√
Marshall Islands				√	√	√	√
Mauritania	√	√	√	√	√	√	√
Mauritius	√	√	√	√	√	√	√
Mexico	√	√	√	√	√	√	√
Micronesia (Federated States of)				√	√	√	√
Moldova	√	√	√	√	√	√	√
Monaco	√	√	√	√	√	√	√
Mongolia	√	√	√	√	√	√	√
Montenegro	√	√	√	√	√	√	√
Morocco	√	√	√	√	√	√	√
Mozambique		√	√	√	√	√	√
Myanmar				√	√	√	√
Namibia	√	√	√	√	√	√	√
Nauru					√	√	√
Nepal	√	√	√	√	√	√	√
Netherlands	√	√	√	√	√	√	√
New Zealand	√	√	√	√	√	√	√
Nicaragua	√	√	√	√	√	√	√
Niger	√	√	√	√	√	√	√
Nigeria	√	√	√	√	√	√	√
Niue					√	√	√
Norway	√	√	√	√	√	√	√
Oman			√	√	√	√	√
Pakistan	√		√	√	√	√	√
Palau					√	√	√
Panama	√	√	√	√	√	√	√
Papua New Guinea	√	√	√	√	√	√	√
Paraguay	√	√	√	√	√	√	√
Peru	√	√	√	√	√	√	√
Philippines	√	√	√	√	√	√	√
Poland	√	√	√	√	√	√	√
Portugal	√	√	√	√	√	√	√
Qatar			√		√	√	√
Republic of Korea	√	√	√	√	√	√	√
Romania	√	√	√	√	√	√	√

Russian Federation	√	√	√	√	√	√	√
Rwanda	√	√	√	√	√	√	√
St. Kitts and Nevis			√	√	√	√	
St. Lucia			√	√	√	√	√
Saintt Vincent and the Grenadines			√	√	√	√	√
Samoa		√		√	√	√	√
San Marino	√	√	√	√	√	√	
São Tomé and Príncipe					√	√	√
Saudi Arabia			√	√	√	√	√
Senegal	√	√	√	√	√	√	√
Serbia	√	√	√	√	√	√	√
Seychelles	√	√	√	√	√	√	√
Sierra Leone	√	√	√	√	√	√	√
Singapore				√	√	√	√
Slovakia	√	√	√	√	√	√	√
Slovenia	√	√	√	√	√	√	√
Solomon Islands	√		√	√	√	√	√
Somalia	√	√	√				
South Africa		√	√	√	√	√	√
Spain	√	√	√	√	√	√	√
Sri Lanka	√	√	√	√	√	√	√
Sudan	√	√	√		√	√	√
Suriname	√	√	√	√	√	√	√
Swaziland	√	√	√	√	√	√	√
Sweden	√	√	√	√	√	√	√
Switzerland	√	√	√	√	√	√	√
Syrian Arab Republic	√	√	√	√	√	√	√
Tajikistan	√	√	√	√	√	√	
Thailand	√	√	√	√	√	√	√
The Former Yugoslav Republic of Macedonia	√	√	√	√	√	√	√
Timor-Leste	√	√	√	√	√	√	
Togo	√	√	√	√	√	√	√
Tonga			√		√	√	√
Trinidad and Tobago	√	√	√		√	√	√
Tunisia	√	√	√		√	√	√
Turkey	√	√	√	√	√	√	
Turkmenistan	√	√	√	√	√		√
Tuvalu				√	√	√	√
Uganda	√	√	√	√	√	√	√
Ukraine	√	√	√	√	√	√	√
United Arab Emirates			√	√	√	√	√
United Kingdom of Great Britain and Northern Ireland	√	√	√	√	√	√	√
United Republic of Tanzania	√	√	√	√	√	√	√
United States of America		√	√			√	
Uruguay	√	√	√	√	√	√	√
Uzbekistan	√	√	√	√	√	√	√

	ICESCR	ICCPR	CERD	CEDAW	CRC	FCCC	KP
Vanuatu		√		√	√	√	√
Venezuela (República Bolivariana de)	√	√	√	√	√	√	√
Viet Nam	√	√	√	√	√	√	√
Yemen	√	√	√	√	√	√	√
Zambia	√	√	√	√	√	√	√
Zimbabwe	√	√	√	√	√	√	

ICESCR-International Covenant on Economic, Social and Cultural Rights
ICCPR-International Covenant on Civil and Political Rights
CERD-Convention on the Elimination of All Forms of Racial Discrimination
CEDAW-Convention on the Elimination of All Forms of Discrimination against Women
CRC-Convention on the Rights of the Child
FCCC – Framework Convention on Climate Change
KP - Kyoto Protocol

NOTES

1. Parts of this introductory sub-section and the next are drawn from Rajamani, Lavanya, *From Berlin to Bali and Beyond: Killing Kyoto Softly*, 57(3) INT'L & COMP. L. Q. 909 (2008).

2. G.A. Res. 44/228, U.N. Doc. A/RES/44/228 (Dec. 22, 1989).

3. United Nations Development Programme, *Human Development Report 2000: Human Rights and Human Development* (2000) [hereinafter Human Development Report 2007/8], *available at* http://hdr. undp.org/en/reports/global/hdr2007-2008/.

4. Intergovernmental Panel on Climate Change, *Climate Change 2007: Fourth Assessment Report* (Susan Solomon et. al., eds., 2007).

5. *Id.*

6. *Id.* Summary for Policy Makers, at 8.

7. *Id.*

8. *Id.*

9. An "emergency summit" of scientists in Copenhagen in March 2009 reported that new data across many fields showed dramatically faster change than they had earlier forecasted. Adam, David, *Stern Attacks Politicians for Climate "Devastation,"* THE GUARDIAN (Mar. 13, 2009), *available at* http://www.guardian.co.uk/environment/2009/mar/13/stern-attacks-politicians-climate-change.

10. The IPCC described climate change as a "massive threat to human development." Human Development Report 2007/8, Summary for Policy Makers, *supra* note 3.

11. *Supra* note 3, at 8.

12. *Id.* at 9.

13. Stern, Nicholas, *Stern Review on the Economics of Climate Change* (Oct. 30, 2006) [hereinafter Stern Review], *available at* http://www.hm-treasury.gov.uk./independent_reviews/ stern_review_economics_climate_change/sternreview_index.cfm, Chapter 4 (Implications of Climate Change for Development).

14. *Id.* at 92.

15. STERN, NICHOLAS, CLIMATE CHANGE AND THE CREATION OF A NEW ERA OF PROGRESS AND PROSPERITY (2009), cited in McKibben, Bill, *Can Obama Change the Climate?* 56(10) N.Y. REV. BOOKS 39 (June 11 – July 1, 2009).

16. On the impacts of the global financial and economic crises on human development, *see* World Bank, *Swimming Against the Tide: How Developing Countries are Coping with the Global Crisis*, (Mar. 2009); Institute for Development Studies, *Voices from the South: the Impact of the Financial Crisis on Developing Countries* (Nov. 2008), *available at* www.ids.ack.uk/go/financial-crisis-impact; and Overseas Development Institute, *Children in Times of Economic Crisis: Past Lessons, Future Policies*, Background Note (Mar. 2009), *available at* http://www.chronicpoverty.org/pubfiles/global-crisis-children%20 printing.pdf. The estimated cost for needed mitigation and adaptation in developing countries is US$100 billion annually: Tearfund, *Adaptation and the Post 2012 Framework* (Nov. 2007) at 7. Yet ODA could suffer steep declines in the economic crisis: United Nations Conference on Trade and Development, *Keeping Aid Afloat: No Stone Unturned, Policy Brief No. 7* (Mar. 2009), *available at* http:// www.unctad.org/en/docs/presspb20092_en.pdf. The World Bank estimates that only one quarter of countries most clearly exposed to the global economic and financial crises have reasonable fiscal capacities to undertake significant counter-cyclical spending on social, let alone environmental, programmes: World Bank, *The Global Economic Crisis: Assessing Poverty with a Vulnerability Lens* (Apr. 2009), *available at* http://siteresources.worldbank.org/NEWS/Resources/WBGVulnerable-CountriesBrief.pdf. On the constraints to the development and deployment of clean technologies *see* Climate Institute, *Breaking Through on Technology: Perspectives for Australia* (June 2009) at 7, *available at* http://www.climateinstitute.org.au/images/reports/techbreakthroughaus.pdf. For arguments and policy recommendations concerning the impacts of the global economic and financial crises on the environment generally, including with respect to the global carbon market, *see* United Nations Environment Programme, *Global Green New Deal, Policy Brief* (Mar. 2009), *available at* http:// www.unep.org/pdf/A_Global_Green_New_Deal_Policy_Brief.pdf.

17. Humphreys, Stephen, THE HUMAN RIGHTS DIMENSIONS OF CLIMATE CHANGE: A ROUGH GUIDE (2008) [hereinafter ROUGH GUIDE]. This book explores in some detail the silence on human rights in climate change discourse, including in page 3, footnote 4, to the limited references in the IPCC's

Fourth Assessment Report to human rights. An explicit reference is found in Intergovernmental Panel on Climate Change, *Climate Change 2007: Fourth Assessment Report* (Susan Solomon et. al., eds., 2007) at 696.

18. *Id.* However for a different view *see* Tully, Stephen, *Like Oil and Water: A Sceptical Appraisal of Climate Change and Human Rights*, 15 AUST. INT'L L. J. 213 (2008). The author analyses human rights-oriented and other litigation strategies in the context of environmental protection, and appraises the typical scheme of remedies flowing from human rights claims. While noting the importance of the human rights paradigm in highlighting the impacts of climate change upon individuals, the author cautions against over-estimating the comparative advantages of legal strategies focused upon human rights litigation *per se*, given the difficulties of establishing clear violations, identifying perpetrators and overcoming the territorial application of international human rights law.

19. *Id.*

20. This term refers to treaties that were entered into post-1972; are international, rather than regional, in scope, impact and interest; and encompass treaties that according to erstwhile UN Secretary General reflect "humanity's efforts to achieve economic advancement while ensuring that the environment will also be preserved for future generations." Letter from the UN Secretary General to Heads of State in the Context of Treaty Event: Focus 2002, Sustainable Development (Apr. 30, 2002), *available at* http://untreaty.un.org/English/TreatyEvent2002/index.htm.

21. The current commitments require industrialized countries to reduce a basket of greenhouse gases (GHG) 5% below 1990 levels in the commitment period 2008-2012, *see* Article 3, Kyoto Protocol to the United Nations Framework Convention on Climate Change, Dec. 11, 1997, 37 I.L.M. 22. The IPCC recommends 25-40% below 1990 levels by 2020 for industrialized countries, *see* Kyoto Protocol to the United Nations Framework Convention on Climate Change, Dec. 11, 1997, 37 I.L.M. 22, Box 13.7 at 776. Two IPCC authors later recommended 15-30% below baseline for developing countries by 2020, *see* den Elzen, Michel, *Emission Reduction Trade-Offs for Meeting Concentration Targets*, Bonn Climate Change Talks, Presentation at the IPCC In-Session Workshop, FCCC SB-STA 28 (June 6, 2008), *available at* http://www.ipcc.ch/graphics/pr-ar4-2008-06-briefing-bonn.htm. However, in June 2009, the World Wildlife Fund estimated that the pledged GHG reductions by industrialised countries amount to a total emissions cut of only 10% compared with 1990 levels. In the view of the Executive Secretary of the UN Framework Convention on Climate Change, Mr. Yvo de Boer: "there is no question that industrialised countries must raise their sights higher." Max, Arthur, *UN Climate Chief Confident of Global Warming Pact*, WASH. POST, June 12, 2009, *available at* http://www.washingtonpost.com/wp-dyn/content/article/2009/06/12/AR2009061201914_2.html.

22. For status of implementation, *see* United Nations Framework Convention on Climate Change, *Annual Compilation and Accounting Report for Annex B Parties under the Kyoto Protocol*, U.N. Doc FCCC/KP/CMP/2008/9/Rev.1. The EU-15 is currently 2.7% below 1990 levels, economies in transition are 30-40% below 1990 levels due to economic restructuring, and other industrialized countries are marginally above 1990 levels. The U.S., as a non-Kyoto Party, is not part of the analysis.

23. World Bank, *World Development Report 2006: Equity and Development* (2006); United Nations Development Programme, *Human Development Report 2005: International Cooperation at a Crossroad: Aid, Trade and Security in an Unequal World* (2005).

24. United Nations Framework Convention on Climate Change, *Report of the Conference of the Parties on its Seventh Session, Addendum*, UNFCCC/CP/2001/13/Add.1 (Jan. 21, 2002) [hereinafter UN-FCCC].

25. Kyoto Protocol to the United Nations Framework Convention on Climate Change, Dec. 11, 1997, 37 I.L.M. 22 [hereinafter Kyoto Protocol].

26. The terms "developing" and "industrialized" or occasionally "developed" are used, for want of more nuanced terms, while acknowledging their reductionist character and their failure to reflect the diversity within and between these groupings.

27. In terms of scientific inputs, the COP relies upon the work of the IPCC as well as national communications from Member States, technical support for which is made available by a COP subsidiary body called the Consultative Group of Experts on National Communications from Non-Annex-I Parties. Subsidiary bodies have also been set up to advise States on scientific, technological and methodological climate change matters, technology transfer to developing countries for mitigation and adaptation, as well as to verify how the convention is being applied. These are the Subsidiary Body for Scientific and Technological Advice (SBSTA), Expert Group on Technology Transfer, and Subsidiary Body for Implementation, respectively.

28. Kyoto Protocol's Status of Ratification, *available at* http://unfccc.int/files/kyoto_protocol/status_ of_ratification/application/pdf/kp_ratification_20090708.pdf. The secretariat, supporting institutions, and subsidiary bodies of the UNFCCC generally serve simultaneously as those of the Kyoto Protocol.

29. *See* Kyoto Protocol, *supra* note 25, Articles 6, 7, and 12 respectively. Under the CDM, States can receive additional emission credits if they set up schemes to combat climate change in developing countries.

30. United Nations Climate Change Conference, Dec. 3-15, 2007, *Report of the Conference of the Parties on its Thirteenth Session*, U.N. Doc FCCC/CP/2007/6/Add.1 (Mar. 15, 2008).

31. *See* Decision 1/CP.13, *Bali Action Plan*, in United Nations Climate Change Conference, Dec. 3-15, 2007, *Report of the Conference of the Parties on its Thirteenth Session*, U.N. Doc FCCC/CP/2007/6/Add.1 (Mar. 15, 2008). There is no agreement as yet on the legal form of this "agreed outcome," but it is widely expected to lead to a new climate agreement either to supplement or replace the Kyoto Protocol.

32. The Copenhagen Conference was the Fifteenth Conference of the Parties to the UNFCCC (COP 15). http://unfccc.int/2860.php.

33. A number of funds have been established under the UNFCCC and elsewhere. In 2001, the UNFCCC secretariat initiated a "National Adaptation Programme of Action" (NAPA) process, under which LDCs may identify priority activities that respond to their urgent and immediate needs to adapt to climate change (those for which further delay would increase vulnerability or costs at a later stage) as a tool for international resource mobilisation. On NAPAs *see* http://unfccc.int/cooperation_support/least_developed_countries_portal/frequently_asked_questions/items/4743txt. php, last visited June 10, 2009. Moreover, a five-year programme of work (Nairobi Programme of Work, 2005-2010) was put in place by States party, international organisations, and other stakeholders to help all States party, and, in particular, LDCs and low-lying countries, improve their understanding and assessment of impacts, vulnerability, and adaptation to climate change as a basis for informed decision-making on climate change adaptation. Decision 2/CP.11, U.N. Doc. FCCC/CP/2005/5/Add.1 at 5. Further information on the Nairobi Programme of Work *available at* http://unfccc.int/adaptation/sbsta_agenda_item_adaptation/items/3633.php, last visited June 10, 2009.

34. This is not to denigrate UN Member States' achievements unfairly. The Kyoto Protocol has arguably proven effective in stimulating and framing domestic action on climate change in a number of industrialised countries, with the EU as, perhaps, the most notable example, as well as facilitating adaptation responses in certain developing countries. There are difficult challenges confronting any serious international regulatory effort in the climate change context, given the complicated inter-governmental politics, high economic stakes and inter-temporal trade-offs involved.

35. United Nations Office of the High Commissioner for Human Rights, *Frequently Asked Question on a Human Rights-Based Approach to Development Cooperation* (2006), *available at* http://www.ohchr. org/Documents/Publications/FAQen.pdf.

36. The philosophical influences within contemporary international human rights instruments reflect a range of traditions. So-called "dignitarian" traditions identify the inherent dignity of the human person, a socially contingent concept, as providing the philosophical underpinnings for equal rights for all human beings. Dignitarian justifications are perceived to sit in tension with more traditional liberal explanations of rights, and the utilitarian associations of the latter. For further discussion *see* A DICTIONARY OF HUMAN RIGHTS (David Robertson ed., 2007).

37. *See* Preamble, Universal Declaration on Human Rights, G.A. Res. 217A, U.N. GAOR, 3d Sess., 1st plen. mtg., U.N. Doc A/810 (Dec. 12, 1948) [hereinafter UDHR]; Preamble, African Charter on Human and People's Rights, June 27, 1981, 21 I.L.M. 58 (also known as the Banjul Charter) [hereinafter African Charter]; and Article 1(1) Vienna Declaration and Programme of Action, June 14-25, 1993, 32 I.L.M. 1661 [hereinafter Vienna Declaration]. On a formal rather than philosophical level, the idea of the universality of human rights is supported by the empirical fact of the universal adherence by all States to the UN international human rights treaty regime, along with the universal application of other sources of law including customary international law and *jus cogens*.

38. Koskenniemi, Martii, The Preamble of the Universal Declaration on Human Rights, in THE UNIVERSAL DECLARATION OF HUMAN RIGHTS (G. Alfredsson & A. Eide eds., 1999).

39. For a listing *see* http://www2.ohchr.org/english/law/index.htm.

40. International Covenant on Civil and Political Rights, Dec. 16, 1966, 6 I.L.M. 368 [hereinafter ICCPR].

41. International Covenant on Economic, Social and Cultural Rights, Dec. 16, 1966, 6 I.L.M. 360 [hereinafter ICESCR].

42. Convention on the Rights of the Child, Nov. 20, 1989, 28 I.L.M. 1448 [hereinafter CRC]. *See* The Major Economies Forum on Energy and Climate was launched on March 28, 2009. 17 major economies participate in the Forum which is intended to facilitate a candid dialogue among major developed and developing economies and help generate the political leadership necessary to achieve a successful outcome at the climate change conference in Copenhagen. http://www.state.gov/g/oes/climate/mem/ visited on 1/19/2010.

43. It is however noteworthy that signature of a treaty creates a presumption that a state will not act in a way that will defeat the treaty's object and purpose.

44. Most, but not all, of the core human rights treaties have optional individual communications procedures, covering the entire range of human rights: civil, social, cultural, political and economic. The CRC is among the notable exceptions.

45. The Committee against Torture, established under the CAT, has the power to undertake country investigations. Other expert bodies established under the 59-member Human Rights Council, known as "Special Procedures," have thematic and country-specific mandates, variously. While Special Procedures do not review States parties' compliance with their treaty obligations, many of them do carry out an independent monitoring function on the invitation of UN Member States as well as help to clarify the normative content of particular human rights. For an overview of the work of Special Procedures *see* http://www2.ohchr.org/english/bodies/chr/special/index.htm, last visited June 10, 2009.

46. "General Comments," sometimes also called "General Recommendations," are issued by treaty bodies to provide guidance to States as to the views of the treaty body on particular provisions or cross-cutting issues under the treaty it supervises. While General Comments are not themselves legally binding, they form a central part of the review process in which States parties' compliance with the treaty obligations is assessed, and have been relied upon by national courts in interpreting constitutional human rights claims in particular cases (*see e.g. infra* note 60). The role of treaty bodies in issuing General Comments which flesh out the meaning of treaty standards is not uncontroversial, to the extent that this might result in obligations unforeseen at the time of ratification. Be that as it may, such concerns have not proven sufficient to unsettle the well-established practice of treaty bodies' in relying upon their own legal interpretations in reviewing States parties' compliance with their treaty obligations, under periodic reviews of national reports as well as under individual communications procedures. For a general outline of the roles and functions of human rights treaty bodies *see* http://www.ohchr.org/EN/HRBodies/Pages/HumanRightsBodies.aspx, last visited June 10, 2009.

47. European Convention for the Protection of Human Rights and Fundamental Freedoms, Nov. 4, 1950, 213 U.N.T.S. 222 [hereinafter European Convention]; American Convention on Human Rights, Nov. 22, 1969, 9 I.L.M. 673 [hereinafter American Convention]; African Charter on Human and People's Rights, June 27, 1981, 21 I.L.M. 58 [hereinafter African Charter].

48. The European Court, the Inter-American Commission, and the African Commission each has the authority to receive communications from individuals claiming a party to the relevant treaty has failed to comply with its obligations. The European Court's decisions bind the state party. The two Commissions may only issue non-binding decisions, but they may also bring a claim to the Inter-American Court of Human Rights or the African Court on Human and Peoples' Rights, which may issue decisions binding on States that have accepted their jurisdiction. American Convention, *supra* note 47, Article 68; Protocol to the African Charter on Human and Peoples' Rights on the Establishment of an African Court on Human and Peoples' Rights, Article 30, June 10, 1998.

49. European Union Charter of Fundamental Rights, Dec. 7, 2000, OJ 2000 C 364 at 1. The Charter was intended by EU Member States as a nonbinding re-affirmation of existing norms, to help the EU promote "fundamental rights" (expressed to embrace all human rights – civil, political, economic, social, and cultural) within all spheres of the EU's competence. For discussions on its history and contemporary normative significance *see* Betten, Lammy, *The EU Charter on Fundamental Rights: A Trojan Horse or a Mouse?* 17 INT'L J. COMP. LAB. L. & INDUS. REL. 151 (2001); de Búrca, Grainne, *The Drafting of the European Union Charter of Fundamental Rights*, 26 EUR. L. REV. 126 (2001); Quinn, Gerard & Leo Flynn, THE U.N. CHARTER ON FUNDAMENTAL RIGHTS (2005); Craig, Paul & Grainne De Búrca, E.U. LAW: TEXT, CASES, Materials (4th ed. 2007). It is worthy of note that under the Lisbon Treaty, which entered into force on December 1, 2009, the Charter of Fundamental Rights of the

European Union has full legal effect as binding treaty law. The Charter referred to in the Lisbon Treaty is an amended version of the Charter "solemnly proclaimed" on December 7, 2000.

50. *See* African Charter, *supra* note 37, Articles 4, 6, 12, 18(1) (referring only to family, not privacy or home); American Convention, *supra* note 47, Articles 4(1), 7, 11(2), 22; ICCPR, *supra* note 40, Articles 6(1), 9, 12, 17(1); European Convention, *supra* note 47, Articles 2(1), 5, 8(1), Protocol No. 4, Article 2.

51. Protocol No. 1 to the European Convention, Article 1; American Convention, *supra* note 47, Article 21; African Charter, *supra* note 37.

52. European Social Charter, Oct. 18, 529 U.N.T.S. 89. The Council of Europe adopted a more detailed and extensive Revised Social Charter in 1996 [hereinafter European Social Charter (Revised)], opened for signature May 3, 1996 (Europ. T.S. No. 163), which has superseded the older version in whole or part for countries that have ratified it. Some important parties to the 1961 Charter, however, including Austria, the Czech Republic, Denmark, Germany, Greece, Poland, Spain, and the United Kingdom, have yet to ratify the 1996 Charter. Further, the EU Charter on Fundamental Rights promotes all kinds of rights equally, subject to ongoing debates regarding the legal status and scope of application of that instrument.

53. Additional Protocol to the American Convention on Human Rights in the area of Economic, Social and Cultural Rights, 1988, *reprinted in* 28 ILM 156 (1989) [hereinafter San Salvador Protocol]. The Protocol has fourteen parties, including Argentina, Brazil, Columbia, Mexico, and Uruguay.

54. African Charter, *supra* note 37, Articles 15-17.

55. ICESCR, *supra* note 41, Articles 6, 7, 9, 11–13, 15(1); European Social Charter, *supra* note 52, Articles 1-4, 11, 12; African Charter, *supra* note 37, Articles 15-17; San Salvador Protocol, *supra* note 53, Articles 6, 7, 9, 10, 12–14.

56. San Salvador Protocol, *supra* note 53, Article 11(1). The African Charter also includes a specific right to a "satisfactory" environment, but as a right of peoples rather than individuals. African Charter, *supra* note 37, Article 24. *See infra* Chapter IV(3).

57. Charter of Fundamental Rights of the European Union, C/364 OJEC, Dec. 18, 2000, *available at* http://www.europarl.europa.eu/charter/pdf/text_en.pdf. Article 37 of the Charter states that: "a high level of environmental protection and the improvement of the quality of the environment must be integrated into the policies of the Union and ensured in accordance with the principle of sustainable development."

58. To this effect *see* Pedersen, Ole W., *European Environmental Human Rights and Environmental Rights: A Long Time Coming?*, 21 GEO. INT'L ENVTL. L. REV. 73 (2008). However as Pedersen observes at page 104: "if the Charter were to become primary Community law, and thus become subject to the jurisdiction of the [European Court of Justice], this could lead to a broadening of the scope of Article 37."

59. The African Commission on Human and Peoples' Rights can hear claims concerning all rights in the African Charter, including economic, social, and cultural rights. African Charter, *supra* note 37, Articles 55–6. Moreover, the UN General Assembly recently approved a draft Optional Protocol to the ICESCR, permitting individual complaints. Optional Protocol to the International Covenant on Economic, Social and Cultural Rights Permitting Individual Complaints, U.N. Doc A/RES/63/117 (Dec. 10, 2008) [hereinafter ICESCR Optional Protocol]. *See* Press Release, Economic, Social and Cultural Rights: Legally Entitlements Rather than Charity, Say U.N. Experts, United Nations (Dec. 10, 2008), *available at*: http://www.unhchr.ch/huricane/huricane.nsf/view01/C5486C42747EC60BC1 25751B005B08B3?opendocument last visited Dec. 11, 2008. For further background on the Optional Protocol to the ICESCR *see* http://www2.ohchr.org/english/issues/escr/intro.htm last visited Nov. 28, 2008. For an extensive comparative analysis of recent trends in the judicial enforcement of socio-economic rights claims in national jurisdictions across all regions *see* SOCIAL RIGHTS JURISPRUDENCE: EMERGING TRENDS IN INTERNATIONAL AND COMPARATIVE LAW (Malcolm Langford ed., 2009).

60. The European Social Charter gives an independent committee of experts the authority to examine States' reports on their own compliance, and an additional protocol to the Charter authorizes the committee to consider "collective complaints" submitted by certain international and national non-governmental organizations. Reports and recommendations of the European Committee on Social Rights (the expert body), and recommendations transmitted to the Council of Europe's Committee of Ministers for a decision. Additional Protocol to the European Social Charter Providing for a System of Collective Complaints, Sept. 11, 1995, 34 I.L.M. 1453. As an illustration of the potential impacts of this protocol, a complaint brought in 2006 against France by a homeless people's federation alleging a violation of the right to housing under Article 31 of the Revised European Social Charter recently resulted in a favourable recommendation by the Committee of Ministers, which

was incorporated within strategic guidelines and budget discussions between central government and certain local governments, as well as being taken up by the *Haute Autorité de Lutte contre les Discriminations et pour l'Egalité* (the national anti-discrimination agency): FEANTSA v. France, 47 Eur. Ct. H.R. 15 (2007). For a summary *see* http://www.escr-net.org/caselaw/caselaw_show.htm?doc_id=939653&country=13532, last visited June 18, 2009. The Inter-American Commission can address the rights protected by the San Salvador Protocol in its country reports. San Salvador Protocol, *supra* note 53, Article 19(7).

61. ICCPR, *supra* note 40, Article 2(1).

62. NOWAK, MANFRED, U.N. COVENANT ON CIVIL AND POLITICAL RIGHTS: CCPR COMMENTARY (2005) "The duty *to respect* . . . means that the States parties must refrain from restricting the exercise of these rights where such is not expressly allowed."

63. *See* JOSEPH, SARAH ET. AL., THE INTERNATIONAL COVENANT ON CIVIL AND POLITICAL RIGHTS: CASES, MATERIALS, AND COMMENTARY (2000). "It is . . . likely that the general duty in Article 2(1) on States to 'ensure' ICCPR rights entails a duty, of perhaps varying degrees of strictness, to protect individuals from abuse of all ICCPR rights by others." Nowak emphasizes that the term "ensure" requires the state to take positive steps to give effect to the rights generally. Nowak, *id.* at 37-39. Among the State's duties of performance are to take "positive measures to protect against private interference" with respect to certain rights. *Id.* at 39.

64. United Nations Human Rights Committee, General Comment No. 31, Nature of the General Legal Obligation on States Parties to the Covenant, U.N. Doc. CCPR/C/21/Rev.1/Add.13 (2004).

65. The non-discrimination requirement should not be read as prohibiting differential treatment between groups of people, however as long as any distinctions are objectively justifiable. Moreover, temporary special measures in favour of women, minorities, people with disabilities, and disadvantaged groups are lawful under relevant international human rights instruments.

66 For illustrations of the "minimum core content" of the rights to adequate food and the highest attainable standard of health, *see* United Nations, Committee on Economic Social and Cultural Rights [hereinafter CESCR], General Comment No. 12: The Right to Adequate Food, E/C.12/1999/5 (1999), and CESCR General Comment No. 14, The right to the highest attainable standard of health, E/C.12/2000/4 (2000), respectively. In terms of the Committee's jurisprudence, the obligation to guarantee "essential minimum levels" and avoid retrogression in the realisation of socio-economic rights are qualified by resource availability: *see* CESCR General Comment No. 3: The Nature of State Parties Obligations, E/C.3/1991/3 (1990), *available at* http://daccessdds.un.org/doc/UNDOC/GEN/N07/394/33/PDF/N0739433.pdf?OpenElement.

67. This obligation of "non-retrogression" operates as a legal presumption, rebuttable on demonstration by the state concerned that it has considered all alternative policy measures and that the retrogression in the achievement of a particular right is justifiable by reference to the totality of rights in the ICESCR in the context of the full use of available resources. CESCR General Comment No. 3 (1990), *id.* For a fuller discussion of these obligations *see* OHCHR, Frequently Asked Questions on Economic, Social and Cultural Rights, Fact Sheet No. 33 (December 2008), *available at* http://www.ohchr.org/Documents/Publications/FactSheet33en.pdf. And for a more contextualised discussion on how these obligations may help to inform and frame economic policy-making *see* Balakrishnan, Radhika, Diane Elson & Raj Patel, *Rethinking Macro Economic Strategies from a Human Rights Perspective (Why MES with Human Rights II)*, Carnegie Policy Innovations (Feb. 2009), *available at* http://www.networkideas.org/featart/mar2009/MES2.pdf.

68. CESCR General Comment No. 12, *supra* note 66.

69. CESCR General Comment No. 14, *supra* note 66, paras. 33, 37.

70. Approximately thirty States have not have ratified the ICESCR, and in many others the Covenant does not have direct effect or has not been fully translated into national law. Yet the ICESCR can still exert influence on national jurisprudence. In the case of South Africa, for instance, fertile ground has existed for socio-economic rights litigation since the late 1990s; the formulation of socio-economic rights in the national constitution is not identical to the ICESCR, yet the jurisprudence under the latter instrument has proven to be a relevant influence on judicial review in that country. And, in FEANTSA v. France, *supra* note 60, the European Committee on Social Rights reportedly used the ICESCR as "a key source of interpretation" of Article 31 of the European Social Charter, as well as the CESCR's General Comment No. 4, The Right to Adequate Housing, E/1992/23 (1991), General Comment No. 7 (1997) on the right to adequate housing (Article 11(1) of the Covenant): Forced evictions, and the work of the UN Special Rapporteur on the Right to Adequate Housing. *See* Langford ed., *supra* note 59, more generally on this theme.

71. Langford, Malcolm, *The Justiciability of Social Rights: From Practice to Theory*, in Langford ed., *supra* note 59, at 14-20. This includes failing to regulate the activities of private companies and to ensure access to affordable services in the context of privatisation.

72. Langford, *Id.* at 22. This analysis of comparative jurisprudence shows, among other things, that so-called "positive" obligations need not necessarily be costly.

73. Langford, *Id.* at 24-7.

74. Langford, *Id.* at 23-4.

75. *See* African Charter, *supra* note 37, Article 2; American Convention, *supra* note 47, Article 1(1); ICCPR, *supra* note 40, Articles 2(1), 26; ICESCR, *supra* note 41, Article 2(2); European Convention, *supra* note 47, Article 14.

76. Convention on the Elimination of All Forms of Discrimination Against Women, U.N. Doc. A/RES/34/180, Dec. 18, 1979 [hereinafter CEDAW]. the Convention on the Elimination of All Forms of Racial Discrimination, Dec. 25, 1965, 5 I.L.M. 352 [hereinafter ICERD], and the Convention on the Rights of Persons with Disabilities, Dec. 13, 2006, U.N. Doc. A/RES/63/192 [hereinafter CPRD].

77. ICCPR, *supra* note 40, Article 27. *See also* International Convention on the Protection of the Rights of All Migrant Workers and Members of Their Families, U.N. Doc. A/RES/45/158 (Dec. 18, 1990) [hereinafter MWC]; and the CRC, *supra* note 42.

78. ICCPR, *supra* note 40, Article 1(1); ICESCR, *supra* note 41, Article 1(1).

79. African Charter, *supra* note 37, Articles 20, 21, 24.

80. *See* Articles 2(1) of the ICCPR and ICESCR, *supra* notes 40-1. General Comment No. 31 of the Human Rights Committee, *supra* note 64, provides that States parties' obligations extend to both individuals within their national territory, and those outside their territory but within their effective control. The CESCR has no equivalent statement but seems to adopt the same position as the Human Rights Committee through its recognition in a number of General Comments that a State party could violate its Covenant obligations if it fails to protect persons "within its jurisdiction" from infringements by third parties. *See also* Bruno Simma, *From Bilateralism to Community Interests in International Law*, in 250 Recueil Des Cours 217, 364-73 (1994) (differentiating human rights treaties from other regimes on the basis that the former treaties aim at protecting citizens from the states parties to the treaty).

81. The recognised bases for so-called "prescriptive" extra-territorial jurisdiction (a case where regulating to protect third parties, including trans-national corporations and business entities is concerned) from violating human rights in third countries under international law include where the perpetrator or victim is a national (the so-called "active" or "passive" nationality principle); where the acts have substantial adverse effects on the State; or where specific international crimes are involved. An overall reasonableness test must also be met, which includes non-intervention in other States' internal affairs, although where human rights are at issue the scope of the non-intervention principle narrows considerably, as discussed in the survey of sources of international law in Chapter II, below. For further discussion of these issues *see e.g.* United Nations High Commissioner for Human Rights, *State Responsibilities to Regulate and Adjudicate Corporate Activities under the United Nations' core Human Rights Treaties*, Individual Report on the ICCPR (June 2007) at 48-52, *available at* http://www.reports-and-materials.org/Ruggie-ICCPR-Jun-2007.pdf; and the corresponding report for the ICESCR, *available at* http://www.reports-and-materials.org/Ruggie-report-ICESCR-May-2007.pdf, at 53-4; de Schutter, Oliver, *Extraterritorial Jurisdiction as a tool for improving the Human Rights Accountability of Transnational Corporations*, Background Paper: Seminar of Legal Experts (Nov. 3-4, 2006), *available at* http://www.reports-and-materials.org/Olivier-de-Schutter-report-for-SRSG-re-extraterritorial-jurisdiction-Dec-2006.pdf.

82. UNFCCC Articles 3(1) & 3(3). A range of preventive measures, including technology transfer, emissions reduction measures, education and scientific studies, are set forth in Articles 4-6 & 9.

83. *See e.g.* Limon, Marc, *Human Rights and Climate Change: Constructing a Case for Political Action*, 33 HARV. ENVTL. L. REV. 439 (2009); Halvorssen, Anita M., *Common, but Differentiated Commitments in the Future Climate Change Regime – Amending the Kyoto Protocol to Include Annex C and the Annex C Mitigation Fund*, 18 Colo. J. Int'l Envtl. L. & Pol'y 247 (2007).

84. *See e.g.* Watt-Cloutier, Sheila, *Climate Change and Human Rights*, in Human Rights Dialogue: "Environmental Rights" (Apr. 22, 2004).

85. Organization of American States, Inter-American Commission on Human Rights, *Petition Seeking Relief from Violations Resulting from Global Warming Caused by Acts and Omissions of the United States* (2005) [hereinafter Inuit Petition], *available at* http://www.inuitcircumpolar.com/files/uploads/icc-files/FINALPetitionICC.pdf.

86. *Id*. American Declaration on the Rights and Duties of Man, Apr. 1948, OAS Resolution XXX, OEA/Ser.L.V/II.82 doc.6 rev.1 [hereinafter American Declaration].

87. Quoted in George, Jane, *ICC Climate Change Petition Rejected*, NUNATSIAQ NEWS (2006), *available at*: http://www.nunatsiaq.com/archives/61215/news/nunavut/61215_02.html.

88. Press Release, Inter-American Commission on Human Rights, IACHR Announces Webcast of Public Hearings of the 127th Regular Period of Sessions, No 8/07 (Feb. 26, 2007), *available at* http://www.cidh.org/Comunicados/English/2007/8.07eng.htm.

89. Harrington, Joanna, *Climate Change, Human Rights and the Right to be Cold*, 18 FORDHAM ENVT'L. L. REV. 513 (2007) (criticizing, on procedural and substantive grounds, the transformation of the ICC petition into a generalized hearing of a particularized claim against an absent state).

90. Articles inspired by the Inuit Case include: Sinden, Amy, *Climate Change and Human Rights*, 27 J. LAND RESOURCES & ENVTL L. 255 (2007) (arguing that thinking of climate change as a human rights issue helps us to see that it is not just a matter of aggregate costs and benefits but of winners and losers, and imbues climate change with a sense of gravity and moral urgency); Osofsky, Hari M., *The Inuit Petition as a Bridge? Beyond the Dialectics of Climate Change and Indigenous Peoples' Rights*, 31 (2), AM. INDIAN L. REV. 675 (2007) (identifying the Inuit case as lying at the intersection of two streams of cases – environmental rights litigation and climate change litigations – occurring at multiple levels of governance, exploring the limits of dialectical analysis with respect to substantive categories, legal structures and legal approaches that occur within the petition, and concluding that such a petition/advocacy strategy can play a useful role in greater protection of indigenous rights); Abate, Randall S., *Climate Change, the United States and the Impacts of Arctic Melting: A Case Study in the Need for Enforceable International Environmental Human Rights*, 26 STAN. ENVTL. L.J. 3 (2007) (listing environmental human rights in international law instruments and national constitutions, exploring the possibility for extraterritorial application of U.S. law to protect the Inuit, in particular under the Alien Tort Claims Act, and arguing *inter alia* for greater linkages between environment and human rights discourses and the use of human rights impact assessments for environmental harms); Koivurova, Timo, *International Legal Avenues to Address the Plight of Victims of Climate Change: Problems and Prospects*, 22 ENVTL. L. & LITIG. 267 (2007) (exploring the prospects and limits of bringing climate change cases before the International Court of Justice, International Tribunal on the Law of the Sea, and the prospects for success in the Inuit Case before the IACHR); Aminzadeh, Sara C., *A Moral Imperative: The Human Rights Implications of Climate Change*, 30(2) HASTINGS INT'L & COMP. L. REV. 231 (2007) (using the Inuit petition as a starting point to list and explore the impacts of climate change on specific human rights, and advocating a human rights based approach to climate change litigation since States have a "moral imperative to act"); and Middaugh, Marguerite E., *Linking Global Warming to Inuit Human Rights*, 8 SAN DIEGO INT'L L.J. 179 (2006) (listing and evaluating specific claims made in the Inuit petition, finding that the evidence the Inuit have presented provides strong support for their allegation of human rights violations, and arguing that the IACHR is an advantageous forum given its progression toward a more expansive interpretation of human rights).

91. *See e.g.* statements made in response to the four-year international study leading to the Arctic Climate Impact Assessment (ACIA). Statement, Representatives of Arctic Indigenous Peoples Organizations on the Occasion of the 11th Conference of Parties to the Framework Convention on Climate Change (Dec. 6, 2005), *available at* http://UNFCCC.int/resource/docs/2005/cop11/stmt/ngo/011.pdf .

92. *See* Note, Secretariat of the UN Framework Convention on Climate Change, *Promoting Effective Participation in the Convention Process*, UNFCCC/SBI/2004/5 (Apr. 16, 2004) para. 39-47. According to the UNFCCC website "over 985 NGOs and 67 IGOs are admitted as observers representing a broad spectrum of interests, and constituency groupings have emerged to facilitate interaction."

93. United Nations Permanent Forum on Indigenous Issues, *Report on the second session*, Economic and Social Council, E/2003/43, E/C.19/2003/22 (May 12-23, 2003), at 10.

94. United Nations Framework Convention on Climate Change, Report of the Subsidiary Body for Implementation on its twentieth session, UNFCCC/SBI/2004/10 (Aug. 31, 2004), para. 105.

95. United Nations Permanent Forum on Indigenous Issues, *Report on the seventh session*, Economic and Social Council, E/2008/43, e/c.19/2008/13 (Apr. 21-May 2, 2008) at 3-4.

96. Malé Declaration on the Human Dimension of Global Climate Change (Nov. 14, 2007), *available at* http://www.meew.gov.mv/downloads/download.php?f=32.

97. United Nations Office of the High Commissioner for Human Rights, *Human Rights and Climate Change*, Resolution 7/23 (Mar. 28, 2008), *available at* http://ap.ohchr.org/documents/E/HRC/resolutions/A_HRC_RES_7_23.pdf.

98. United Nations Office of the High Commissioner for Human Rights, *Report on the Relationship Between Climate Change and Human Rights*, U.N. Doc. A/HRC/10/61 (Jan. 15, 2009).

99. *Id.*

100. United Nations Human Rights Council Resolution 10/4 para. 3 [hereinafter Res. 10/4], in United Nations Human Rights Council, *Draft Report of the Human Rights Council on its Tenth Session*, U.N. Doc A/HRC/10/L.11 (Mar. 31, 2009). This resolution was adopted by consensus with 88 co-sponsors. In the resolution, the Council decided to hold a panel discussion on the relationship between climate change and human rights during its eleventh session. The resolution welcomed the decision of the Special Rapporteur on adequate housing to prepare a thematic report on the impact of climate change of the right to adequate housing and also encouraged OHCHR to participate at a senior level at the Secretary-General's High-Level meeting on climate change on September 22, 2009 at UN Headquarters in New York and at the UN Climate Change Conference (COP15) on December 7-18, 2009 in Copenhagen, Denmark. For an overview of Special Procedures' and human rights treaty bodies' efforts to date to address the human rights implications of climate change and further recommendations along these lines *see* Limon, *supra* note 83, at 463-6.

101. Organization of American States, Human Rights and Climate Change in the Americas, Resolution 2429, AG/RES. 2429 (XXXVIII-O/08) (June 3, 2008).

102. Press Release, Centre for Human Rights and Environment, OAS Approves Human Rights and Climate Change Resolution (June 4, 2008).

103. Res. 10/4 (Mar. 2009), *supra* note 100.

104. At the Fifth Session (Mar. 29-Apr. 8, Bonn) of the Ad-Hoc Working Group on Long-Term Cooperative Action under the Convention (a subsidiary body of the UNFCCC tasked under the Bali Action Plan to pursue the full, effective, and sustained implementation of the Convention) [hereinafter AWG-LCA], the Maldives delegation began the process of trying to integrate human rights language into the draft negotiating text being prepared by the Chair of the AWG-LCA. *See e.g.* Maldives Delegation to the Fifth Session of the Ad-Hoc Working Group on Long-Term Cooperative Action, *Proposed Draft Wording to Be Sent as National Submission to Be Included in the Negotiating Text Under Shared Vision* (Apr. 2009), *available at* http://www.maldivesmission.ch/fileadmin/ Pdf/Environment/Maldives_wording_AWG-LCA_April_09.pdf. A text dated June 22, 2009 (FCCC/ AWGLCA/2009/INF.1) which was prepared by the chair of the AWG-LCA and aimed to provide a starting point for the negotiations towards an Agreed Outcome at COP15 in Copenhagen, reflecting ideas and proposals submitted by Parties to the UNFCCC. The two draft provisions were: paragraph 2, reflecting proposals made by small island States, stating that adverse effects of climate change "have a range of direct and indirect implications for the full and effective enjoyment of human rights including the right to self determination, statehood, life, food and health and the right to a people not to be deprived of its own means of subsistence, particularly in developing countries; and paragraph 22 (a)(iii) adding a new criterion or guiding principle for adaptation measures: "The respect for, protection and promotion of fundamental human rights and basic rights as outlined in the Universal Declaration of Human Rights, International Covenant on Economic, Social and Cultural Rights, International Covenant on Civil and Political Rights and other relevant conventions and treaties." The text also explicitly incorporated the recognition reflected in the UN Human Rights Council's resolution 10/1 (March 2009) that the adverse "effects of climate change will be felt most acutely by those segments of the population who are already in vulnerable situations owing to such factors as geography, poverty, gender, age, indigenous or minority status and disability," helping to turn attention from governments and economies to individuals and communities affected by climate change.

105. Limon, *supra* note 83, at 461.

106. *Id.* at 460-1, citing submissions of the U.S. and the UK to the UN Office of the High Commissioner for Human Rights in connection with the report of the latter to the Human Rights Council in 2009.

107. OHCHR Report, *supra* note 98, para. 70.

108. *Id.* For an extensive discussion of these and other challenges to litigating human rights claims in respect to climate change harms *see* Tully, *supra* note 18.

109. For a discussion of the latter *see* Rough Guide, *supra* note 17, at 55-77.

110. General typologies and indicative contours of human rights obligations under international human rights treaties were outlined in Chapter I(3) above, and are elaborated further in Part IV below in specific application to environmental harms including, potentially, and with several important qualifications, harms attributable to climate change.

111. *See* Vienna Convention on the Law of Treaties May 23, 1969, 8 I.L.M. 679 [hereinafter Vienna Convention] stating that "every treaty in force is binding upon the parties to it and must be performed by them in good faith."

112. ICCPR, Article 6; American Convention, Article 4; European Convention, Article 2; African Charter, Article 4.

113. The Committee re-affirmed in its General Comment No. 31, *supra* note 64, para. 6, that States parties' duties are of both a positive and negative kind. Moreover, the Committee has interpreted the right to life flexibly to include, for example, threats to life caused by health risks as well as dangers emanating from nuclear waste. *See* Nowak, *supra* note 62, at 124-5. By way of further example, in its General Comment No. 28, the Committee highlighted family planning and reproductive health as significant factors in the context of Article 6, and asked that States' national reports under the ICCPR include information on the "particular impact on women of poverty and deprivation that may pose a threat to their lives." *See* United Nations Human Rights Committee, General Comment No. 28, Equality of Rights Between Men and Women (Article 3), U.N. Doc. CCPR/C/21/Rev.1/Add.10 (Mar. 29, 2000), para. 10. This principle has not necessarily been reflected consistently in the Committee's jurisprudence under the First Optional Protocol (the ICCPR's complaints mechanism) however. *See e.g.* Plotnikov v. Russian Federation, Communication No. 784/1997, U.N. Doc. CCPR/C/65/D/784/1997 (May 5, 1999), inadmissibility decision of March 25, 1999, discussed in SEPÚLVEDA, MAGDALENA, THE NATURE OF THE OBLIGATION UNDER THE COVENANT ON ECONOMIC, SOCIAL AND CULTURAL RIGHTS (2003) at 150, note 155 and accompanying text. But generally, the Committee has interpreted Article 6 purposively, and has not apparently relied to any great extent upon arbitrary distinctions as to sources of threats to the right to life.

114. *See* Chapter IV infra.

115. OHCHR Report, *supra* note 98, paras. 22-23.

116. Parsons, Claudia, *Small Islands Win U.N. Vote on Climate Change Security*, REUTERS (June 3, 2009), *available at* http://www.reuters.com/article/environmentNews/idUSTRE5525W920090603. By resolution, the UN General Assembly invited all relevant UN bodies to intensify efforts to address climate change and asked the UN Secretary General to submit a report on possible security implications.

117. *See* Brown, Oli & Elec Crawford, *Rising Temperatures, Rising Tensions: Climate Change and the Risk of Violent Conflict in the Middle East*, International Institute for Sustainable Development (2009), *available at* http://www.iisd.org/pdf/2009/rising_temps_middle_east.pdf; United Nations Environment Programme, *From Conflict to Peace-Building: The Role of Natural Resources and the Environment* (Feb. 2009), *available at* http://postconflict.unep.ch/publications/pcdmb_policy_01.pdf; Mabey, Nick, *Delivering Climate Security: International Security Responses to a Climate Changed World*, Royal United Services Institute, Whitehall Papers No. 69 (Apr. 23, 2008), *available at* http://www.tandf.co.uk/journals/spissue/rwhi-si1.asp; Chellaney, Brahma, *Climate Change and Security in Southern Asia: Understanding the National Security Implications*, 152(2) ROYAL UNITED SERVICES INST. J. 63 (Apr. 2007).

118. Center for Naval Analyses Corporation, *National Security and the Threat of Climate Change* (2007), *available at* http://securityandclimate.cna.org/report/National%20Security%20and%20the%20Threat%20of%20Climate%20Change.pdf. *See also* Johnson, Douglas, *Global Climate Change: National Security Implications*, Strategic Studies Institute Colloquium Brief (May 2007), *available at* http://www.strategicstudiesinstitute.army.mil/pubs/display.cfm?pubID=779.

119. Inuit Petition, *supra* note 85, at 90.

120. *Id.* at 91.

121. Intergovernmental Panel on Climate Change, *Climate Change 2007: Fourth Assessment Report* (Susan Solomon et. al., eds., 2007), at 689.

122. Views regarding the work programme of the United Nations Framework Convention on Climate Change, Ad Hoc Working Group on Long Term Cooperative Action under the Convention, *Submission of the Maldives on behalf of the Least Developed Countries*, UNFCCC/AWGLCA/2008/MISC.1 (Mar. 3, 2008) at 19.

123. *Id.* at 20.

124. *Id.* at 21.

125. ICESCR Article 11(1). Article 11 provides, in full: "(1) The States parties to the present Covenant recognize the right of everyone to an adequate standard of living for himself and his family, including adequate food, clothing and housing, and to the continuous improvement of living conditions. The States parties will take appropriate steps to ensure the realization of this right,

recognizing to this effect the essential importance of international co-operation based on free consent. (2) The States parties to the present Covenant, recognizing the fundamental right of everyone to be free from hunger, shall take, individually and through international co-operation, the measures, including specific programmes, which are needed: (a) To improve methods of production, conservation and distribution of food by making full use of technical and scientific knowledge, by disseminating knowledge of the principles of nutrition and by developing or reforming agrarian systems in such a way as to achieve the most efficient development and utilization of natural resources; (b) Taking into account the problems of both food-importing and food-exporting countries, to ensure an equitable distribution of world food supplies in relation to need."

126. UDHR Article 25, ICESCR Article 11, CEDAW Article 12(2), CRC Articles 24(2)(c) & 27. In addition, the right to food has been incorporated or read into many national constitutions including those of Bangladesh, Brazil, Colombia, India, Iran, Pakistan, South Africa, and Sri Lanka. There is also considerable constitutional case law; *See e.g.* India People's Union for Civil Liberties v. Union of India, 1997, A.I.R. 1997 S.C. 568 (India).

127. CESCR General Comment No. 12, Right to Adequate Food, *supra* note 66.

128. *Id.* para. 4. *See also* Food and Agriculture Organization, *Voluntary Guidelines to Support the progressive realization of the right to adequate food in the context of national food security* (Nov. 2004), *available at* http://www.fao.org/docrep/meeting/009/y9825e/y9825e00.htm.

129. CESCR, General Comment No. 12, *supra* note 66, para. 28.

130. de Schutter, Olivier, *Report of the Special Rapporteur on the Right to Food: Building Resilience: a Human Rights Framework on World Food and Nutrition Security*, U.N. Doc A/HRC/9/23 (Sept. 8, 2008).

131. Statement, Olivier de Schutter, Special Rapporteur on the Right to Food, Interactive Thematic Dialogue of the UN General Assembly on the Global Food Crisis and the Right to Food (Apr. 6, 2009).

132. de Schutter, Olivier, United Nations Special Rapporteur on the Right to Food, *Contribution to the UN Commission on Sustainable Development at its 17th Session* (Apr. 5, 2009) at 3 & 6, *available at* http://www.srfood.org/images/stories/pdf/otherdocuments/19-srrtfsubmissioncsd-01-05-09-1.pdf.

133. UNFCCC Article 2.

134. *See generally* BALS, CHRISTOPH ET. AL., CLIMATE CHANGE, FOOD SECURITY AND THE RIGHT TO ADEQUATE FOOD (2008), *available at* http://www.germanwatch.org/klima/climfood.pdf; *See also* Söllner, Sven, *The Breakthrough of the Right to Food*, 11 MAX PLANCK YEARBOOK OF UN LAW 391 (2007).

135. *Supra* note 4.

136. *Id.* at 11.

137. *Id.* at 12.

138. Stern Review, *supra* note 13, at 72.

139. United Nations Development Programme, *Human Development Report 2006: Beyond Scarcity: Power, Poverty and the Global Water Crisis* (2006), at 275.

140. Stern Review, *supra* note 13, at 97.

141. *See* European Union, *An EU Strategy for Biofuels*, COM (2006) 34 final (Mar. 18, 2006) (aiming to increase biofuels to 10% of total energy sources by 2020); *See* Caney, Simon, *Climate Technology Transfer: A Derivation of Rights- and Duty-Bearers from Fundamental Human Rights*, Background Paper, International Council on Human Rights Policy (July 9-10, 2009), at 33-36 for further details and references.

142. *See generally* NAYLOR, ROSAMOND L. ET. AL., THE RIPPLE EFFECT: BIOFUELS, FOOD SECURITY AND THE ENVIRONMENT (2007).

143. Christian Aid, *Growing Pairs: The Possibilities and Problems of Biofuels* (2009), *available at* http://www.christianaid.org.uk/images/biofuels-report-09.pdf. The report's author claims that "[v]ast sums of European and American taxpayers' money are being used to prop up industries which are fuelling hunger, severe human rights abuses and environmental destruction – and failing to deliver the benefits claimed for them." The report urges governments to adopt a new vision on biofuels, seeing them as a force for rural development in poor countries, rather than a silver bullet solution to climate change.

144. Article 11 is set out *supra* note 125. Article 2(1) provides, materially that: "Each State Party to the present Covenant undertakes to take steps, *individually and through international assistance and co-operation*, especially economic and technical, to the maximum of its available resources, with a view to achieving progressively the full realization of the rights recognized in the present Covenant by all appropriate means..." Article 23 provides: "The States parties to the present Covenant agree that international action for the achievement of the rights recognized in the present Covenant includes such methods as the conclusion of conventions, the adoption of recommendations, the

furnishing of technical assistance and the holding of regional meetings and technical meetings for the purpose of consultation and study organized in conjunction with the Governments concerned."
145. CESCR, General Comment No. 12, *supra* note 66, paras. 36-42. To similar effect, the UN Special Rapporteur on the Right to Food has argued that: "[International assistance] should be understood as having three implications, corresponding respectively to (a) an obligation not pursue policies which have a negative impact on the right to adequate food [respect], (b) an obligation to ensure that third parties, including private actors, do not interfere with the enjoyment of the right to food [protect]; and (c) an obligation to cooperate internationally in order to contribute to the fulfilment of the right to food [fulfil]." *See generally* Narula, Smita, *The Right to Food: Holding Global Actors Accountable under International Law*, 44 Colum. J. Transnat'l L. 691 (2006).
146. Article 12 of the ICESCR provides: "(1) The States parties to the present Covenant recognize the right of everyone to the enjoyment of the highest attainable standard of physical and mental health. (2) The steps to be taken by the States parties to the present Covenant to achieve the full realization of this right shall include those necessary for: (a) The provision for the reduction of the stillbirth-rate and of infant mortality and for the healthy development of the child; (b) The improvement of all aspects of environmental and industrial hygiene; (c) The prevention, treatment and control of epidemic, endemic, occupational and other diseases; (d) The creation of conditions which would assure to all medical service and medical attention in the event of sickness."
147. CESCR General Comment No. 14, *supra* note 66.
148. UDHR Article 25, ICESCR Article 12, ICERD 5(e)(iv), CEDAW Articles 11(1)(f) & 12, CRC Article 24, European Social Charter Article 11, African Charter on Human and Peoples' Rights Article 16, The American Declaration Article XI, San Salvador Protocol Article 10, and Arrondelle v. United Kingdom, 5 Eur. Ct. H.R. 118 (1983) (reading a right to health into Article 8 of the European Convention on Human Rights).
149. As of 2004, 73 national constitutions contained a right to health care. *See* Gauri, Varun, *Social Rights and Economics: Claims to Health Care and Education in Developing Countries*, 32(3) World Development 465 (2004). *See e.g.* Brigido Simon v. Commission on Human Rights, G.R. No. 100150, 229 SCRA 17 (Jan. 5, 1994) (Phil.); Mariele Cecilia Viceconte v. Ministry of Health and Social Welfare, Poder Judicial de la Nación, Causa no 31.777/96 (June 2, 1998) (Argentina); Consumer Education and Research Centre v. Union of India, 1995, 3 S.C.C. 42 (India), paras. 24 and 25; and Paschim Banga Khet Mazdoor Samiti v. State of West Bengal, (1996) AIR SC 2426 (India).
150. CESCR General Comment No. 14, *supra* note 66 and for a discussion on the sources and content of this right *see* Hunt, Paul, *Report of the Special Rapporteur on the Right of Everyone to the Highest Attainable Standard of Physical and Mental Health*, U.N. Doc. E/CN.4/2003/58 (2003), paras. 10-36.
151. World Health Organization, Protecting Health From Climate Change (2008) at 6, *available at* http://www.who.int/world-health-day/toolkit/report_web.pdf.
152. *Supra* note 20.
153. *See e.g.* Convention on Long-Range Transboundary Air Pollution, Nov. 13, 1979, 18 I.L.M. 1442 Article 2; Basel Convention on the Control of Transboundary Movements of Hazardous Wastes and their Disposal, Mar. 22, 1979, 28 I.L.M. 656; and Rotterdam Convention on the Prior Informed Consent Procedure for Certain Hazardous Chemicals and Pesticides in International Trade, Sept. 10, 1998, 38 I.L.M. 1; *See also* Need to Ensure a Healthy Environment for the Well-being of Individuals, G.A. Res. 45/94, U.N. Doc. A/RES/45/94 (Dec. 14, 1990) (recognizing that "all individuals are entitled to live in an environment adequate for their health and well being").
154. UNFCCC Article 1(1).
155. UNFCCC Article 4(1)(f).
156. CRC Article 14, para. 2(c).
157. *Supra* note 4, Chapter 8 (Human Health) at 393. *See also* Stern Review, *supra* note 13, Chapter II, Chapter 3 (How Climate Change will Affect People around the World).
158. *Id.*
159. *Supra* note 4; *See also* World Health Assembly, Resolution on Climate Change and Health, WHA61.19 (May 24, 2008) *available at* http://www.who.int/gb/ebwha/pdf_files/A61/A61_R19-en.pdf.
160. OHCHR Report (2009), *supra* note 98, para. 32.
161. Inuit Petition, *supra* note 85, at 87-88.
162. Declaration of Alma-Ata, International Conference on Primary Health Care, Alma-Ata, USSR, 6-12 September 1978, Art. II, *available at* http://www.who.int/hpr/NPH/docs/declaration_almaata.pdf.

163. *See generally* CESCR, General Comment No. 15: The Right to Water, E/C.12/2002/11 (2003). Although the ICESCR does not explicitly include the right to water, the Committee decided that the right falls within "the category of guarantees essential for securing an adequate standard of living" and is "also inextricably related to the right to the highest attainable standard of health…and the rights to adequate housing and adequate food." *Id.* para. 3. *See also* General Comment No. 14, *supra* note 66, para. 11 (stating that the right to health extends "not only to timely and appropriate health care but also to the underlying determinants of health, such as access to safe and potable water and adequate sanitation"). For a discussion *see* SALMAN, SALMAN & SIOBHÁN MCINERNEY-LANKFORD, THE HUMAN RIGHT TO WATER, LEGAL AND POLICY DIMENSIONS (2004).

164. CEDAW Article 14(2)(h), CRC Article 24(2)(c), Geneva Convention relative to the Treatment of Prisoners of War Articles 20, 26, 29 & 46, Geneva Convention relative to the Treatment of Civilian Persons in Time of War Articles 85, 89 & 127. *See generally id.* CESCR General Comment No. 15; Guissé, El Hadji, *Report of the Special Rapporteur of the Sub-Commission on the Right to Drinking Water Supply and Sanitation on the relationship between the enjoyment of economic, social and cultural rights and the promotion of the realization of the right to drinking water supply and sanitation* U.N. Doc E/CN.4/Sub.2/2002/10 (2002); *See also* Preamble, United Nations Water Conference, Mar. 14-25, 1977, *Mar Del Plata Action Plan* (Mar. 1977); Paragraph 18.47 of Agenda 21, Rio Declaration on Environment and Development, U.N. Doc. A/CONF.151/26 (Vol. 1) (Aug. 12, 1992); United Nations International Conference on Population and Development, Sept. 5-13, 1994, *Program of Action Report*, 5-13 September 1994, U.N. Doc DPI/1618/POP (March 1995); and Resolution 2002/6 of the United Nations Sub-Commission on the Promotion and Protection of Human Rights on the promotion of the realization of the right to drinking water.

165. CESCR, General Comment No. 15, *supra* note 163.

166. Stern Review, *supra* note 13, Chapter II, Chapter 3 (How Climate Change will Affect People Around the World).

167. OHCHR Report (2009), para. 29.

168. UNFCCC Article 3.

169. UNFCCC Article 4.

170. CESCR General Comment No. 12, *supra* note 66, para. 6.

171. *See* CESCR General Comment No. 7 on Forced Evictions, *supra* note 70; and CESCR General Comment No. 12, *supra* note 66, para. 8.

172. OHCHR Report (2009), *supra* note 98, para. 36.

173. *See* Stern Review, *supra* note 13, at 77 describing 250 million as a "conservative" assumption and, more generally, McAdam, Jane & Ben Saul, *Weathering Insecurity: Climate-Induced Displacement and International Law*, in HUMAN SECURITY AND NON-CITIZENS: LAW, POLICY AND INTERNATIONAL AFFAIRS (Alica Edwards & Carla Ferstman eds., 2009). Such calculations are controversial, however, in view of the difficulty in predicting the rate of sea level rise, and in agreeing on how the phenomenon of climate-induced displacement is to be defined. *See* Saul, Ben & Jane McAdam, *An Insecure Climate for Human Security? Climate-Induced Displacement and International Law*, Legal Studies Research Paper 08/131 (Oct. 2008).

174. Brown, Oli, *Migration and Climate Change*, International Organization for Migration, Migration Research Series No. 31 (2008) at 9.

175. Saul, *supra* note 173, at 2.

176. OHCHR Report (2009), *supra* note 98, para. 38. In this respect the report notes further that the Guiding Principles on Internal Displacement (E/CN.4/1998/53/Add.2, annex) provide that, "at the minimum, regardless of the circumstances, and without discrimination, competent authorities shall provide internally displaced persons with and ensure safe access to: … basic shelter and housing" (Principle 18).

177. Rolnik, Raquel, *Report of the Special Rapporteur on Adequate Housing as a Component of the Right to an Adequate Standard of Living, and on the Right to Non-Discrimination in this Context*, U.N. Doc. A/HRC/10/7/Add.4 (Mar. 3, 2009).

178. *Id.* para 7.

179. Human Development Report 2007/8, *supra* note 3, at 31. As the authors of Human Development Report observe, "[o]ne section of humanity – broadly the poorest 2.6 billion – will have to respond to climate change forces over which they have no control, manufactured through political choices in countries where they have no voice."

180. UDHR Article 12, ICCPR Article 17, CRC Article 16, European Convention Article 8 and American Declaration Article V.

181. UDHR Article 17, American Declaration Article XXIII and American Convention Article 21. For a more detailed discussion *see infra* notes 289 & 339-43 and accompanying text.

182. ICCPR Article 1(2).

183. UDHR Article 13.

184. *Id.*

185. Convention Concerning Indigenous and Tribal Peoples, June 27, 1989, 28 I.L.M. 1382; United Nations Declaration on the Rights of Indigenous Peoples, G.A. Res. 61/295, A/RES/61/295 (Oct. 2, 2007); ICCPR Article 27; CERD Article 5; Organization of American States, Proposed American Declaration on the Rights of Indigenous Peoples (Mar. 1997), *available at* http://www.oas.org/ and CERD General Recommendation No. 23, Article 5, A/52/18, Annex V (1997) (calling upon States to recognize and protect "the rights of indigenous peoples to own, develop, control and use their communal lands, territories and resources").

186. UDHR Article 27, ICESCR Article 15 and American Declaration Article XIII.

187. ICCPR Article 1, ICESCR Article 1, Decision Regarding Communication 155/96 (Social and Economic Rights Action Center/Center for Economic and Social Rights v. Nigeria), 96 AJIL 937 (2002).

188. A plan for negotiating positive incentives for reducing emissions for deforestation and forest degradation in developing countries was one of the key features of the Bali Road Map negotiated at the Thirteenth Conference of the Parties (COP13) to the UNFCCC in December 2007. *See* United Nations Collaborative Programme on Reducing Emissions for Deforestation and Forest Degradation in Developing Countries (REDD) Framework Document (June 20, 2008) *available at* unfccc.int/resource/docs/2007/cop13/eng/06a01.pdf#page=8. Under a REDD regime, industrialized countries would make financial transfers to developing countries – through market and/or fund-based mechanisms – to compensate them for the opportunity and other costs of avoiding emissions from deforestation. At COP-14 in Poznan in December 2008, the U.S., Canada, New Zealand and Australia reportedly deleted lines relating to indigenous peoples rights in the text on REDD. *See* Adam, David, *Indigenous Rights Row threatens Rainforest Protection Plan*, THE GUARDIAN (Dec. 9, 2008).

189. UDHR Article 13, ICCPR Articles 1 & 12(1), ICESCR Article 1, American Convention Article 22(1), and American Declaration Article VIII. In the Human Rights Committee's view, States should refrain from interfering in the internal affairs of other States in a way that adversely affects the exercise of the right to self-determination. *See* United Nations Human Rights Committee, General Comment No. 12, The Right of Self-Determination of Peoples (1984), para. 14, *available at* http://www.unhchr.ch/tbs/doc.nsf/(Symbol)/f3c99406d528f37fc12563ed004960b4?Opendocument. *See* discussion in the OHCHR Report (2009), *supra* note 98, paras. 39-41.

190. Human Development Report 2007/8, *supra* note 3, at 79.

191. Human Development Report 2007/8, *supra* note 3, at 80, citing Intergovernmental Panel on Climate Change, *Climate Change 2007: Fourth Assessment Report* (Susan Solomon et. al., eds., 2007); Warren, R. et. al, *Understanding the Regional Impacts of Climate Change*, Research Report Prepared for the Stern Review on the Economics of Climate Change. Research Working Paper No. 90, Tyndall Centre for Climate Change (Sept. 2006); and ROBERTS, TIMMONS & BRADLEY C. PARKS, A CLIMATE OF INJUSTICE: GLOBAL INEQUALITY, NORTH-SOUTH POLITICS AND CLIMATE POLICY (2007).

192. OHCHR Report (2009), *supra* note 98, para. 42.

193. Gender and Climate Change documents, *available at* http://www.gencc.interconnection.org/.

194. Gender and Climate Change Network, *Women for Climate Justice Position Paper* (Dec. 2007).

195. *Id.*

196. The Committee expressed its concern "about the absence of a gender perspective in the [UNFCCC] and other global and national policies and initiatives on climate change." Drawing from its examination of State parties' reports to CEDAW, the Committee observed that that "climate change does not affect women and men in the same way and has a gender-differentiated impact. However, women are not just helpless victims of climate change – they are powerful agents of change and their leadership is critical." The CEDAW committee called upon States parties to include gender eq.uality as an overarching guiding principle in the agreement emanating from the 15th Conference of Parties in Copenhagen. *Statement of the Committee on the Elimination of Discrimination Against Women on Gender and Climate Change*, Sept. 2009 (on file with authors).

197. OHCHR Report (2009), *supra* note 98, para. 48.

198. SAVE THE CHILDREN UK, THE LEGACY OF DISASTERS: THE IMPACT OF CLIMATE CHANGE ON CHILDREN 4 (2007), *available at* http://www.savethechildren.org.uk/en/docs/legacy_of_disasters.pdf. The authors argue, citing data in the World Disasters Report 2006, Annex 11: "While not all natural di-

sasters are directly linked to climate change, of the total number of people affected by disasters, an overwhelming majority (98 per cent in the last decade) is affected by disasters that are influenced by climate change, such as floods or droughts."

199. United Nations Children's Fund, *Climate Change and Children: A Human Security Challenge* (Nov. 2008), *available at* http://www.unicef-irc.org/publications/pdf/climate_change.pdf; United Nations Children's Fund, *Our Climate, Our Children, Our Responsibility* (2008), *available at* http://www.unicef.org.uk/campaigns/publications/pdf/climate-change.pdf.

200. The main recognised sources of international law are codified in the Statute of the International Court of Justice, 39 AJIL Supp. 215 (1945), Article 38(1): "The Court, whose function is to decide in accordance with international law such disputes as are submitted to it, shall apply: (a) international conventions, whether general or particular, establishing rules expressly recognized by the contesting States; (b) international custom, as evidence of a general practice accepted as law; (c) the general principles of law recognized by civilized nations; and (d) subject to the provisions of Article 59, judicial decisions and the teachings of the most highly qualified publicists of the various nations, as subsidiary means for the determination of rules of law." The present discussion focuses upon Article 38(1)(a)-(c) as the primary sources.

201. For illustrations of tensions between international human rights treaty obligations and those arising under the trade, intellectual property and investment regimes, respectively, *see* Howse, Robert & Ruti G. Teitel, *Beyond the Divide: The Covenant on Economic, Social and Cultural Rights and the World Trade Organisation*, in Dialogue on Globalization, Occasional Paper No. 30 (Apr. 2007); Stiftung, Friedrich Ebert & Center For International Environmental Law, Human Rights and Climate Change: Practical Steps for Implementation (2009), *available at* http://library.fes.de/pdf-files/iez/global/04572.pdf; 3D & Associates, Menace sur le droit à l'alimentation de l'enfant : la protection intellectuelle des semences (Burkina Faso), Report submitted to the Committee on the Rights of the Child (Oct. 2009); and Peterson, Luke & Kevin Gray, International Human Rights in Bilateral Treaty and Investment Treaty Arbitration, International Institute for Sustainable Development Research Paper (2003), *available at* http://www.iisd.org/pdf/2003/investment int human rights bits.pdf.

202. *See* International Law Commission, *Conclusions of the Work of the Study Group on the Fragmentation of International Law: Difficulties Arising from the Diversification and Expansion of International Law, Report of the International Law Commission to the General Assembly*, 61 U.N. GAOR Supp. (No. 10) U.N. Doc. A/61/10 (2006).

203. *See id. See also* McLachlan, Campbell, *The Principle of Systemic Integration and Article 31(3)(c) of the Vienna Convention*, 54(2) I.C.L.Q. 279 (2005); Pauwelyn, Joost, *Bridging Fragmentation and Unity: International Law as a Universe of Inter-Connected Islands*, 25 Mich. J. Int'l L. 903, 904-5 (2004).

204. International Law Commission, *Conclusions, supra* note 202, at note 406: "That two norms are *valid* in regard to a situation means that they each cover the facts of which the situation consists. That the two norms are *applicable* in a situation means that they have binding force in respect to the legal subjects finding themselves in the relevant situation."

205. On the fragmentation problems arising from the proliferation of specialised international courts and tribunals *see* Guillaume, Gilbert, *The Future of International Judicial Institutions*, 44 INT'L COMP. L. Q. 848, 861-2 (1995); Spelliscy, Shane, *The Proliferation of International Tribunals: A Chink in the Armor*, 40 Colum. J. Transnat'l L. 143 (2002); Dupuy, Pierre-Marie, *The Danger of Fragmentation or Unification of the International Legal System and the International Court of Justice*, 31 N.Y.U. J. Int'l L. & Pol. 791 (1999).

206. *Supra* notes 24-5.

207. *See* the UNFCCC website, *available at* http://www.UNFCCC.int.

208. The UNFCCC and the Kyoto Protocol are serviced by a Secretariat based in Bonn, Germany staffed with over 250 international civil servants. *See* http://UNFCCC.int/secretariat/items/1629.php.

209. Through Joint Implementation, the Clean Development Mechanism and Emissions Trading, Protocol Articles 6, 12 and 17, and the Kyoto Protocol.

210. At the seventh UNFCCC Conference of the Parties, Parties adopted the Marrakech Accords which laid down operating rules for the mechanisms and accounting procedures for emissions reduction credits. They established a compliance system and set out the consequences for non-compliance. *See* United Nations Framework Convention on Climate Change, *Report of the Conference of the Parties on its Seventh Session, Addendum*, Volume I, UNFCCC/CP/2001/13/Add.1 (Jan. 21, 2002); *See also* Volume II UNFCCC/CP/2001/13/Add.2 (2002); Volume III UNFCCC/CP/2001/13/Add.3

(2002); and Volume IV UNFCCC/CP/2001/13/Add.4 (2002). By the standards of MEAs general-ly, the Kyoto compliance procedure is noteworthy in including both "compliance facilitation" as well as enforcement mechanisms. DOELLE, MEINHARD, FROM HOT AIR TO ACTION? CLIMATE CHANGE, COMPLIANCE AND THE FUTURE OF INTERNATIONAL ENVIRONMENTAL LAW (2005).

211. *Supra* note 39.

212. For a discussion of the role of the treaty monitoring bodies [hereinafter treaty bodies] *see* http://www2.ohchr.org/english/bodies/treaty/index.htm, and for the monitoring mechanisms under the Human Rights Council, *see* http://www2.ohchr.org/english/bodies/hrcouncil/.

213. The new compliance committee under Kyoto has an "enforcement branch" whose decisions are not, strictly speaking, legally binding, *see* BODANSKY, DANIEL, THE ART AND CRAFT OF INTERNA-TIONAL ENVIRONMENTAL LAW (2009) at 23. When discussing the non-compliance procedure under the Montreal Protocol on Substances That Deplete the Ozone Layer, 26 I.L.M. 1550 (Sept. 16, 1987), Birnie and Boyle remark: "the supervisory body, whether a meeting of the parties or a Commis-sion, is in substance no more than a diplomatic conference of States, and the existence ... of a sepa-rate legal personality does not alter the reality that the membership of these institutions is in no sense independent of the States they represent." BIRNIE, PATRICIA W. & A. E. BOYLE, INTERNATIONAL LAW AND THE ENVIRONMENT 165 (2nd ed., 2002). There has been considerable resistance by States to the idea of legal or quasi-legal mechanisms of compliance and adjudication in international environmental treaties, in comparison with the compliance and complaint procedures under inter-national and regional human rights treaties. The collective nature of global environmental interests is no doubt one of the main explanations for this, notwithstanding the existence of human rights obligations owed by States to the world at large (obligations *erga omnes*, discussed below), result-ing in softer or more diplomatic compliance mechanisms. This is not to say that human rights treaty bodies or national courts are inherently apolitical or function in a political vacuum; indeed, Gauri & Brinks argue that the positive impacts of human rights adjudication depend to some ex-tent upon the capacity and inclination of national courts to take account of and operate within the prevailing political and institutional setting. *See* GAURI, VARUN & DAN BRINKS, COURTING SOCIAL JUSTICE: JUDICIAL ENFORCEMENT OF SOCIAL AND ECONOMIC RIGHTS IN THE DEVELOPING WORLD (2008). However, there do remain important differences in the nature of the interests and claim-duty rela-tionships regulated by global environmental and human rights treaties, as well as the composition and typical functions of their respective compliance mechanisms. For an illustrative discussion of these themes in connection with the 1987 Montreal Protocol on Substances that Deplete the Ozone Layer, grounded in a deeper analysis of evolving norms of state responsibility in connection with MEAs, *see* Koskenniemi, Martii, *Breach of Treaty or Non-Compliance? Reflections on the Enforcement of the Montreal Protocol*, 3 Y.B. INT'L ENVTL. L. 123, 125-34, 136, 147 (1992). For a deeper analysis of compliance theory design relating to the Kyoto compliance system specifically, *see* Doelle *supra* note 210, at 69-108.

214. SANDS, PHILIPPE, PRINCIPLES OF INTERNATIONAL ENVIRONMENTAL LAW 143-50 (2nd ed., vol. 1, 2003). This view is hotly debated. For example, Handl argues: "A multilateral treaty that addresses fundamental concerns of the international community at large and that, as such, is strongly sup-ported by the vast majority of States, by international organizations and other transnational actors – and this is, of course, precisely the case with the biodiversity, climate, and ozone regimes, among others – may indeed create expectations of general compliance, in short such a treaty may come to be seen as reflecting legal standards of general applicability ... and as such must be deemed capable of creating rights and obligations both for third States and third organizations." Handl, Gunther, *The Legal Mandate of Multilateral Development Banks as Agents for Change Toward Sustainable Develop-ment*, 92 AM. J. INT'L L. 642, 660-2 (1998). But, in Bodansky's view, "[i]nternational environmental norms reflect not how States regularly behave, but how States speak to each other." Calling such law "declarative law," part of a "myth system" representing the collective ideals and the "verbal practice" of States, Bodansky argues that "our time and efforts would be better spent attempting to translate the general norms of international environmental relations into concrete treaties and ac-tions." Bodansky, Daniel, *Customary (and Not So Customary) International Environmental Law*, 3 IND. J. GLOBAL LEGAL STUD. 105, 110-9 (1995).

215. *See e.g.* Wiener, Jonathan, *Precaution*, in OXFORD HANDBOOK OF INTERNATIONAL ENVIRONMENTAL LAW 604-7 (Daniel Bodansky et. al., eds., 2007).

216. McIntyre, Owen & Thomas Mosedale, *The Precautionary Principle as a Norm of Customary In-ternational Law*, 9 J. ENVTL. L. 221 (1997); and TROUWBORST, ARIE, EVOLUTION AND STATUS OF THE PRECAUTIONARY PRINCIPLE IN INTERNATIONAL LAW 284 (2002); *cf.* Bodansky, Daniel, *Deconstructing*

the Precautionary Principle, in Bringing New Law To Ocean Waters 381-91 (D.D. Caron & H.N. Schieber eds., 2004).

217. Universal Declaration on Human Rights, G.A. Res. 217A, U.N. GAOR, 3d Sess., 1st plen. mtg., U.N. Doc A/810 (Dec. 12, 1948).

218. Proclamation of Teheran, Final Act of the International Conference on Human Rights, U.N. Doc. A/Conf. 32/41 at 3 (1968).

219. For a discussion of customary human rights law *see* Simma, Bruno & Philip Alston, *The Sources of Human Rights Law: Custom, Jus Cogens and General Principles*, 12 Aust. Y.B. Int'l L. 82 (1992); Akehurst, Michael, A Modern Introduction To International Law (5th ed. 1984). For a general discussion of the normative significance of the UDHR *see* Sohn, Louis, *The New International Law: Protection of the Rights of Individuals Rather than States*, 32 Am. U. L. Rev. 1 (1982); Hannum, Hurst, *The Status of the Universal Declaration of Human Rights in National and International Law*, 25 GA. J. Int'l & Comp. L. 287 (1995-6).

220. *See e.g.* Schachter, Oscar, *International Law in Theory and Practice: General Course in Public International Law*, 178 Receuil Des Cours 21, 333-42 (1982); Hannum, Hurst, *Human Rights*, in The United Nations and International Law 149-51 (Christopher Joyner ed., 1997).

221. Cassese, Antonio, *The Self-Determination of Peoples*, in The International Bill Of Rights – The Covenant on Civil and Political Rights 111 (Louis Henkin ed., 1981).

222. For further arguments in this direction *see* Buergenthal, Thomas, *The World Bank and Human Rights*, in The World Bank and International Financial Institutions and the Development of International Law 95,96 (Edith Brown Weiss et. al., eds., 1999).

223. Gauri, *supra* note 149, at 465.

224. *Supra* note 59 and accompanying text.

225. Alston, Philip, *Ships Passing in the Night: The Current State of the Human Rights and Development Debate as Seen Through the Lens of the Millennium Development Goals*, 27 Hum. Rts. Q. 755 (2005).

226. Article 53, Vienna Convention: "A treaty is void if, at the time of its conclusion, it conflicts with a peremptory norm of general international law. For the purposes of the present Convention, a peremptory norm of general international law is a norm accepted and recognized by the international community of States as a whole as a norm from which no derogation is permitted and which can be modified only by a subsequent norm of general international law having the same character." Moreover, Article 64 of the Vienna Convention provides: "If a new peremptory norm of international law emerges, any existing treaty which is in conflict with that norm becomes void and terminates."

227. Ragazzi, Maurizio, The Concept of International Obligations Erga Omnes 47 (1997); Gaja, Giorgio, *Jus Cogens Beyond the Vienna Convention*, 172 Hague Recueil 1981-III, 290-301 (1981).

228. For an outline of the consequences of inconsistency between jus cogens norms and other sources of international law, *see* International Law Commission, *Conclusions of the Work of the Study Group on the Fragmentation of International Law: Difficulties Arising from the Diversification and Expansion of International Law, Report of the International Law Commission to the General Assembly*, 61 U.N. GAOR Supp. (No. 10) U.N. Doc. A/61/10 (2006). However, for a more sceptical view on the probative value and practical importance of *jus cogens see e.g.* Linderfalk, Ulf, *The Effects of* Jus Cogens *Norms: Whoever Opened the Pandora's Box, Did You Ever Think About the Consequences*, 18(5) Eur. J. Int'l L. 853 (2007); Weisburd, A. Mark, *The Emptiness of the Concept of Jus Cogens, As Illustrated by the War in Bosnia-Herzegovina*, 17 Mich. J. Int'l L. 1 (1995-96).

229. For example, States may choose to exclude themselves from the application of an emerging customary human rights rule by persistently objecting to it. This is not possible for *jus cogens* norms.

230. Ragazzi, *supra* note 227, at 189. The International Law Commission, in its commentary on draft Article 50 of the Draft Articles on the Law of Treaties, stated that it was the "particular nature of the subject matter" that confers peremptory character upon a given norm. Fitzmaurice, summarising the International Law Commission's work, wrote that a common feature of peremptory norms is that they involve "not only legal rules but considerations of morals and of international good order." Ragazzi, *supra* note 227, at 49.

231. For a recent discussion on the nature of the disagreements *see* Criddle, Evan & Evan Fox-Decent, *A Fiduciary Theory of Jus Cogens*, 34 Yale J. Int'l L. 331 (2009).

232. *Id.* at 103. On the problem of demonstrating compliance, Herrmann remarks: "Although it is possible to identify violations of normative principles, it is more difficult to demonstrate compliance. The empirical problem is quite similar in this domain to the problem plaguing successful

deterrence. When a State complies with a normative principle, it might be doing this for several reasons. One of these reasons may be that they saw no material payoff for violating the norm. Politicians have many motives to mislead observers on this score. For bargaining purposes, for example, leaders may want to claim they gave up an easy gain in the name of justice and now want reciprocation ... [L]eaders also have plenty of reasons to mislead themselves and to believe in normatively self-serving stories. How to establish what sort of mindset was active in decision-making and which beliefs were decisive is an empirical challenge quite similar to that faced by rationalists when attempting to determine motives and beliefs." Herrmann, Richard, *Linking Theory to Evidence in International Relations*, in Handbook Of International Relations 119 (Walter Carlsnaes et. al., eds., 2002).

233. Waldock, Humphrey, 'Second Report on the Law of Treaties' Doc.A/CN.4/156 at pp 52 and 53. *See generally* Seiderman, Ian, Hierarchy in International Law: The Human Rights Dimension chap. 3 (2001).

234. Inter-American Commission on Human Rights, *Report* 62/02, *Case* 12.285, *Michael Domingues*, (Oct. 15, 2001) (finding that there was a *"jus cogens* norm not to impose capital punishment on individuals who committed their crimes when they had not yet reached 18 years of age"); Prosecutor v. Furundzija, Case No. ICTR IT-95-17/1-T, Judgement, (Dec. 10, 1998) (finding that there is a jus cogens norm prohibiting torture). However, for a critique of the gender bias of *jus cogens see* Charlesworth, Hilary & Christine Chinkin, *The Gender of Jus Cogens*, 15 Hum. Rts. Q. 63 (1993).

235. *See e.g.* United Nations Human Rights Committee, *Concluding Observations of the Human Rights Committee: Israel*, U.N. Doc. CCPR/CO/78/ISR (Aug. 21, 2003), para. 16; Tanase and others v. Romania, Eur. Ct. H.R., Application no. 62954 (May 26, 2009), *available at* http://www.unhcr.org/refworld/docid/4a535d4d2.html (finding that forced eviction in the circumstances of the latter case contravened the prohibition on "cruel, inhuman or degrading treatment or punishment" under Article 3 of the ECHR). Forced eviction has been condemned as a "gross violation of human rights" by the former UN Commission on Human Rights on several occasions. *See e.g.* United Nations Commission on Human Rights Res. 1993/77 on Forced Evictions (Mar. 10, 1993); United Nations Commission on Human Rights Res. 2004/28 on the Prohibition of Forced Evictions (Apr. 16, 2004).

236. The situation is not static, however. Pavoni suggests, for example, that "[i]nternational law is rapidly evolving in the area of environmental security, and celebrated legal doctrines, such as jus cogens and obligations *erga omnes*, are increasingly advocated as including the basic norms aimed at the preservation of global environmental resources (climate, ozone layer, biodiversity)." Pavoni, Riccardo, *Biosafety and Intellectual Property Rights: The Jurisprudence of the European Patent Office as a Paradigm of an International Public Policy Issue*, in Environment, Human Rights and International Trade (Francesco Francioni, ed., 2001).

237. Ragazzi, *supra* note 227, at 18-73.

238. Barcelona Traction (Belgium v. Spain), 1970 I.C.J. 4, 33-4 (Feb. 1970).

239. International State responsibility attaches to breaches of international obligations contained in treaties, custom and other recognised sources of international law, including MEAs and human rights treaties. The nature of the secondary norms of State responsibility, as reflected in the ILC's Articles on the Responsibility of States for Internationally Wrongful Acts (concluded in 2001), is independent of the content of applicable primary rules under environmental, human rights or other sources of law. The ILC's Articles offer an authoritative source of law on these secondary norms and, with the agreement of the concerned parties, were even invoked by the ICJ in draft form to support its decision in the *Gabcikovo/Nagymaros* case between Hungary and Slovakia, in relation to the state of necessity and the environmental circumstances of the case. *See* Gabcíkovo-Nagymaros (Hungary v. Slovakia), 1997 I.C.J. 7 (Sept. 1997). Under the ILC's Articles, States other than an injured State may invoke international responsibility with respect to *inter alia*, obligations *erga omnes*, although they may only claim cessation of wrongful acts, assurances of non-repetition, and reparation "in the interest of the beneficiaries of the obligation breached." The ILC Articles attach particular consequences to the violation of *jus cogens* obligations, including the duty to cease any serious breach and the duty neither to recognize as lawful a situation created by the serious breach, nor render aid or assistance in maintaining such a situation. *See* The International Law Commission's Articles on State Responsibility: Introduction, Text and Commentaries (James Crawford ed., 2002), Articles 41(1)-(2); and Orellana, Marcos A., *Criminal Punishment for Environmental Damage: Individual and State Responsibility at a Crossroad*, 17 Geo. Int'l Env. L. REV. 673, 685-8 (2005).

240. Ragazzi, *supra* note 227, at 194.

241. Birnie, Patricia W. & A. E. Boyle, International Law and the Environment (2nd ed., 2002).

242. International Law Commission, *Fragmentation of International Law: Difficulties Arising from Diversification and Expansion of International Law: Report of the Study group of the International Law Commission*, U.N. Doc. A/CN.4/L.682 (Apr. 13, 2006), 1-25, para.154. *See generally supra* note 202 and accompanying text.

243. *Id.*

244. *Id.* The authors are grateful to Stephen Humphreys and participants at the workshop of the International Council on Human Rights Policy, "Climate Change: Technology Policy and Human Rights," in Geneva, July 9-10, 2009, for discussions on this theme. ICHRP, *Human Rights and Climate Change Technology Policy: The Roles of Technology in Ensuring Basic Human Rights in a Climate Constrained World* – draft report (2011) available at http://www.ichrp.org/en/projects/138. See also, CIEL / ICHRP, *Technology Transfer in the UNFCCC and Other International Legal Regimes: The Challenge of Systemic Integration* working paper (2010) available at http://www.ichrp.org/en/projects/138.

245. The general rule of interpretation is contained in Article 31 of the 1969 Vienna Convention on the Law of Treaties, *supra* note 111, the provisions of which are generally considered to be declaratory of customary international law: Akehurst, *supra* note 219, at 121; Brownlie, Ian, Principles of Public International Law 632 (1998). Article 31 provides, relevantly: "(1) A treaty shall be interpreted *in good faith* in accordance with the ordinary meaning to be given to the terms of the treaty in their context and in the light of its object and purpose... (3) There shall be taken into account, together with the context: (a) Any subsequent agreement between the parties regarding the interpretation of the treaty or the application of its provisions; (b) Any subsequent practice in the application of the treaty which establishes the agreement of the parties regarding its interpretation; (c) Any relevant rules of international law applicable in the relations between the parties." For a discussion *see* McLachlan, *supra* note 203.

246. Koskenniemi et. al., *supra* note 213.

247. Article 48 of the Articles on State Responsibility recognizes that States, by virtue of their participation in a multilateral regime or as a consequence of their membership in the international community, have a legal interest in the performance of certain multilateral obligations. As such, it recognizes the right of States to protect and enforce obligations entered into in the collective interest. Moreover, environmental treaties under which accountability or compliance mechanisms have been created, such as the Kyoto Protocol, recognize the right of every state to report a defaulting state to the compliance committee. Formal inter-state compliance mechanisms exist in human rights treaties as well, albeit optional in nature and requiring a State's express consent to be bound. Both have proven to be dead letters in practice, however, a reflection no doubt of the preference of States to resolve disputes, as far as possible, through diplomatic rather than legal means.

248. For an argument to this effect *see* Dupuy, René-Jean, *Humanity and the Environment*, 2 Colo. J. Int'l Envtl. L. & Pol'y 202 (1991).

249. United Nations Human Rights Committee, General Comment No. 31, Nature of the General Legal Obligation on States Parties to the Covenant, U.N. Doc. CCPR/C/21/Rev.1/Add.13 (2004), para. 2 interpreting Article 2(1) of the ICCPR in light of the inter-state compliance mechanism under Article 41 of the Covenant and UN Charter-based obligations of States to promote universal respect for and observance of "human rights and fundamental freedoms." To similar effect *see* Institut de Droit International, *Obligations Erga Omnes in International Law*, First and Second Report of the Special Rapporteur Giorgio Gaja, 71 Y.B. Inst. Of Int'l L. (2005), Part I, Session of Krakow, 2005 – First part, Preparatory Work, 119-51, 189-202. Cf. Ragazzi, *supra* note 227, at 145 & 163, noting the ICJ's distinction between "basic" and other human rights. Moreover, Prosper Weil has cautioned against arbitrary expansion of *erga omnes* obligations, fearing that it could get "out of hand," and any state could "appoint itself avenger of the international community" and "thus under the banner of law, chaos and violence would come to reign among States." Weil, Prosper, *Towards Relative Normativity in International Law*, 77 Am. J. Int'l L. 413, 431-33 (1983).

250. Socio-economic rights law and doctrine have advanced considerably since that date, with many obligations now understood to be of a prohibitive or essentially "negative" character, immediately implementable irrespective of national conditions and resource constraints, in like manner to "basic" civil and political rights. United Nations, Committee on Economic Social and Cultural Rights, General Comment No. 3: The Nature of State Parties Obligations, E/C.3/1991/3 (1990). For a theoretical exposition of a concept of "basic rights" that transcends traditional dichotomies between negative and positive obligations, *see* Shue, Henry, Basic Rights (1996); *cf.* Caney, Simon,

Cosmopolitan Justice, Responsibility and Global Climate Change, 18 Leiden J. Int'l L. 747 (2005), and for more general support for broadening and aligning the concept of *erga omnes* with contemporary human rights values *see* Carrillo-Salcedo, Juan-Antonio, *Book Reviews and Notes: The Concept of International Obligations Erga Omnes. By Maurizio Ragazzi*, 92 Am. J. Int'l L. 791, 793 (1998).

251. Picone, P., *Obblighi reciproci ed obblighi erga omnes delgli Stati nel campo della protezione internazionale dell'ambiente marino dall'inquinamento*, in Diritto Internazionale E Protezione E Protezione Dell'ambiente Marino 94-135 (V. Starace, ed., 1983), discussed and critiqued in Ragazzi, *supra* note 227, at 158-60.

252. *See* Article 198 of the UN Convention on the Law of the Sea.

253. Ragazzi, *supra* note 227, at 82-91.

254. Picone, *supra* note 251, at 125-35, cited and discussed in Ragazzi, *supra* at 227. *See also* Sands, *supra* note 214, at 188 and citations referred therein.

255. *See contra* Fitzmaurice, Malgosia, International Protection of the Environment, 293 Recueil Des Cours 165, 165-86 (2001); Arsajani, Mahnoush H. & W. Michael Reisman, *The Quest for an International Liability Regime for the Protection of the Global Commons*, in International Law Theory and Practice, Essays In Honour of Eric Suy 485 (K. Wellens ed.,1998).

256. *Id.*

257. Brownlie, Ian, Principles of Public International Law (7th edn. 2008) 19.

258. *Id.* at 789.

259. Bassiouni, M. Cherif, *A Functional Approach to General Principles of International Law*, 11 MICH. J. INT'L L. 768 (1989-90).

260. *Id.* at 768-72. Simma and Alston suggest that general principles of law correspond more closely than custom to a situation where "a norm invented with strong inherent authority is widely accepted even though widely violated." Simma and Alston, *supra* note 219, at 102. *Cf.* Lammers, J. G., *General Principles of Law Recognised by Civilised Nations*, in Essays In The Development of the International Legal Order 53, 56-7 (F. Kalshoven, P.J. Kuyper & J. G. Lammers eds., 1980).

261. Rosenne, Shabtai, Practice and Methods of International Law (1984). Some commentators have even suggested that general principles constitute a higher source of law than treaties or custom, although this is certainly a minority view. *See e.g.* Rhyne, Charles, International Law: The Substance, Process, Procedures and Institutions for World Peace With Justice 54-69 (1971).

262. Article 102(4) Restatement (Third) of the Foreign Relations Law of the United States (1987), 258, formalises this hierarchy, listing as an accepted source of international law "[g]eneral principles common to the major legal systems, even if not incorporated or reflected in customary law or international agreement, may be invoked as supplementary rules of international law where appropriate."

263. S Carlston, S., Law And Organization In World Society 216 (1962).

264. Bassiouni, *supra* note 259, at 775-81. Along similar lines *see* Cheng, Bin, General Principles Of Law As Applied By International Courts And Tribunals 390 (1953).

265. Bassiouni, *supra* note 259, at 769.

266. Bassiouni, *supra* note 259, at 774.

267. The ICJ and its predecessor, the Permanent Court of International Justice (PCIJ), have identified "general principles through the examination of many manifestations of state conduct, policy and practice at the international level, including foreign policies, bilateral and multilateral treaties, international pronouncements, collective declarations, writings of scholars, international case law, and international customs, even when unperfected." Bassiouni, *supra* note 266, at 789.

268. In Lauterpacht's assessment, the main function of general principles has been "a safety value to be kept in reserve rather than a source of law of frequent application." Lauterpacht, H., The Development of International Law by The International Court 166 (rev. ed. 1958). For a useful overview of the ICJ's and PCIJ's jurisprudence *see* Bassiouni, *supra* note 266, at 791-801.

269. Hunter, David et. al., International Environmental Law and Policy 316 (1998). On the "good faith" or *pacta sunt servanda* principle *see* Nuclear Tests (Australia. v. France), 1974 I.C.J. 253 (Dec. 20, 1974), and *supra* note 111.

270. On self-determination, *see* Advisory Opinion on Western Sahara, 1975 I.C.J. 12 (Oct. 16, 1975), 30-3, a finding no doubt facilitated by the pre-existence of the right to self-determination in treaty law. In his dissenting opinion in the South West Africa case, Judge Tanaka argued that all human rights, as part of natural law, could be regarded as "general principles" of international law. South West Africa Cases (Ethiopia v. South Africa; Liberia v. South Africa), 1966 I.C.J. 6 (July 18, 1966). But there is little support elsewhere either for this finding or the basis upon which it was made.

271. These principles emerged from German and U.S. municipal law, respectively.

272. *See* Chapter IV below.

273. So-called "soft" law can interact with and influence the development of "hard" law. The normative influence of the UDHR was mentioned above in this connection, insofar as the development of treaty and customary human rights law is concerned. For further arguments to this effect *see* Charney, Jonathan I., *Universal International Law*, 87 AM. J. INT'L L. 529 (1993); Yoshida, O., *Soft Enforcement of Treaties: The Montreal Protocol's Noncompliance Procedure and the Functions of Internal International Institutions*, 10 COLO. J. INT'L ENVTL. L. & POL'Y 95, 120-1 (1999); Bodansky, *supra* note 213, at 25-6. However, for a more critical appraisal of the importance of soft law *see* d'Aspremont, Jean, *Softness in International Law: A Self-Serving Quest for New Legal Materials*, 19(5) EUR. J. INT'L L. 1075 (2008), and in the context of compliance regimes in environmental law more particularly, *see* Handl, Gunther, *Controlling Implementation of and Compliance with International Environmental Commitments: The Rocky Road from Rio*, 5 COLO. J. INT'L ENVTL. L. & POL'Y 305, 330 (1994).

274. *See e.g.* Marong, Alhaji, *From Rio to Johannesburg: Reflections on the Role of International Legal Norms in Sustainable Development*, 16 GEO. INT'L ENVTL. L. REV. 21, 44-5 (2003); Toope, Stephen J., *Confronting Indeterminacy: Challenges to International Legal Theory*, 19 C.C.I.L. PROCS. 209, 211 (1990), arguing that "[l]aw emerges in a constant interplay between norm and fact and between means (process) and ends (substance). On this view, international law is best treated as a particular form of practical reasoning..."

275. Lowe, Vaughan, *Sustainable Development and Unsustainable Arguments*, in INTERNATIONAL LAW AND SUSTAINABLE DEVELOPMENT: PAST ACHIEVEMENTS AND FUTURE CHALLENGES 19, 31 (Alan Boyle & David Freestone eds., 1999). As Lowe notes in discussing the normative status of 'sustainble development' "Internatioanl lawyers are perhaps excessively concerned with the aspect of the norm whch demands that states and other legal persons bound by the norm conduct themselves in compliance with it. There are other aspects of normativit. Norms may function primarily as rules for decision, of concern to judicial tribunals, rather than as rules of conduct."

276. Judge Weeramantry referred to "sustainable development" as a "principle of normative value," in Gabcíkovo-Nagymaros (Hungary v. Slovakia), 1997 I.C.J. 97, 98 (Sept. 1997) (separate opinion of Judge Weeramantry) and the discussion in Marong, *id.* at 44. As to the distinction between "rules" and "principles," Dworkin argues that rules require specific courses of action, whereas a principle "states a reason that argues in one direction, but does not necessitate a particular decision." DWORKIN, RONALD, TAKING RIGHTS SERIOUSLY 24 (1999). *See generally* Marong, *id.* at 57-8.

277. Lowe, Vaughan, Sustainable Development and Unsustainable Arguments, *Supra* note 275 at 31 Alternatively, principles lacking the status of "hard law" can operate as "legitimate expectations" or objectives, exerting influence on discourse and legal regimes and influencing the evolution of customary and other rules. As Marong argues with reference to the "sustainable development" concept, "the legal notion of sustainable development implies a legitimate expectation, derived from international discourse since 1972, that States and other actors should conduct their affairs in a manner consistent with the pursuit of economic development, social development and environmental protection as equal objectives. The legitimate expectation argument does not require sustainable development norms to be binding international law. Rather, it envisages that it is both possible and legitimate for some norms to only be at the pre-legal stage of development yet provide moral suasion for particular types of behavior or serve as steps towards development of substantive legal norms." Marong, *supra* note 274, at 45.

278. While such an interpretation may sit uncomfortably with the realist school of international relations, the constructivist school of thought furnishes useful explanations of how state behaviour can be influenced, if not always determined, by factors such as those outlined above. For fuller discussion *see* OXFORD HANDBOOK ON INTERNATIONAL RELATIONS (Christian Reus-Smit & Duncan Snidal, eds, 2008); Schmitz, Hans-Peter & Kathryn Sikkink, *International Human Rights*, in HANDBOOK ON INTERNATIONAL RELATIONS 520 (Walter Carlsnaes et. al., eds., 2002), 517-37; Mitchell, Ronald B., *International Environment*, in HANDBOOK ON INTERNATIONAL RELATIONS 500-16 (Walter Carlsnaes et. al., eds., 2002).

279. The right to property is set out in Article 17 of the UDHR: "(a) Everyone has the right to own property alone or in association with others; (b) No one shall be arbitrarily deprived of his property." While neither the ICCPR nor the ICESCR expresses a human right of this kind, the right to property is reflected in Article 21 of the American Convention on Human Rights, the First Protocol to the European Convention on Human Rights, as well as many national constitutions. However,

where it exists, the right to property is heavily qualified, a reflection of the depth of political and philosophical disagreement on the status of property as a human right, as distinct from an instrumental means to achieving human rights, as well as the broad range of legitimate limitations on property rights, for example taxation, compulsory acquisition of land for public purposes, and environmental and public health restrictions on the use of property. David Robertson ed., *supra* note 36, at 163-4. Property rights have nevertheless assumed importance in connection with indigenous peoples' human rights claims, including in the climate change context. Carbon trading schemes rely upon a system of enforceable property rights, and proponents of such schemes may describe these in generic terms as "rights based approaches." However, whatever the instrumental importance that may flow from property rights protections in particular contexts, from a normative standpoint it is important not to confuse the "right to property" as expressed in the UDHR and regional instruments with the comparatively well established human rights under international law.

280. It should be noted that the international human rights legal framework and the human rights principle of "non-discrimination and equality" do not necessarily cover the field of equity and justice concerns in the climate change context. "Can we really equate the carbon dioxide guzzling automobiles in Europe and North America or, for that matter, anywhere in the Third World with the methane emissions of draught cattle and rice fields of subsistence farmers in West Bengal or Thailand? Do these people not have a right to live?" Agarwal, Anil & Sunita Narain, Global Warming in an Unequal World: A Case of Environmental Colonialism 3 (1991). To the same extent, are all industrialized country inhabitants to share in the responsibility? What about rights within states?

281. Convention on Access to Information, Public Participation in Decision-making and Access to Justice in Environmental Matters [hereinafter Aarhus Convention], June 25, 1998, 38 I.L.M. 517, *available* at http://www.unece.org/env/pp/documents/cep43e.pdf.

282. United Nations Conference on Environment and Development, June 3-14, 1992, *Report Annex I: Rio Declaration on Environment and Development*, U.N. Doc A/CONF.151/26/Rev.1 (Aug. 12, 1992). Principle 10 provides: "Environmental issues are best handled with participation of all concerned citizens, at the relevant level. At the national level, each individual shall have appropriate access to information concerning the environment that is held by public authorities, including information on hazardous materials and activities in their communities, and the opportunity to participate in decision-making processes. States shall facilitate and encourage public awareness and participation by making information widely available. Effective access to judicial and administrative proceedings, including redress and remedy, shall be provided."

283. *See e.g.* Kravchenko, Svitlana, *Right to Carbon or Right to Life: Human Rights Approaches to Climate Change*, 9 VT. J. Of Envtl. L. 513 (2008).

284. Two regional agreements do recognize environmental rights: the African Charter states that "[a]ll peoples shall have the right to a general satisfactory environment favorable to their development," and Article 11 of the San Salvador Protocol recognizes the right of "everyone…to live in a healthy environment." *Supra* note 53.

285. As Koskenniemi observes: "The exercise of constraint over States – as over individuals – is always in need of justification. Law's special kind of justifying power lies in the formulation which submits the exercise of constraint to previously agreed rules, institutions and procedural safeguards against its use for external purposes. Though the formalism may not always be 'effective,' and it can sometimes, perhaps often, be replaced by less formal procedures, it cannot be done away with altogether without serious difficulties regarding the political acceptability of the whole regime." Koskenniemi, *supra* note 213, at 147.

286. *See e.g.* Woodcock, Andrew, *Jacques Maritain, Natural Law and the Universal Declaration of Human Rights*, 8 J. History of Int'l L. 245 (2006). Recognising the richness and complexity of the underlying philosophical and ethical claims about rights serves a vital function in creating space for a critical assessment of existing international law free from the constraints of positivism and undue formalism. It is worth noting in this context that as international lawyers engage more extensively on issues such as climate change and human rights, tensions may emerge between the formalism and positivism attributable to the structure of international legal argument, on the one hand, and critical legal orientations and argumentation grounded in ethics and philosophy, on the other. These kinds of tensions are inevitable in any inter-disciplinary undertaking and, to the extent that they are acknowledged and accommodated through open debate, could be viewed as potentially fruitful or even indispensible, rather than as a risk factor.

287. These elements of a human rights approach draw from and elaborate upon Oxfam, *Climate Wrongs and Human Rights: Putting People at the Heart of Climate-Change Policy*, Oxfam Briefing Paper 3 (Sept. 2008); and Human Rights and Equal Opportunity Commission of Australia, *Background Paper: Human Rights and Climate Change* (2008), *available at* http://www.hreoc.gov.au/pdf/about/media/papers/hrandclimate_change.pdf.

288. As was seen in Section 3 of Chapter I, above, the jurisprudence under the ICESCR, drawing from the pioneering work of legal philosopher Henry Shue, has generated a tripartite typology of human rights obligations applicable to States parties to that Covenant to "respect" (do no harm, or not violate), "protect" (prevent third parties from interfering with the right, and provide appropriate mechanisms for redress) and "fulfil" (budget and plan for the progressive realisation of human rights above an immediately binding minimum "core" threshold). This should be seen principally as a heuristic device rather than a normative straitjacket. While of less direct application to the nature of obligations under the ICCPR, CRC and other international treaties, this typology has proven influential in international human rights scholarship and practice. For an extensive comparative analysis of the manner in which regional and national courts adjudicate socio-economic rights obligations *see* Langford, ed., *supra* note 59.

289. *See* CESCR, General Comment No. 3, *supra* note 67. As discussed in Chapter I, Section 3 above, there is an immediate obligation under the ICESCR, which does not depend upon available resources, to "take steps" – deliberate, concrete and targeted – towards meeting the obligations recognized in the Covenant. The "minimum core" content of particular socio-economic rights has been defined by the CESR in terms of immediate obligations and a minimum package of survival needs. Beyond this threshold, the rights in the ICESCR are to be realised progressively, subject to national resource constraints and appropriately tailored benchmarks. *See e.g.* CESCR, General Comments No. 12 (1999) and 14 (2000), *supra* note 66.

290. *See* the "do no harm" discussion in Chapter V below.

291. Certain minimal obligations to prevent transboundary harm can readily be identified under custom or general principles of international law, along with general obligations to cooperate in both international human rights and environmental law. However quantifying, adjudicating and enforcing obligations of a more positive kind, beyond "do no harm," remain very significant challenges, as the discussion in Parts IV and V suggest.

292. This section is drawn from Knox, John H., *Climate Change and Human Rights Law*, 50 VA. J. INT'L L. __ (forthcoming 2009). There is a large literature on the intersections between human rights and environmental protection. It includes LINKING HUMAN RIGHTS AND THE ENVIRONMENT (Romina Picolotti & Jorge D. Taillant eds., 2003); HUMAN RIGHTS AND THE ENVIRONMENT: CONFLICTS AND NORMS IN A GLOBALIZING WORLD (Lyuba Zarsky ed., 2002); HUMAN RIGHTS APPROACHES TO ENVIRONMENTAL PROTECTION (Alan Boyle & Michael Anderson eds., 1996); Boyle, Alan, *Human Rights or Environmental Rights? A Reassessment*, 18 FORDHAM ENVTL. L. REV. 471 (2007); Merrills, J.G., *Environmental Rights*, in THE OXFORD HANDBOOK OF INTERNATIONAL ENVIRONMENTAL LAW (Daniel Bodansky et. al., eds., 2007); Rajamani, Lavanya, *The Right to Environmental Protection in India: Many a Slip between the Cup and the Lip?*, 16(3) REV. EUR. CMTY. & INT'L ENVTL. L. 274 (Dec. 2007); Ebeku, Kaniye S.A., *Constitutional Right to a Healthy Environment and Human Rights Approaches to Environmental Protection in Nigeria: Gbemre v. Shell Revisited*, 16(3) REV. EUR. CMTY. & INT'L ENVTL. L. 312 (Dec. 2007); Kotzé, Louis J., *The Judiciary, the Environmental Right and the Quest for Sustainability in South Africa: A Critical Reflection*, 16(3) REV. EUR. CMTY. & INT'L ENVTL. L. 298 (Dec. 2007); Shelton, Dinah, *Background Paper 2: Human Rights and the Environment: Jurisprudence of Human Rights Bodies*, UNEP-OHCHR Expert Seminar on Human Rights and the Environment (2002). Osofsky, Hari M., *Learning from Environmental Justice: A New Model for International Environmental Rights*, 24 STAN. ENVTL. L.J. 71, 79 (2005); Shelton, Dinah, *Human Rights and the Environment: Jurisprudence of Human Rights Bodies*, UNEP-OHCHR Expert Seminar on Human Rights and the Environment (2002); Cook, Kate, *Environmental Rights as Human Rights*, 2 EUR. HUM. RTS. L. REV. 196 (2002); Atapattu, Sumundu, *The Right to a Healthy Life or the Right to Die Polluted? The Emergence of a Human Right to a Healthy Environment under International Law*, 17 TUL. ENVTL. L.J. 65, 74-8 (2002); Malone, Linda A. & Scott Pasternack, *Exercising Environmental Human Rights and Remedies in the United Nations System*, 27 WM. & MARY ENVTL. L. & POL'Y REV. 365 (2002); Popovic, Neil A.F., *In Pursuit of Environmental Human Rights: Commentary on the Draft Declaration of Principles on Human Rights and Environment*, 27 COLUM. HUM. RTS. L. REV. 487 (1996); Sands, Philippe, *Human Rights, Environment and the Lopez Ostra Case: Context and Consequences*, 6 EUR. HUM. RTS. L. REV. 597 (1996); McGoldrick, Dominic, *Sustainable Development and Human Rights: An Integrated Conception*, 45 INT'L & COMP. L.Q. 796

(1996); Handl, Gunther, *Human Rights and Protection of the Environment: A Mildly Revisionist View*, in Human Rights, Sustainable Development and the Environment (Antônio Augusto Cancado Trindade ed., 1992).

293. *See generally* Shelton, *supra* note 292 (noting that nearly all global and regional human rights bodies have considered the link between environmental degradation and internationally-guaranteed human rights; the complaints brought have been based upon rights to life, property, health, information, family and home life, but underlying the complaints are instances of pollution, deforestation, water pollution, and other types of environmental harm). Relevantly, in the *Gabcíkovo Nagymoros* case, Judge Weeramantry recognized the protection of the environment as a "*sine qua non* for numerous human rights such as right to health and the right to life itself." Gabcíkovo-Nagymaros (Hungary v. Slovakia), 1997 I.C.J. 7 (Sept. 1997) (separate opinion of Judge Weeramantry).

294. For the ICCPR, the duty to protect has been traced to the requirement in Article 2(1) for States to "ensure" the rights recognized in the treaty. *See* Human Rights Committee, General Comment No. 31, *supra* note 64, para. 8. The Committee on Economic, Social and Cultural Rights has also derived a duty to protect from the language of the ICESCR. *See* CESCR, General Comment No. 12, *supra* note 66, para. 15. Regional tribunals have interpreted the regional agreements to include the duty as well. *See e.g.* Commission Nationale de Droits de l'Homme et des Libertés v. Chad, Comm. No. 74/92, 2000 Afr. H.R.L. Rep. 66, 68, para. 20 (1995) ; Velásquez Rodríguez v. Honduras, Inter-Am. Ct. H.R. (ser. C) No. 4, para. 172 (July 29, 1988); Z and Others v. United Kingdom, 34 Eur. Ct. H.R. 3, para. 73 (2002). *See generally* Knox, John H., *Horizontal Human Rights Law*, 102 AM. J. INT'L L. 1, 20-3 (2008).

295. Decision Regarding Communication 155/96 (Social and Economic Rights Action Center/Center for Economic and Social Rights v. Nigeria) (African Commission on Human & People's Rights, Oct. 2001), 96 AJIL 937, para. 2 (2002) [hereinafter Ogoniland case].

296. *Id.* para. 67.

297. *Id.* para. 57. Continued social mobilisation and campaigning resulted in a US$15.5M out-of-court settlement of claims against Shell Oil in connection with human rights violations in the Nigeria delta. Walker, Andrew, *Will Shell payout change the Nigeria Delta?*, BBC NEWS, June 9, 2009, *available at* http://news.bbc.co.uk/2/hi/africa/8090822.stm.

298. The Commission said that according to the government itself, "billions of gallons of untreated toxic wastes and oil have been discharged directly into the forests, fields and waterways of the Oriente. Organization of American States, Inter-American Court of Human Rights, *Report on the Situation of Human Rights in Ecuador*, OEA/Ser.L./V/II.96, Doc. 10, Rev. 1, 90-1 (Apr. 24, 1997) [hereinafter *Ecuador Report*]. The Commission received evidence that residents were "exposed to levels of oil-related contaminants far in excess of internationally recognized guidelines," which posed significantly increased risks of cancer and other health problems. *Id.* A survey of communities in the area found that roughly three-quarters of the residents had gastro-intestinal problems, half had headaches, and one-third had skin problems. *Id.* at 90.

299. *Id.* at 88, 92.

300. *See* Oneryildiz v. Turkey, 2004-XII Eur. Ct. H.R. 79, 117, para. 89-90 (2004).

301. Fadeyeva v. Russia, 45 Eur. Ct. H.R. 10, para. 88 (2005); Lopez Ostra v. Spain, 20 Eur. Ct. H.R. 277, para. 51 (1994); Taskin v. Turkey, 2004-X Eur. Ct. H.R. 1149, para. 113 (Nov. 10, 2004).

302. Fadeyeva v. Russia, 45 Eur. Ct. H.R. 10, para. 69 (2005). "The assessment of that minimum is relative and depends on all the circumstances of the case, such as the intensity and duration of the nuisance, its physical or mental effects [and] ... [t]he general environmental context ..." *Id.*

303. Lopez Ostra v. Spain, 20 Eur. Ct. H.R. 277, para. 51 (1994). *See also* Hatton and Others v. United Kingdom, 34 Eur. Ct. H.R. 1, para. 96 (2002). "There is no explicit right in the Convention to a clean and quiet environment, but where an individual is directly and seriously affected by noise or other pollution, an issue may arise under Article 8."

304. Hatton *id.* para. 96.

305. *Id.* para. 98.

306. *Id.*; Lopez Ostra v. Spain, 20 Eur. Ct. H.R. 277, para. 51 (1994).

307. CESCR General Comment No. 14, *supra* note 66, para. 4. "[T]he right to health embraces a wide range of socio-economic factors that promote conditions in which people can lead a healthy life, and extends to the underlying determinants of health, such as ... a healthy environment."; Marangopoulos Foundation for Human Rights v. Greece, Eur. Comm. of Social Rights, Complaint No. 30/2005, Decision on the Merits, para. 195 (Dec. 6, 2005) [hereinafter *Marangopoulos Foundation*] holding that the right to protection of health "includ[es] the right to a healthy environment."

308. CESCR General Comment No. 15, *supra*, note 164.

309. Ogoniland Case, *supra* note 295, paras. 64–5. The African Commission accepted the claimants' argument that the right to food, while not mentioned explicitly in the African Charter, is essential for the fulfilment of other rights, such as rights to health, education, and work.

310. CESCR General Comment No. 15, *supra* note 164, para. 21.

311. *Id.* para. 23.

312. *Id.* para. 28.

313. CESCR General Comment No. 14, *supra* note 66, para. 34.

314. *Id.* para. 36.

315. Importantly, these procedural rights are an integral part of the normative framework for all rights, whether civil, political, economic, social or cultural. *See e.g.* Foti, J. Et. Al., Voice and Choice: Opening The Door to Environmental Democracy (2008).

316. Hatton and Others v. United Kingdom, 34 Eur. Ct. H.R. 1, para. 98 (2002); Fadeyeva v. Russia, 45 Eur. Ct. H.R. 10, para. 105 (2005); Lopez Ostra v. Spain, 20 Eur. Ct. H.R. 277, para. 51 (1994); *see* Taskin v. Turkey, 2004-X Eur. Ct. H.R. 1149, para. 116 (Nov. 10, 2004).

317. *See* Fadeyeva v. Russia, 45 Eur. Ct. H.R. 10, para. 87 (2005); Lopez Ostra v. Spain, 20 Eur. Ct. H.R. 277, para. 49 (1994). In *Fadeyeva*, the State also failed to implement its legislation providing for a residence-free zone around the polluting facility. *See* Fadeyeva v. Russia, 45 Eur. Ct. H.R. 10, paras. 116, 132 (2005).

318. *See* Taskin v. Turkey, 2004-X Eur. Ct. H.R. 1149, paras. 26, 117 (Nov. 10, 2004); Giacomelli v. Italy, 45 Eur. Ct. H.R. 38, paras. 92-3 (2006).

319. Nevertheless, the Court has said that "domestic legality should be approached not as a separate and conclusive test, but rather as one of many aspects which should be taken into account in assessing whether the State has struck a 'fair balance.' " Fadeyeva v. Russia, 45 Eur. Ct. H.R. 10, para. 98 (2005).

320. *See* Hatton and Others v. United Kingdom, 34 Eur. Ct. H.R. 1, para. 120 (2002).

321. Fadeyeva v. Russia, 45 Eur. Ct. H.R. 10, para. 105 (2005).

322. Taskin v. Turkey, 2004-X Eur. Ct. H.R. 1149, para. 119 (Nov. 10, 2004). The Court has said that these requirements apply to the right to life as well as to the right to privacy. Oneryildiz v. Turkey, *supra* note 300 at para. 90; Budayeva v. Russia, Application No. 15339/02, para. 133 (Eur. Ct. H.R. Mar. 20, 2008).

323. Fadeyeva v. Russia, 45 Eur. Ct. H.R. 10, para. 105 (2005). *See also* Giacomelli v. Italy, 45 Eur. Ct. H.R. 38, para. 80 (2006); Hatton and Others v. United Kingdom, 34 Eur. Ct. H.R. 1, para. 100 (2002) (stressing that States have a "wide margin of appreciation" to set substantive standards).

324. Budayeva v. Russia, Application No. 15339/02, para. 132 (Eur. Ct. H.R. Mar. 20, 2008); Oneryildiz v. Turkey, *supra* note 300, paras. 89-90 (2004).

325. *See* Budayeva v. Russia, Application No. 15339/02, paras. 147-58 (Eur. Ct. H.R. Mar. 20, 2008).

326. *Id.* paras. 159–60. The Court also held that Russia's failure to conduct any investigation of the causes of the mudslide violated its duty to ensure that the framework set up to protect the right to life is properly implemented and that breaches of the right are adequately addressed. *Id.* paras. 172-76.

327. *Ecuador Report, supra* note 298, at ch. VIII. The same rights also appear in international environmental instruments, including the 1998 Aarhus Convention and Principle 10 of the 1992 Rio Declaration, *supra* notes 281 and 164 respectively. The European Court of Human Rights has interpreted Article 6 of the ECHR, a provision guaranteeing a fair and public hearing in the determination of civil rights and obligations, as implying a similar set of rights. *See e.g.* Kreuz v. Poland, 12 Eur. Ct. H.R. 371 (2001).

328. E.g. Inter-American Commission on Human Rights, *Third Report on the Situation of Human Rights in Paraguay*, OEA/Ser/L/VII.110, doc. 52, ch. 9, para. 50 (2001) (recommending that Paraguay "[a]dopt the necessary measures to protect the habitat of the indigenous communities from environmental degradation, with special emphasis on protecting the forests and waters, which are fundamental for their health and survival as communities"). The Human Rights Committee has also heard complaints from indigenous people about development that adversely affects the environment on which they depend. In Sara et. al. v. Finland, Comm. No. 431/1990, Hum. Rts. Comm., U.N. Doc. CCPR/C/50/D/431/1990 (1994), Finnish citizens of Sami origin, reindeer herders of Lapland, who were opposed to the passing of the Wilderness Act which extended State ownership to wilderness areas of Lapland, complained that logging and development of the area would make reindeer herding impossible, and that their rights under Article 27 of the ICCPR to enjoy

their culture had been violated. The Human Rights Committee held that the Samis should have taken recourse to domestic tribunals first but directed that Finland stop development activities until such recourse is concluded. In an earlier case, Lubicon Lake Band v. Canada, U.N. Doc. Supp. No. 40 (A/45/40) (1990), the leader of the Lubicon Lake Band, an indigenous tribe living in Alberta, Canada that had initiated several legal actions to halt industrial development on land which on it claimed to have traditional rights, alleged violations of the Band's right to self determination and pursuit of economic and social development contrary to Articles 1-3 of the ICCPR. It was argued that the development threatened the existence of the indigenous people. The Committee found that there were no effective domestic remedies available to the Band. However, it also observed that the Band could not bring a claim arising under Article 1 of the Covenant, but directed that it could still seek relief under Article 27. They found violations of Article 27 but also that Canada's proposal on how to correct the situation was admissible.

329. *See* Saramaka People v. Surin, 2007 Inter-Am. Ct. H.R. (ser. C) No. 172, para. 95 (Nov. 28, 2007); Indigenous Cmty. Yakye Axa v. Para., Inter.-Am. Ct. H.R. (ser. C) No. 146, para. 143 (June 17, 2005); Maya Indigenous Cmty. of the Toledo Dist. v. Belize, Case 12.053, Inter-Am.C.H.R., Report No. 40/04, OEA/Ser.L/V/II.122 doc. 5 rev., para. 113 (2004); Indigenous Community of Awas Tingni v. Nicaragua, Inter-Am. Ct. H.R. (Ser. C) No. 79, para. 148 (Aug. 31, 2001). For discussion on the status of the right to property in international law *see supra* note 289 and accompanying text.

330. Saramaka People v. Surin, 2007 Inter-Am. Ct. H.R. (ser. C) No. 172, para. 121 (Nov. 28, 2007); *see* Indigenous Community of Awas Tingni v. Nicaragua, Inter-Am. Ct. H.R. (Ser. C) No. 79, para. 149 (Aug. 31, 2001) ("[T]he close ties of indigenous people with the land must be recognized and understood as the fundamental basis of their cultures, their spiritual life, their integrity, and their economic survival."); United Nations Human Rights Committee, General Comment No. 23, The Rights of Minorities, para. 3.2 (1994) (stating that the right of members of minorities to enjoy their own culture "may consist in a way of life which is closely associated with territory and use of its resources").

331. Saramaka People v. Surin, 2007 Inter-Am. Ct. H.R. (ser. C) No. 172, para. 121 (Nov. 28, 2007). "[T]he natural resources found on and within tribal people's territories that are protected under Article 21 are those natural resources traditionally used and necessary for the very survival, development and continuation of such people's way of life." *Id.* para.122.

332. *Id.* para. 61.

333. African Charter, *supra* note 37, Article 24.

334. Ogoniland Case, *supra* note 295, para. 2.

335. *Id.* para. 52.

336. *Id.* para. 53.

337. *See id.* para. 54 ("Undoubtedly and admittedly, the government of Nigeria … has the right to produce oil, the income from which will be used to fulfill the economic and social rights of Nigerians.").

338. *Id.* para. 65.

339. Specifically, States must take appropriate steps "(1) to remove as far as possible the causes of ill-health; (2) to provide advisory and educational facilities for the promotion of health…; [and] (3) to prevent as far as possible epidemic, endemic and other diseases." European Social Charter, *supra* note 52, Article 11.

340. *Marangopoulos Foundation, supra* note 307, paras. 216-20.

341. *Id.* para. 204.

342. *See id.* paras. 208-10, 215.

343. *Id.* para. 221. In January 2008, the ministerial committee echoed the conclusion that Greece had violated the Social Charter but made no recommendations, instead only "welcom[ing] the measures already taken by the Greek authorities as well as further measures envisaged in order to ensure the effective implementation of the rights protected by the European Social Charter." Council of Europe Committee of Ministers, *Resolution on Complaint No. 30/2005 by the Marangopoulos Foundation for Human Rights (MFHR) against Greece*, Res. CM/ResChS(2008)1 (Jan. 16, 2008).

344. CESCR General Comment No. 15, *supra* note 164, para. 56.

345. Core obligations listed by the CESCR include ensuring "access to the minimum essential amount of water that is sufficient and safe for personal and domestic uses to prevent disease." *Id.* para. 37(a). To be safe, the water must be "free from micro-organisms, chemical substances and radiological hazards that constitute a threat to a person's health." *Id.* para. 12. In other words, the minimum substantive standard is that States must protect water used for domestic purposes from

pollution that rises to the level of threatening personal health. On minimum substantive standards pertaining to the rights to adequate food and health, *see* CESCR, General Comment Nos. 12 & 14, *supra* note 66, outlining a range of qualitative standards and substantive criteria concerning accessibility, affordability, cultural acceptability and freedom from contaminants, and non-discrimination, among others. The CESCR is increasingly taking into account quantitative data addressing the "core content" of socio-economic rights in its periodic reviews of national reports, including indicators such as maternal mortality, primary school completion rates, availability of essential drugs as defined by the WHO, among others. *See* United Nations Office of the High Commissioner for Human Rights, *Frequently Asked Question on Economic, Social and Cultural Rights, Fact Sheet No. 33* (2008).

346. United Nations, Committee on Economic Social and Cultural Rights, General Comment No. 15: The Right to Water, E/C.12/2002/11, para. 40 (2003). General Comment No. 15 departs from the Committee's previous jurisprudence in arguing that a lack of resources may not justify non-fulfilllment of "essential minimum levels" of the right in question. For critical discussion on this question *see* United Nations Office of the High Commissioner for Human Rights, *Frequently Asked Question on a Human Rights-Based Approach to Development Cooperation* (2006), *available at* http://www.ohchr.org/Documents/Publications/FactSheet33en.pdf.

347. *See generally* Langford ed., *supra* note 59. Surveying global social rights jurisprudence, Langford (at 21-4) observes that no single uniform approach to adjudicating claims entailing positive rights includes substantive minimum guarantees. However, two broad types of obligations can be noted: (1) the obligation to "take steps" to progressively realise social rights within maximum resources available to the State (in line with the CESCR's jurisprudence); and (2) the implicit obligation to realise a minimum core level of social rights. However, reviewing experience in jurisdictions as diverse as Colombia, Finland, South Africa, New York State, Switzerland and Gambia – along with the European and African regional systems – Langford suggests (at 24) "the distinction between the more conduct-oriented duty to *take steps* and the result-oriented duty to *immediately realise* some aspect of the right is not always apparent in practice" particularly where it is evident that the state has had ample time and resources to address the alleged violation. Beyond the cases surveyed by Langford, in June 2009 the European Committee on Social Rights handed down its decision in the FEANTSA case, *supra* note 60, concerning an alleged violation by France of the right to housing under Article 31 of the Revised European Social Charter. While the Committee found that the wording of Article 31 cannot be interpreted as imposing an "obligation of results," it emphasized that Charter rights must take a "practical and effective" form. Therefore, compliance with the Charter requires States parties to: adopt the necessary legal, financial and operational means of ensuring steady progress towards achieving the goals; maintain meaningful statistics on needs, resources and results; undertake regular reviews of the impact of the strategies adopted; establish a timetable; and pay close attention to the impact of the policies adopted on each of the categories of persons concerned, particularly the most vulnerable. The Committee used the ICESCR as "a key source of interpretation" of Article 31, as well as the CESCR's General Comments No. 4 and No. 7 on forced evictions and the right to adequate housing. For a summary *see* http://www.escr-net.org/caselaw/caselaw_show.htm?doc_id=939653&searchstring=feantsa. The Committee's findings of substantive non-compliance, and its affirmation of a range of procedural obligations pertaining to the right to housing, are consistent with the observations noted above on the emerging trends in environmental human rights jurisprudence more specifically. In a similar vein, the Colombian Constitutional Court has issued rulings on the right to health with very significant implications for restructuring the health sector in response to reported structural obstacles to access. Yamin, A.E. & O. Parra-Vera, *How do Courts set Health Policy? The Case of the Colombian Constitution Court*, 6(2) PLoS Medicine (2009), *available at* www.PLoSMedicine.org.

348. ICCPR, Article 1(2); ICESCR, Article 1(2).

349. To this effect, *see* Cassese, *supra* note 221, at 106, citing the instance of the commercial and environmental exploitation of Nauru. *See also* Nowak, *supra* note 62, at 24-6, and the caution shown by the Human Rights Committee in addressing issues concerning economic self-determination.

350. *Supra* note 281.

351. *See e.g.* Kreuz v. Poland, 12 Eur. Ct. H.R. 371 (2001).

352. Musungu, Sisule F., *Health: Human Rights, Climate Vulnerability and Access to Technology*, Background Paper (draft), International Council on Human Rights Policy (July 2009).

353. For a more cautious assessment of the judicial role, *see* Boyle, Alan, *Human Rights or Envi-*

ronmental Rights? A Reassessment, 18 FORDHAM ENVTL. L. REV. 471 (2007). Boyle (at 498) describes environmental human rights jurisprudence as suggesting that the contribution of international law to environmental protection is chiefly "the empowerment of individuals and groups most affected by environmental problems," and for whom the opportunity to participate in decisions is the most useful and direct means of influencing the balance of environmental, social and economic interests. He describes (at 508) the two-pronged standard of review developed by the human rights bodies—i.e., strict procedural requirements, including prior assessment and public participation in the decision-making process, but deference to the substantive decisions that result—"tenable and democratically defensible." However, the extent of judicial deference to the executive and legislature in any given setting is obviously a context-specific – and often complex and controversial – inquiry.

354. *See* d'Aspremont, *supra* note 273.

355. On the political dimensions and recent legal developments concerning this issue, with a cautious prognosis on the practical utility of a self-standing right, *see* Limon, *supra* note 83, at 468-73.

356. *See e.g.* United Nations General Assembly Resolution, Problems of the Human Environment, G.A. Res. 2398 (XXIII), U.N. Doc. A/ Res/2398/23 (Dec. 3, 1968); Stockholm Declaration on the Human Environment of the United Nations Conference on the Human Environment, June 16, 1972, 11 I.L.M. 1416 (1972) [hereinafter Stockholm Declaration]; Hague Declaration on the Environment, Mar. 11, 1989, 28 I.L.M. 1308; and Need to Ensure a Healthy Environment for the Well-being of Individuals, G.A. Res. 45/94, U.N. Doc. A/RES/45/94 (Dec. 14, 1990).

357. *See e.g.* Aarhus Convention and Principle 10 of the Rio Declaration, *supra* notes 281 and 164.

358. *See e.g.* Article 24, African Charter, *supra* note 37; and Article 11, San Salvador Protocol, *supra* note 53. Article 24, African Charter reads:

> All peoples shall have the right to a general satisfactory environment favourable to their development.

Article 11, San Salvador Protocol reads:

> 1. Everyone shall have the right to live in a healthy environment and to have access to basic public services.
>
> 2. The States Parties shall promote the protection, preservation, and improvement of the environment.

A procedural (and by extension a substantive right) in relation to the environment can be found in the Aarhus Convention. Article 1, Aarhus Convention reads:

> In order to contribute to the protection of the right of every person of present and future generations to live in an environment adequate to his or her health and well-being, each Party shall guarantee the rights of access to information, public participation in decision-making, and access to justice in environmental matters in accordance with the provisions of this Convention, *supra* note 281.

Explicit references to the environment and natural resources in the context of other rights can be found in Article 24 of the CRC and Articles 2, 4, 7 and 15 of the Convention Concerning Indigenous and Tribal Peoples, June 27, 1989, 28 I.L.M. 1382 [hereinafter Convention Concerning Indigenous and Tribal Peoples]. Article 24 (2) CRC reads:

> States Parties recognize the right of the child to the enjoyment of the highest attainable standard of health and to facilities for the treatment of illness and rehabilitation of health. States Parties shall strive to ensure that no child is deprived of his or her right of access to such health care services...
>
> (c) To combat disease and malnutrition, including within the framework of primary health care, through, inter alia, the application of readily available technology and through the provision of adequate nutritious foods and clean drinking-water, taking into consideration the dangers and risks of environmental pollution.

Convention Concerning Indigenous and Tribal Peoples in Independent Countries Article 4 (1) reads:

> Special measures shall be adopted as appropriate for safeguarding the persons, institutions, property, labour, cultures and environment of the peoples concerned;

Article 7(3) reads:

> Governments shall ensure that, whenever appropriate, studies are carried out, in co-operation with the peoples concerned, to assess the social, spiritual, cultural and environmental impact on them of planned development activities. The results of these studies shall be considered as fundamental criteria for the implementation of these activities;

Article 15 (1) reads:

> The rights of the peoples concerned to the natural resources pertaining to their lands shall be specially safeguarded. These rights include the right of these peoples to participate in the use, management and conservation of these resources.

359. *Supra* note 57 and accompanying text.

360. *See e.g.* Section 24, Constitution of the Republic of South Africa, 1996. *See generally* Ksentini, Fatma Zohra, *Report of the Special Rapporteur on Human Rights and the Environment*, E.CN.4/Sub.2/1994/9, Annex III, 81-89 (July 1994) [hereinafter Ksentini Report]. *See generally* Issue 16(3), Rev. Eur. Cmty. & Int'l Envtl. L. 298 (Dec. 2007) for articles on Environmental Rights in India, South Africa and Nigeria.

361. *See* Pedersen, *supra* note 58, at 82.

362. Fitzmaurice, Gerald, *The General Principles of International Law Considered from the Standpoint of the Rule of Law*, extract from Recueil des Cours 1957 at 96-108, and also Evans, Malcolm D. ed., *International Law* (OUP 2003) at 129.

363. Pedersen, *supra* note 58, at 82; Holwick, Scott, *Transnational Corporate Behavior and Its Disparate and Unjust Effects on the Indigenous Cultures and the Environment of Developing Nations: Jota v. Texaco, a Case Study*, 11 Colo. J. Int'l Envtl. L. & Pol'y 183, 218 (2000).

364. *See e.g.* European Parliamentary Assembly Recommendation on the Environment and Human Rights, Rec. 1614 (June 27, 2003). This recommendation urges Member States to recognize a human right to a healthy, viable, decent environment, and to safeguard individual procedural rights. It also recommends that the Committee of Ministers draw up an additional protocol to the ECHR concerning the recognition of individual procedural rights that enhance environmental protection.

365. Examples include European Community Directives concerning environmental impact assessments, access to information on the environment, and public participation in drawing up certain plans and programs relating to the environment. *See* Pedersen, *supra* note 58, at 104-9.

366. For arguments in this direction *see* Rodriguez-Rivera, Luis E., *Is the Human Right to Environment Recognized Under International Law? It Depends on the Source*, 12 Colo. J. Int'l Envtl. L. & Pol'y 1 (2001).

367. Environmental human rights jurisprudence has mostly concerned itself with pollution claims. Shelton argues that "issues such as resource management and nature conservation or biodiversity [and, one may venture – climate change] are more difficult to bring under the human rights rubric, absent a right to a safe and ecologically-balanced environment." Shelton, *supra* note 292, at 230. On the moral case for a self-standing "right to clean technology transfer" *see* Caney, *supra* note 141.

368. On the risks of conceptual lassitude in so-called "third generation" or "solidarity rights" projects, Brownlie has warned: "It is, of course, easy to be sceptical about experimental views and forward thinking. However, the type of reasoning deployed in some of the "forward thinking" literature may have results which are negative in terms of the practical advancement of good purposes. As policy goals, as standards of morality, the so-called new generation of human rights would be acceptable and one could sit round a table with non-lawyers and agree on practical programmes for attaining these good ends. What concerns me as a lawyer is the casual introduction of serious confusions of thought, and this is in the course of seeking to give the new rights an actual legal context. Many points could be made, one of which would be the tendency of what may be called the enthusiastic legal literature to develop as an isolated genre, with the select few repetitiously citing one another and the same materials, completely outside the main stream of diplomacy and international law... It will be said that we have to start somewhere, and that pioneers are by definition isolated. But that is not what is happening here. The type of law invention about which I have reservations involves a tendency to cut out the real pioneering – the process of persuasion and diplomacy – and to put in its place the premature announcement that the new settlement is built." Brownlie, Ian, *The Rights of Peoples in Modern International Law*, in The Rights Of Peoples, 14-5 (James Crawford ed., 1988). However, for a rejection of superficial categories or "generations" of human rights *see* Alston, Philip, *A Third Generation of Solidarity Rights: Progressive Development or Obfuscation of International Human Rights Law*, 29 Neth. Int'l L. Rev. 307, 316-7 (1982).

369. Oposa et. al. v. Factoran, G. R. No. 101083, 224 S.C.R.A. 792 (S.C., July 30, 1993) (Phil.), reprinted in 33 I.L.M. 173 (1994). *See* the discussion in Kravchenko, *supra* note 283, at 539, and below in Chapter V in connection with the "do no harm" and precautionary principles.

370. Taskin v. Turkey, 2004-X Eur. Ct. H.R. 1149, 209-10 (Nov. 10, 2004). In this case, the Court examined, among other things, the extent to which individuals' views were taken into account in the decision-making process and the procedural safeguards available. In the face of inaction from the executive in response to clear environmental hazards, the Court said the decision-making process

must be based upon appropriate investigations and studies, emphasised the importance of public access to information and access to justice, thereby aligning the ECHR's requirements with Aarhus standards.

371. *Supra* note 295.

372. *Id.* para. 52.

373. *Id.* para.53.

374. Liebenberg, Sandra, *Adjudicating Social Rights Under a Transformative Constitution*, in Social Rights Jurisprudence: Emerging Trends in International and Comparative Law, 75-101 (Malcolm Langford ed., 2009).

375. La Constitution (Fr.), Charter for the Environment, Article 1, *available at* http://www.legifrance. gouv.fr/html/constitution/const03.htm. For discussions *see* Marrani, David, *The Second Anniversary of the Constitutionalisation of the French Charter for the Environment: Constitutional and Environmental Implications*, 10 Envtl. L. Rev. 9 (2008); Pedersen, *supra* note 58, at 108-9.

376. Pedersen, *supra* note 58, at 109.

377. *Id.* The court reportedly found that the Charter constituted a "fundamental freedom" of constitutional value allowing for the suspension of the administrative permission under French procedural law.

378. For a range of arguments on the possible advantages of a self-standing environmental human right *see* Atapattu, Sumundu, *The Public Health Impact of Global Environmental Problems and the Role of International Law*, 30 Am. J. L. & Med. 283, 296-302 (2004).

379. *Supra* note 241, at 254-9. On the anthropocentricity objection, *see* Redgwell, Catherine, *Life, the Universe and Everything: A Critique of Anthropocentric Rights*, in Human Rights Approaches to Environmental Protection 87 (Alan Boyle & Michael Anderson eds., 1996 (discussing such critiques, and arguing that, given the increasing awareness of the interconnectedness of human beings and the environment and of the intrinsic value of the latter, it is unlikely that the recognition of a human right to a clean, healthy or decent environment will have as its necessary corollary the denial of non-human "rights").

380. Anderson, Michael R., *Human Rights Approaches to Environmental Protection: An Overview*, in Human Rights Approaches to Environmental Protection (Alan Boyle & Michael Anderson eds., 1996).

381. du Bois, Francois, *Social Justice and the Judicial Enforcement of Environmental Rights and Duties*, in Human Rights Approaches to Environmental Protection 157 (Alan Boyle & Michael Anderson eds., 1996).

382. Handl, Gunther, *Human Rights and Protection of the Environment: A Mildly Revisionist View*, in Human Rights, Sustainable Development And The Environment 117 (Antônio Augusto Cancado Trindade ed., 1992).

383. *See* Boyle, Alan, *The Role of International Human Rights Law in the Protection of the Environment*, in Human Rights Approaches to Environmental Protection (Alan Boyle & Michael Anderson eds., 1996); McGoldrick, *supra* note 292, at 811.

384. United Nations General Assembly Resolution, Setting International Standards in the Field of Human Rights, G.A. Res. 41/120, U.N. Doc. A/RES/41/120 (Dec. 4, 1986). Recognising that standard-setting should proceed with "adequate preparation," the General Assembly decided that additional human rights instruments should: (i) be consistent with the existing body of international human rights law; (ii) be of fundamental character and derive from the inherent dignity and worth of the human person; (iii) be sufficiently precise to give rise to identifiable and practicable rights and obligations; (iv) provide, where appropriate, realistic and effective implementation machinery, including reporting systems; [and] (v) attract broad international support. *See also* Alston, Philip, *Conjuring Up New Human Rights: A Proposal for Quality Control*, 78 Am. J. Int'l L. 607 (1984). Certain States cited G.A. Res. 41/120 as grounds for their objections in the course of negotiations towards the UN Declaration on the Rights of Indigenous Peoples, for example.

385. Even limiting global warming to 2 degrees centigrade temperature increase, the most ambitious limit on the table, proposed by the EU, would result in serious climatic changes. *See* European Union, Communication from the Commission to the Council, the European Parliament, the European Economic and Social Committee, and the Committee of the Regions, Limiting Global Climate Change to 2° Celsius: The way ahead for 2020 and beyond, COM/2007/0002 final (Oct. 1, 2007).

386. For critiques of these rights *see* Alston, *supra* notes 368 & 384; Brownlie, *supra* note 368.

387. For authoritative discussions on this broad topic *see* Non-State Actors and Human Rights (Philip Alston ed., 2005); Clapham, Andrew, Human Rights Obligations of Non-State Actors

(2006); TRANSNATIONAL CORPORATIONS AND HUMAN RIGHTS (Olivier de Schutter ed., 2006); Kinley, David & Junko Tadaki, *From Talk to Walk: The Emergence of Human Rights Responsibilities for Corporations Under International Law*, 44 VA. J. INT'L L. 931 (2004).

388. Lee, John, *The Underlying Legal Theory to Support a Well-Defined Human Right to a Healthy Environment as a Principle of Customary International Law*, 25 COLUM. J. ENVTL. L. 283, 308-9 (2000).

389. This section generally draws on Knox, *supra* note 293 and Knox, John H., *Linking Human Rights and Climate Change at the United Nations*, 33 HARV. ENVTL. L. REV. 477 (2009).

390. *See e.g.*, Hatton and Others v. United Kingdom, 34 Eur. Ct. H.R. 1, para. 98 (2002); CESCR General Comment No. 15, *supra* note 164, paras. 21, 23 (2002); Ogoniland Case (Social and Economic Rights Action Center v. Nigeria), Communication 155/96 (African Commission on Human & Peoples' Rights, Oct. 2001) para. 57; Lopez Ostra v. Spain, 20 Eur. Ct. H.R. 277, para. 51 (1994). For further discussion in the context of corporate regulation *see* United Nations High Commissioner for Human Rights, *State Responsibilities to Regulate and Adjudicate Corporate Activities under the United Nations' core Human Rights Treaties*, Individual Report on the ICCPR (June 2007), *available at* http://www.reports-and-materials.org/Ruggie-ICCPR-Jun-2007.pdf; and the corresponding report for the ICESCR, *available at* http://www.reports-and-materials.org/Ruggie-report-ICESCR-May-2007.pdf.

391. General Comment No. 14, *supra* note 66, para. 40 ("[With respect to the right to health,] [S]tates parties [to the ICESCR] have a joint and individual responsibility . . . to cooperate in providing disaster relief and humanitarian assistance in times of emergency, including assistance to refugees and internally displaced persons.") In *Budayeva v. Russia*, for example, the European Court of Human Rights found that Russia had not implemented policies to protect the inhabitants of a region prone to deadly mudslides; it had not maintained dams, for example, and observation posts to provide timely warnings. The court concluded that Russia had failed to "discharge the positive obligation to establish a legislative and administrative framework designed to provide effective deterrence against threats to the right to life as required by Article 2" of the European Convention on Human Rights, and had thereby violated the Convention.

392. *See* discussion, *supra* pages 47–49.

393. Massachusetts v. EPA, 549 U.S. 497 (2007).

394. ICCPR, Article 2(1) (emphasis added).

395. *See* Dennis, Michael J., *Application of Human Rights Treaties Extraterritorially in Times of Armed Conflict and Military Occupation*, 99 AM. J. INT'L L. 119, 122-5 (2005).

396. International Court of Justice, Advisory Opinion on the Legal Consequences of the Construction of a Wall in the Occupied Palestinian Territory, 2004 ICJ REP. 136, para. 88, 154-60 (July 9, 2004), at 180; López v. Uruguay, (Communication No. 52/1979), Human Rights Committee, U.N. Doc. CCPR/C/OP/1 (1981 & 1985), para. 12.3, at 182; Buergenthal, Thomas, *To Respect and to Ensure: State Obligations and Permissible Derogations*, in THE INTERNATIONAL BILL OF RIGHTS 74 (Louis Henkin ed., 1981); Meron, Theodor, *Extraterritoriality of Human Rights Treaties*, 89 AM. J. INT'L L. 78, 79 (1995).

397. UNHRC General Comment No. 31, *supra* note 64, para.10 (emphasis added). Martin Scheinin, a former member of the Human Rights Committee, has argued for an expansive interpretation of the "effective control" test that would look at whether the State has effective control over the situation that causes a violation of the human right, rather than over the *individual* whose right is violated. Scheinin, Martin, *Extraterritorial Effect of the International Covenant on Civil and Political Rights*, in EXTRATERRITORIAL APPLICATION OF HUMAN RIGHTS TREATIES 76-7 (Fons Coomans & Menno T. Kamminga eds., 2004). This test may go too far, however; it risks finding that Article 2(1) is satisfied whenever a chain of causation exists between a State's actions and extraterritorial harm, which would effectively write the limitation out of Article 2(1).

398. *See* McGoldrick, Dominic, *Extraterritorial Application of the International Covenant on Civil and Political Rights*, in EXTRATERRITORIAL APPLICATION OF HUMAN RIGHTS TREATIES (Fons Coomans & Menno T. Kamminga eds., 2004), *supra* note 397, at 41, 63-65 (discussing the Committee's application of the ICCPR to occupying forces in Somalia, Croatia, and the West Bank and Gaza Strip), and also the United Nations Human Rights Committee, *Concluding Observations for the United States*, U.N. Doc. CCPR/C/USA/CO/3/Rev.1 (Dec. 18, 2006), para. 10, in which the State party was encouraged to "acknowledge the applicability of the Covenant with respect to individuals under its jurisdiction but outside its territory" (in response to reported abuses of Guantanamo detainees).

399. Legal Consequences of the Construction of a Wall, *supra* note 396.

400. One might be tempted to argue that transboundary environmental harm such as climate change raises no issues of extraterritorial duties, because the source of the harm is within the territory and jurisdiction of the originating State. Writing of the European Convention on Human Rights, which has a jurisdictional limit similar to that of the ICCPR, Alan Boyle suggests that "the Convention could arguably have extra-territorial application if a State's failure to control activities causing environmental harm affects life, private life or property in neighbouring countries," because "[t]hese activities are within [States'] jurisdiction in the obvious sense of being subject to their own law and administrative controls. Only the effects are extraterritorial." Boyle *supra* note 292, at 500. The problem is that the European Convention, like the ICCPR, makes clear that the question is not whether the *actions taken* by the State are within its jurisdiction, but whether the *individuals affected* by those actions are within its jurisdiction. If they are not, then the State apparently owes them no duties, whether or not it has jurisdiction over the sources of harm.

401. *Compare* ICCPR, Article 2(1) ("Each State Party to the present Covenant undertakes to respect and to ensure to all individuals within its territory and subject to its jurisdiction the rights recognized in the present Covenant. . . ."), *with* European Convention, Article 1 ("The High Contracting Parties shall secure to everyone within their jurisdiction the rights and freedoms defined in Section I of this Convention."), *and* American Convention, Article 1(1) ("The States Parties to this Convention undertake to respect the rights and freedoms recognized herein and to ensure to all persons subject to their jurisdiction the free and full exercise of those rights and freedoms . . . ").

402. Bankovi? et. al. v. Belgium, 12 Eur. Ct. H.R. 333 (2001).

403. *Id.* at 356-57.

404. Alejandre v. Cuba, Case86/99, Inter-Am. C.H.R. OEA/Ser.L/V/II.106, doc. 3, para. 25 (1999).

405. ICESCR Article 2(1) (emphasis added).

406. The drafting history of Article 2(1) suggests that this provision was never intended to provide a basis for a (richer) country to be held accountable for another State's failure to protect human rights which the latter blamed on lack of international assistance. *See* Craven, Mathew R., The International Covenant on Economic, Social and Cultural Rights: A Perspective on its Development (1995). However, many, if not most, developed countries would presumably not contest the proposition that they have a general obligation under ICESCR to cooperate for the global implementation of the Covenant.

407. Admittedly, the Committee's approach to extra-territorial obligations has not always been consistent and clear. However, the Committee has regularly questioned States about their fulfillllment of their extraterritorial duties without undue objection, and has included its assessment of States' compliance with these duties in its concluding observations on the States' reports. Skogly, Sigrun, Beyond National Borders: States' Human Rights Obligations in International Cooperation 152 (2006).

408. The Committee on the Elimination of Racial Discrimination is another example of a treaty body encouraging States to take steps to prevent abuse by companies abroad even if that Committee does not concretely recognize that they are required to do so. *See e.g.* United Nations Human Rights Committee, *Concluding Observations for Canada*, U.N. Doc. CERD/C/CAN/CO/18, para. 17 (May 2007); and United Nations Human Rights Committee, *Concluding Observations for the United States*, U.N. Doc. CERD/C/USA/CO/6, para. 30 (Feb. 2008).

409. For a detailed description of the views of the first Rapporteur on the Right to Health, Paul Hunt, on this topic, *see* Bueno de Mesquita, Judith & Paul Hunt, *The Human Rights Responsibility of International Assistance and Cooperation in Health*, in Universal Human Rights and Extraterritorial Obligations (Mark Gibney & Sigrun Skogly eds., 2009).

410. *See* OHCHR Report (2009), *supra* note 98, paras. 69-74, 79. For an indication of UN Member States' responses to this element of the report *see* Limon, *supra* note 83, at 455.

411. Legal Consequences of the Construction of a Wall, *supra* note 396, at 180 para.112.

412. For example, with respect to the rights to food and to health, the CESCR has said that States should facilitate access to food and to essential health facilities, goods, and services, and provide the necessary aid when required. States also have the "responsibility... to cooperate in providing disaster relief and humanitarian assistance in times of emergency, including assistance to refugees and internally displaced persons." CESCR General Comment No. 12, *supra* note 66, paras. 36, 38; CESCR General Comment No. 14, *supra* note 66, paras. 39, 40. More generally, the Committee has regularly emphasized that it is "particularly incumbent on States parties and other actors in a position to assist, to provide "international assistance and cooperation, especially economic and

technical" which enable developing countries to fulfill their core and other obligations." *Id.* para. 45; *see also* CESCR General Comment No. 3, *supra* note 66, para. 14.

413. CESCR General Comment No. 12, para. 38; CESCR General Comment No. 14, para. 39. In its review of States' reports, the CESCR asks developed States about their levels of official development assistance. Similarly, the Special Rapporteur on the Right to Health has taken the position that "[t]he human rights responsibility of international assistance and cooperation includes a duty on high-income States to urgently take deliberate, concrete and progressive measures toward devoting a minimum of 0.7 per cent of their gross national product (GNP) to development assistance." Bueno de Mesquita & Hunt, *supra* note 409, at 15.

414. *See* Craven, Matthew, *The Violence of Dispossession: Extra-Territoriality and Economic, Social, and Cultural Rights*, in Economic, Social And Cultural Rights In Action 71 (Mashood A. Baderin & Robert McCorquodale eds., 2007). The 2005 report of the working group charged with negotiating the optional protocol to the ICESCR, for example, included a statement by Canada, the Czech Republic, France, Portugal, and the United Kingdom that they "believed that international cooperation and assistance was an important moral obligation but not a legal entitlement, and did not interpret the Covenant to impose a legal obligation to provide development assistance or give a legal title to receive such aid." *Id.* at 77 (quoting United Nations Economic and Social Council, Commission on Human Rights, Working Group to Consider Options Regarding the Elaboration of an Optional Protocol to the International Covenant on Economic, Social, and Cultural Rights, *Report on Economic, Social and Cultural Rights*, U.N. Doc. E/CN.4/2005/52, para. 76 (Feb. 10, 2005); *see also* Narula, *supra* note 145, at 737: "The articulation of the obligation [of international cooperation] in a manner that includes a duty to fulfill social and economic rights in other countries may also be met with a great deal of political resistance by States that do not wish to cast their aid-giving in legal obligation terms."

415. Alston, *supra* note 225, at 777.

416. *See* Skogly, *supra* note 407, at 71.

417. *See* Vandenhole, Wouter, *EU and Development: Extraterritorial Obligations under the International Covenant on Economic, Social and Cultural Rights*, in Casting The Net Wider: Human Rights, Development And New Duty-Bearers 85, 97 (Margot E. Salomon et al., eds., 2007). The CESCR clearly views the extra-territorial obligation to "protect" more positively under the ICESCR and general international law, however: "States parties should extra-territorially *protect* the right to social security by preventing their own citizens and national entities from violating this right in other countries. Where States parties can take steps to influence third parties (non-State actors) within their jurisdiction to respect the right, through legal or political means, such steps should be taken in accordance with the Charter of the United Nations and applicable international law." United Nations, Committee on Economic Social and Cultural Rights, General Comment No. 19, The Right to Social Security, U.N. Doc. E/C/12/CG/19, para. 54 (Feb. 2008).

418. Craven, *supra* note 406, at 253.

419. *See* Skogly, *supra* note 407, at 68-9.

420. *See* CESCR General Comment No. 14, para. 41; CESCR General Comment No. 12, para. 37; CESCR General Comment No. 15, para. 31.

421. Skogly, *supra* note 407, at 70. Although a State's duty to protect those within its own jurisdiction is well-established, its duty to protect others has received less attention. *But see* CESCR General Comment No. 14, para. 39: "States parties have to respect the enjoyment of the right to health in other countries, *and to prevent third parties from violating the right in other countries*, if they are able to influence these third parties by way of legal or political means" (emphasis added). Similar language is found in CESCR General Comment No. 15: The Right to Water, *supra* note 163, para. 33, and CESCR General Comment No. 19: The Right to Social Security, *supra* note 417, para. 45. Whatever the ambiguities as to the extent to which States are required to prevent abuse by such parties (*e.g.* on the meaning of "legal or political means" in CESCR General Comments No. 14 and No. 19), it seems safe to conclude that States are at the very least *permitted* (subject to satisfying the jurisdictional criteria outlined *supra* note 81), even if not legally *obliged*, to protect against corporate-related rights abuses overseas, and there are certainly strong policy reasons to do so. *See e.g.* United Nations Human Rights Council, *Report of the Special Representative of the Secretary-General on the issue of human rights and transnational corporations and other business enterprises*, U.N. Doc. A/HRC/11/13, paras. 15-6 (Apr. 22, 2009), *available at* http://www2.ohchr.org/english/bodies/hrcouncil/docs/11session/A.HRC.11.13.pdf.

422. *Supra* note 113.

423. Some of the resistance may stem from the CESCR's application of the duty to international economic sanctions. United Nations, Committee on Economic Social and Cultural Rights, General Comment No. 8: The Relationship between Economic Sanctions and Respect for Economic, Social and Cultural Rights, E/C.12/1997/8, para. 7 (1997): With respect to economic sanctions, the "international community" as well as the State concerned must "do everything possible to protect at least the core content of the economic, social and cultural rights of the affected peoples of that State."

424. For a more extensive discussion along these lines *see* Limon, *supra* note 83, at 450-6.

425. *Supra* notes 203, 248-51 and accompanying text. It is not only the climate change and human rights treaty regimes that need to be interpreted and implemented consistently with each other. In the context of clean technology transfer, for example, one of the four "pillars" of the 2007 Bali Action Plan, the international trade, investment and intellectual property regimes must also be reconciled. For a more extensive discussion of the tensions and relationships between the latter regimes, *see* Center for International Environmental Law, *Technology Transfer in the UNFCCC and Other International Legal Regimes: The Challenge of Systemic Integration*, Background Paper, International Council on Human Rights Policy Review Meeting, 9-10 (July 2009).

426. *See* Annex II to this Report which identifies States that are parties to the core human rights treaties as well as the UNFCCC and Kyoto Protocol. As of April 2009, there were 192 States parties to the UNFCCC and 176 to the Kyoto Protocol. The core human rights treaties enjoying the highest levels of subscription are the CRC (191), the ICCPR (164), the ICESCR (160), the ICERD (173) and the CEDAW (186).

427. For a discussion *see* Bodansky et. al. eds., *supra* note 215, at 9-10. On its status as a customary rule of international law *see* Beyerlin, Ulrich, *Different Types of Norms in International Environmental Law: Policies, Principles and Rules*, in Oxford Handbook Of International Environmental Law 439 (Daniel Bodansky et. al., eds., 2007).

428. Trail Smelter Case (United States v. Canada), 3 R.I.A.A. 1905 (1938 & 1941). For further support for this principle *see* International Court of Justice, The Legality of the Threat or Use of Nuclear Weapons, Advisory Opinion, 1996 ICJ REP. 241, 241-2 (July 8, 1996). A "no significant harm" principle was codified specifically in the United Nations Convention on the Law of the Non-Navigable Uses of International Watercourses, May 21, 1997, 36 I.L.M. 700, Article 7.

429. The ICJ in The Legality of the Threat or Use of Nuclear Weapons Case held: "[t]he existence of the general obligation of States to ensure that activities within their jurisdiction and control respect the environment of other States or of areas beyond national control is now part of the corpus of international law relating to the environment." *Id.* at 241, para. 29.

430. Stockholm Declaration on the Human Environment of the United Nations Conference on the Human Environment, June 16, 1972, 11 I.L.M. 1416 (1972) and Rio Declaration, *supra* note 164, Principle 2. *See also* Draft Articles on the Prevention of Transboundary Harm from Hazardous Activities, Nov. 30, 2001, 53rd Sess., Int'l L. Comm'n, Supp. No. 10, ch. V.E.1, Articles III, IV, U.N. Doc. A/56/10, requiring States to *inter alia* "take all appropriate measures to prevent, or to minimize the risk of, significant transboundary harm."

431. *See e.g.* Hunter, David et. al., International Environmental Law and Policy 321-45(1998); Weiss, Edith Brown et. al., International Environmental Law and Policy 317 (1998); Kiss, Alexandre & Dinah Shelton, International Environmental Law 130 (1991); Sands, *supra* note 214.

432. *Supra* note 111 and accompanying text.

433. Schachter, Oscar, *The Emergence of International Environmental Law*, 44 J. INT'L AFF. 457, 462 (1991): "On its own terms, [the "do no harm" principle] has not become State practice: States generally do not "ensure that the activities within their jurisdiction do not cause damage" to the environments of others." Bodansky, *supra* note 214, at 110-1: "Although I am unaware of any systematic empirical study of this issue, transboundary pollution seems much more the rule than the exception in interstate relations. Pollutants continuously travel across most international borders through the air and by rivers and ocean currents."

434. Kravchenko, *supra* note 283, at 523.

435. Bodansky et. al. eds., *supra* note 215, at 9-10.

436. Klein, Pierre, *La responsabilité des organizations financiers et les droits de la personne*, Revue Belge De Droit International 97, 113 (1999); Simma & Alston, *supra* note 219, at 104-6. Due diligence can be understood as "the diligence reasonably expected from, and ordinarily exercised by, a person who seeks to satisfy a legal requirement or discharge an Obligation." BLACK'S LAW DICTIONARY (8th ed., 2006).

437. For a philosophical justification of "do no harm" *see* Pogge, Thomas, World Poverty and Human Rights 132 (2002). On its relevance in the humanitarian aid setting *see* Anderson, Mary, DO NO HARM: HOW AID CAN SUPPORT PEACE – OR WAR (1999). The "do no harm" requirement has also moved into the international aid policy lexicon. Recent policy guidance from the Organisation for Economic Coooperation and Development's Development Assistance Committee (OECD-DAC) provides: " 'Donors' actions may affect human rights outcomes in developing countries in positive and negative ways. They can inadvertently reinforce societal divisions, worsen corruption, exacerbate violent conflict, and damage fragile political coalitions if issues of faith, ethnicity and gender are not taken fully into consideration. Donors should promote fundamental human rights, equity and social inclusion, respect human rights principles in their policies and programming, identify potential harmful practices and develop short, medium and long-term strategies for mitigating the potential for harm." Organization for Economic Co-operation and Development, Development Assistance Committee, *Action-Oriented Policy Paper on Human Rights and Development* (2007), *available at* http://www.oecd.org/dataoecd/50/7/39350774.pdf.

438. Exchange of Letters Constituting an Agreement Between the United Nations and Belgium Relating to the Settlement of Claims Filed Against the United Nations in the Congo by Belgian Nationals, 1965 U.N. Jurid. Y.B. 39 (Feb. 20, 1965).

439. *See e.g.* United Nations, Committee on Economic Social and Cultural Rights, General Comment No. 17: The Right of Everyone to Benefit from the Protection of the Moral and Material Interests Resulting from any Scientific, Literary or Artistic Production of which he or she is the Author, E/C.12/GC/17 para. 56 (2006), postulating that States parties to the ICESCR have obligations as members of relevant international organizations to "take whatever measures they can to ensure that the policies and decisions of those organizations are in conformity with their obligations under the Covenant."

440. Salmon, Jean J. A., *De Quelques Problemes poses aux tribunaux belges par les actions de citoyens belges contre l'O.N.U. en raison de faits survenus sur le territoire de la Republique Democratique du Congo*, 81 J. TRIB. 713 (1966); de Visscher, Paul, *De l'Immunite de juridiction de l'Organisation des Nations Unies et du caractere discretionnaire de la competence de protection diplomatique*, 25 Revue Critique De Jurisprudence Belge 449 (1971) (note on the decision of Sept. 15, 1969 by the Brussels Court of Appeals).

441. United Nations Human Rights Council, *Report of the Special Representative of the Secretary-General on the issue of human rights and transnational corporations and other business enterprises*, U.N. Doc. A/HRC/11/13 (Apr. 22, 2009), *available at* http://www2.ohchr.org/english/bodies/hrcouncil/8session/reports.htm. The 2000 revision of the OECD's Guidelines for Multinational Enterprises, while of a "soft law" character, provide in para. 2 of the chapter on "General Policies," a general obligation of multinational enterprises to "respect the human rights of those affected by their activities consistent with the host government's international obligations and commitments." For a discussion on the international human rights framework in its application to corporations *see* references note 411.

442. Beyerlin, *supra* note 427, at 440. Query Author.

443. Such States include Brazil, AOSIS, Micronesia and Venezuela.

444. *See e.g.* United Nations, Agreement for the Implementation of the Provisions of the United Nations Convention on the Law of the Sea of 10 December 1982 Relating to the Conservation and Management of Straddling Fish Stocks and Highly Migratory Fish Stocks, 34 I.L.M. 1542 (1995); Cartagena Protocol on Biosafety to the Convention on Biological Diversity, Jan. 29, 2000, 39 I.L.M. 1027; Convention on Biological Diversity, June 5, 1992, 31 I.L.M. 818, and the UNFCCC. *See also* references to "prudence and caution" by the International Tribunal on the Law of the Sea in Southern Bluefin Tuna (Austl. & N.Z. v. Japan), Jurisdiction and Admissibility (LOS Convention Annex VII Arb. Trib. Aug. 4, 2000), 39 I.L.M. 1359 (2000), para. 77, and MOX Plant Case (Ireland v. U.K.), Order No. 3, 42 I.L.M. 1187 (2003), para. 84. *See* McIntyre & Mosedale, *supra* note 216. For an extensive list of references, *see* De Sadeleer, Nicholas, Environmental Principles: From Political Slogans to Legal Rules (2002).

445. *See* Sunstein, Cass, *Beyond the Precautionary Principle*, University of Chicago Legal Theory and Public Law Working Paper No. 38 (2003), *available at* http://www.law.uchicago.edu/Lawecon/WkngPprs_126-150/149.crs.precaution-new.pdf.

446. *See* European Communities, *Measures Affecting the Approval and Marketing of Biotech Products – Dispute Settlement*, WT/DS291, WT/DS292, WT/DS293 (Sept. 29, 2006), para. 7.89 (noting, whilst side-stepping the question, that the question of whether the precautionary principle is a general principle of international law is a "complex" and "unsettled" one). To similar effect *see* Bratspies, Rebecca, *Rethinking Decisionmaking in International Environmental Law: A Process-Oriented Inquiry*

into Sustainable Development, 32 YALE J. INT'L L. 363 (2007) (noting that the status of the precautionary principle is unsettled). For contrasting views *see* Bodansky, *supra* note 214 (arguing that the precautionary principle lacks the requisite determinacy expected of a norm of customary international law); *Contra* Freestone, David, *The Precautionary Principle*, in INTERNATIONAL LAW AND GLOBAL CLIMATE CHANGE 23-30 (Robin Churchill & David Freestone eds., 1991); TROUWBORST, ARIE, EVOLUTION AND STATUS OF THE PRECAUTIONARY PRINCIPLE IN INTERNATIONAL LAW 284 (2002) (concluding that "the precautionary principle is not only a general, perhaps even universal custom in that it binds, in principle, all governments of the world, but also in that it aims for comprehensive environmental protection"); Yoshida, *supra* note 273, at 122-3 especially notes 129-33 and accompanying text (relating the precautionary principle in the context of the 1987 Montreal Protocol, *supra* note 213, to Principle 21 of the 1972 Stockholm Declaration, and arguing that the latter has force as a general principle of international law); and McIntyre & Mosedale, *supra* note 216, especially at 223, note 13, and the various references referred thereto. McIntyre & Mosedale describe the precautionary principle as a putative norm of international law requiring environmental harm to be prevented, whereas a precautionary *approach* is required in order to avoid, as far as possible, that harm occurring inadvertently. These authors further contend (*id.* at 241) that the "effective and satisfactory implementation of the principle can be achieved, *inter alia*, by means of, where appropriate, precautionary assessment, the setting of precautionary standards and the discharge of ancillary informational obligations."

447. European Commission, Communication from the Commission on the Precautionary Principle, COM (2000)1 (Feb. 2, 2000). The Council adopted a resolution endorsing the broad lines of the Commission's communication in December 2000.

448. *Id.*

449. It acknowledges however that the precautionary principle must be submitted to the principles of proportionality and non-discrimination, to cost-benefit analysis and to review. *Id.*

450. For example, UNHRC General Comment No. 31, *supra* note 64, refers (at para 8) to States parties' obligations to "prevent, punish, investigate or redress the harm caused ... by private persons or entities," and (at para 17) "to take measures to prevent a recurrence of a violation of the Covenant." Moreover, the decision of the European Court of Human Rights in the case of Oneryildiz v. Turkey, *supra* note 300, suggests that the obligations under Article 2 of the ECHR have a preventive dimension, in view of the finding that the respondent in that case failed to take preventive measures in order to mitigate foreseeable risks.

451. CESCR, General Comment No. 12, *supra* note 66, para. 7.

452. Brinks, Daniel M. & Varun Gauri, *A New Policy Landscape: Legalizing Social and Economic Rights in the Developing World*, in COURTING SOCIAL JUSTICE: JUDICIAL ENFORCEMENT OF SOCIAL AND ECONOMIC RIGHTS IN THE DEVELOPING WORLD 303 (Varun Gauri & Daniel Brinks 2008). One must be wary of drawing categorical conclusions in this regard, however, mindful that empirical observation of human rights claims is in its relative infancy, and a variety of preconditions may be called for to make such claims effective. These results and preconditions are analysed at length in Gauri & Brinks eds., *Id.* and Langford ed., *supra* note 59.

453. *See e.g.* the recent reports of the Special Representative of the UN Secretary General on the Issue of Human Rights and Transnational Corporations and other Business Enterprises on state responsibilities to regulate under the ICCPR and the ICESCR.

454. There is no free-standing right to information on climate change issues or environment questions more broadly, under international human rights law, as was seen in Chapter IV. However, a free-standing right to information in connection with environmental issues has emerged from recent jurisprudence of the Inter-American Court of Human Rights and, to some extent, the European Court of Human Rights in relation to claims under Article 2 of the ECHR (concerning the right to life) connected with environmental harms: Marcel Claude Reyes v. Chile, Inter-Am. Ct. H.R. (ser. C) No. 151 (2006); Oneryildiz v. Turkey, *supra* note 300.

455. Of course, these claims are not straightforward. An issue as complex as climate change requires expertise to make the best decisions and it will not always be the case that those most affected are necessarily best placed to know the answers. Undue or categorical reliance upon participatory processes might in some circumstances slow down policy processes and notionally "democratic" debates can be corralled by special interests, populism or lowest-common-denominator political compromises, on both climate change and human rights issues. These are hard questions, the complexity of which much be recognized.

456. Oposa et. al. v. Factoran, *supra* note 369. *See also* Indigenous Community of Awas Tingni v. Nicaragua, Inter-Am. Ct. H.R. (Ser. C) No. 79 (Aug. 31, 2001), *available at* http://www.escr-net.org/usr_doc/seriec_79_ing.pdf, a case challenging large-scale deforestation in which the Court (and previously the Inter-American Commission) found that the logging permit at issue not only violated certain civil and economic rights of the Awas Tingni community, but was also likely to cause harm to future generations of Awas Tingni.

457. *See e.g.* Bodansky, *supra* notes 214 & 216.

458. *See generally* Boyle, Alan, *Principle of Cooperation: the Environment*, in UNITED NATIONS AND THE PRINCIPLES OF INTERNATIONAL LAW 120 (Vaughan Lowe & Colin Warbrick eds.,1994).

459. UNFCCC Preamble.

460. UNFCCC Article 3(5).

461. For an overview of adaptation activities under the climate treaties *see* http://UNFCCC.int/adaptation/items/4159.php.

462. UNFCCC Article 4(1)(c).

463. UNFCCC Article 4(1)(d).

464. UNFCCC Article 4(1)(g).

465. UNFCCC Article 4(1)(h).

466. UNFCCC Article 4(1) (i).

467. *See e.g.*, United Nations Framework Convention on Climate Change, *Report of the Conference of the Parties on its Eleventh Session*, Addendum, FCCC/CP/2005/5/Add.1 (Mar. 30, 2006) including dialogue on long-term cooperative action to address climate change by enhancing implementation of the Convention.

468. *See* Charter of the United Nations, June 26, 1945, 59 Stat. 1031, T.S. 993, 3 Bevans 1153, Articles 1(3), 55 and 56.

469. Article 55 also requires the United Nations to promote "solutions of international economic, social, health, and related problems," which is sufficiently broad in scope to include climate change.

470. In CESCR General Comment No. 3, *supra* note 66, paras. 13 and 14, the CESCR notes that "maximum resources," within the meaning of Article 2(1), includes both those "existing within a State and those available from the international community through international cooperation and assistance," and moreover that "[i]t is particularly incumbent upon those States which are in a position to assist others in this regard... [The Committee] emphasises that, in the absence of an active programme of international assistance and cooperation on the part of all those States that are in a position to undertake one, the full realisation of economic, social and cultural rights will remain an unfulfillled aspiration in many countries."

471. For example, *see* CESCR General Comment No. 12, *supra* note 66, paras. 36 and 37.

472. *Supra* note 42. Article 4 of the CRC provides, *inter alia*: "With regard to economic, social and cultural rights, States parties shall undertake such measures to the maximum extent of their available resources and, where needed, within the framework of international co-operation." Other provisions outlining obligations of international cooperation include Article 11 (measures to combat the illicit transfer and non-return of children abroad), Article 23 (children with disabilities), Article 24 (right to the highest attainable standard of health), and Article 28 (right to education).

473. *Supra* note 43. Article 4(2) provides: "With regard to economic, social and cultural rights, each State Party undertakes to take measures to the maximum of its available resources and, where needed, within the framework of international cooperation, with a view to achieving progressively the full realization of these rights, without prejudice to those obligations contained in the present Convention that are immediately applicable according to international law." Article 32(1) outlines more detailed stipulations for international cooperation in the fields including capacity building, research and access to scientific knowledge and transfer of technology, while Article 32(2) makes it clear that "[t]he provisions of this Article are without prejudice to the obligations of each State Party to fulfill its obligations under the present Convention."

474. For an analysis of this provision and its possible implications, *see* Pogge, Thomas, *Human Flourishing and Universal Justice*, in HUMAN FLOURISHING 333 (E. F. Paul et. al. eds., 1999).

475. The more pertinent political declarations include the United Nations Millennium Declaration, G.A. Res. 55/2, U.N. Doc. A/RES/55/2 (Sept. 6-8, 2000); the United Nations, World Summit on Sustainable Development, Aug. 26 – Sept. 4, 2002, *Report*, U.N. Doc. A/56/19 (Jan. 8, 2003); and the Monterrey Consensus, Mar. 22, 2002, 3 U.N. Doc. A/CONF.198/3. The MDGs, including MDG 8 (global partnership for development), have generated particular interest in this connection. *See* Alston, *supra* note 225.

476. G.A. Res. 41/128 (Dec. 4, 1986). After the adoption of the Declaration on the Right to Development in 1986, the Vienna Declaration and Programme of Action in 1993 and the Cairo Principles in 1994, the right to development as a universal and inalienable right was reasserted as an integral part of fundamental human rights. *See* Vienna Declaration and Programme of Action, June 14-25, 1993, 32 I.L.M. 1661; Cairo Principles, G. A. Res. 48/141 (1994), paras. 3 (c) and 4 (c); United Nations Fourth World Conference on Women, *Platform for Action*, U.N. Doc A/CONF.177/20 (Sept. 1995) at Chapter I, Resolution 1, Annex II, *inter alia*, paras. 42, 216 and 231; and the Copenhagen Declaration on Social Development, U.N. Doc A/CONF.166/9 (1995) at Chapter I, Resolution 1, Annex I.

477. G.A. Res. 41/128 (1986), Article 1(1).

478. *See generally* BROWNLIE, IAN, THE HUMAN RIGHT TO DEVELOPMENT (1989); and Orford, Anne, *Globalization and the Right to Development*, in Peoples' Rights (Philip Alston, ed., 2001).

479. The International Council on Human Rights Policy identifies four kinds of justice claims that have arisen in the context of climate change: (a) corrective justice, a concept familiar to criminal and tort law, focusing on State responsibility and redress for harmful actions; (b) substantive justice, focusing upon disparities in economic and social attainments between different States, without necessary regard to formal norm compliance; (c) distributional justice, combined with procedural justice, ensuring that decisions about costs and benefits associated with emissions reduction are arrived at through fair processes; and (d) formal justice, relying upon a strict reading of existing legal norms irrespective of substantive justice perspectives. ROUGH GUIDE, *supra* note 17, at 55-9.

480. ROUGH GUIDE, *supra* note 17, at 59.

481. *See generally* Rajamani, Lavanya, *Differential Treatment in the International Climate Regime*, 2005 Y.B. INT'L ENVTL. L. 81 (2007); RAJAMANI, LAVANYA, DIFFERENTIAL TREATMENT IN INTERNATIONAL ENVIRONMENTAL LAW (2006) and references therein.

482. So far as it can be characterized as a human rights treaty, the Genocide Convention is one exception.

483. Provisions in MEAs containing differential treatment can be divided into three main categories: (1) provisions that differentiate between industrial and developing countries with respect to the central obligations contained in the treaty, such as emissions reduction targets and timetables; (2) provisions that differentiate between industrial and developing countries with respect to implementation, such as delayed compliance schedules, permission to adopt subsequent base years, delayed reporting schedules, and softer approaches to non-compliance; and (3) provisions that grant assistance, *inter alia*, financial and technological.

484. Article 5 of the 1987 Montreal Protocol on Substances that Deplete the Ozone Layer constitutes another noteworthy instance of legislated differentiation. The Montreal Protocol gave developed countries five years to decrease pollution to a specified level, while allowing "developing countries" – defined in terms of per capita consumption of ozone-depleting substances – ten years to reach the same goal. However, creating different compliance schedules is not the same thing as different core obligations. For discussion *see* Magraw, Daniel Barstow, *Legal Treatment of Developing Countries: Differential, Contextual and Absolute Norms*, 69(1) COLO. J. INT'L ENVTL. L. & POL'Y 69 (1990), 73-6, distinguishing "differential norms" (such as that reflected in the Montreal Protocol, Article 5) from "contextual norms" (standards permitting wide latitude or margin of appreciation for compliance to take account of scientific uncertainty and context-specific circumstances and thus facilitate agreement on broad parameters or bounds of accepted behaviour while deferring agreement on specifics) and "absolute norms" (norms establishing clear and standardised obligations for all countries whatever their circumstances).

485. *Id.*

486. *See* Rajamani, Lavanya, *Differentiation in the Post-2012 Climate Regime*, 4(4) POL'Y Q. 48 (2008) for an overview of the debate on differentiation in the current negotiations.

487. *See* Redgwell, Catherine, *The Law of Reservation in Respect of Multilateral Conventions*, in HUMAN RIGHTS NORMS AS GENERAL NORMS AND A STATE'S RIGHT TO OPT OUT 13 (Gardner et. al., eds., 1997) (noting that very few human rights treaties prohibit reservations altogether and presenting the "rare example" of Article 9 of the Supplementary Convention on the Abolition of Slavery, the Slave Trade, and Institutions and Practices Similar to Slavery, 1956, which does so).

488. For an argument to this effect *see* Baxi, Upendra, *Voices of Suffering and the Future of Human Rights*, 8 TRANSNT'L & CONTEMP. PROBS. 125, 149-50 (1998).

489. *Supra* note 43.

490. A full list of the reservations and declarations to CEDAW *available at* http://www.un.org/womenwatch/daw/cedaw/reservations.htm. There has been an energetic debate on the applicability to

human rights treaties of ordinary rules of international law concerning reservations embodied in the Vienna Convention on the Law of Treaties. The Human Rights Committee, in particular, has argued that the special subject matter of human rights treaties requires the lifting of the strictures of State consent, and that the Human Rights Committee itself should be authorized to pronounce on the validity or otherwise of reservations to the ICCPR. *See* United Nations Human Rights Committee, General Comment No. 24, Issues relating to reservations made upon ratification or accession to the Covenant or the Optional Protocols thereto, or in relation to declarations under article 41 of the Covenant (1994). *Cf.* International Law Commission, *Conclusions of the Work of the Study Group on the Fragmentation of International Law: Difficulties Arising from the Diversification and Expansion of International Law, Report of the International Law Commission to the General Assembly*, 61 U.N. GAOR Supp. (No. 10) U.N. Doc. A/61/10 (2006) at 113-5. There has been no consistent approach to this issue by the various treaty bodies, however. For a discussion *see* Reservations to Human Rights Treaties and the Vienna Convention Regime (Ineta Ziemele ed., 2004).

491. *See* ICESCR. *See also* Article 4 of the CRC, *supra* note 42 (specifying that with regard to economic, social and cultural rights, States shall take measures "to the maximum extent of their available resources").

492. *Id.*

493. CESCR General Comment No. 3, *supra* note 66 noting that, at a minimum, States are required to provide for the basic needs of the population. For arguments that even the "minimum core" socio-economic rights require sensitivity to national resource constraints *see* Eide, Asbjörn, *Economic, Social and Cultural Rights as Human Rights*, in Economic, Social and Cultural Rights: A Textbook 27 (Asbjörn Eide, Catarina Krause & Allen Rosas eds., 2001); and Scott, Craig & Philip Alston, *Adjudicating Constitutional Priorities in a Transnational Context: A Comment on Soobramoney's Legacy and Grootboom's Promise*, 16 S. AFR. J. Hum. Rts. 206, 250 (2000), positing a distinction between absolute core minimums (applicable to all States) and relative (State-specific) core minimums in which some degree of differentiation is warranted.

494. *Id.*

495. *Id.*

496. Optional Protocol to the International Covenant on Economic, Social and Cultural Rights Permitting Individual Complaints, U.N. Doc A/RES/63/117 (Dec. 10, 2008), Article 14(4).

497. *See generally* Craven, *supra* note 414, at 106-52.

498. *Supra* note 77. The Convention entered into effect on July 1, 2003 but is currently in force in only 42 States.

499. *See* ICCPR Article 2.

500. ICESCR Article 17(2).

501. ICCPR Article 40(2).

502. CEDAW Article 18(2).

503. CRC Article 44(2).

504. *See* Brems, Eva, Human Rights: Universality and Diversity 346-52 (2001).

505. *Id.* at 349 (noting that in the majority of cases the committee "notes" the factors and difficulties asserted, in some cases it "recognizes" or "acknowledges" them, and in others it refers to the difficulties "as asserted by the state" indicating disagreement).

506. The precise language of the permissible limitation varies from right to right and agreement to agreement. For example, the European Convention generally, and the ICCPR and the American Convention with respect to some of the rights, also require limits to be "necessary in a democratic society." See Kiss, Alexandre Charles, Permissible Limitations on Rights, in THE INTERNATIONAL BILL OF RIGHTS: THE COVENANT ON CIVIL AND POLITICAL RIGHTS 290 (Louis Henken ed., 1981); Higgins, Rosalyn, Derogations Under Human Rights Treaties, 48 BRIT. Y.B. INT'L L. 281, 283-5 (1978). The term "ordre public," derived from French law, is not an easy term to translate into English, and therefore the original French term is used in some contexts, such as in the TRIPS agreement. It expresses concerns about matters threatening the social structures which tie a society together (i.e. matters that threaten the structure of civil society as such). For a discussion see Goodwin-Gill, Guy, Ordre Public Considered and Developed, 94 LQR 354 (1978). On the lawful conditions for limitations under the ICCPR see Human Rights Committee, General Comment No. 31, supra note 64, para. 6, noting, in particular, the requirements for necessity and proportionality of any measure limiting the enjoyment of a particular right.

507. For further discussion on derogations *see supra* notes 419-24 and accompanying text.

508. Vienna Declaration *supra* note 37, para. 5.

509. UNFCCC Article 3(1). This principle originated in the 1972 Stockholm Declaration and has been restated in subsequent international agreements including, most notably, Principle 7 of the Rio Declaration, as well as the 2002 World Summit on Sustainable Development. Principle 7, regarded as the definitive statement, provides: "States shall cooperate ... to conserve, protect and restore the health and integrity of the Earth's ecosystem. In view of the different contributions to global environmental degradation, States have common but differentiated responsibilities. The developed countries acknowledge the responsibility that they bear in the international pursuit of sustainable development in view of the pressures their societies place on the global environment and of the technologies and financial resources they command." For a discussion *see* ROUGH GUIDE, *supra* note 17, at 62-4.

510. *See* Chapter V below for discussion of how a term like equity can be rendered more concrete in the context of the "Common but Differentiated Responsibility" concept and related UNFCCC standards.

511. *See* Kellersmann, Bettina, *Die Gemeinsame, Aber Differenzierte Verantwortlichkeit Von Industriestaaten Und Entwicklungsländern Für Den Schutz Der Globalen Umwelt* (English Summary) 335 (2000).

512. International Law Association, International Committee on Legal Aspects of Sustainable Development, *Report Of The Sixty-Sixth Conference* 116 (1995).

513. Principle 16 of the Rio Declaration (1992) reads: "National authorities should endeavour to promote the internalization of environmental costs and the use of economic instruments, taking into account the approach that the polluter should, in principle, bear the cost of pollution, with due regard to the public interest and without distorting international trade and investment." *Supra* note 164. *See also* Environment and Economics: Guiding Principles Concerning International Economic Aspects of Environmental Policies, OECD Recommendation, C (72) 128 (1972). *See generally* PHILIPPE SANDS, PRINCIPLES OF INTERNATIONAL ENVIRONMENTAL LAW, Volume I, 279-81(2nd ed., 2003).

514. *See* International Court of Justice, The Legality of the Threat or Use of Nuclear Weapons, Advisory Opinion, 1996 ICJ REP. 241, para. 29 (July 8, 1996).

515. Words used are "should endeavor to promote" and "in principle."

516. *See* Wirth, David A., *The Rio Declaration on Environment and Development: Two Steps Forward and One Back, or Vice Versa?*, 29 GA. L. REV. 599, 640-5 (1995).

517. These countries include Pakistan, Switzerland, AOSIS, and Ghana.

518. Part III, *supra* note 100 and accompanying text.

519. *See supra* notes 100-4 and accompanying text.

520. *See supra* note 100 and accompanying text.

521. *Id.*

522. The right to development has featured in certain of the human rights claims set forth so far by developing countries, consistent with many developing countries claims for differential treatment based upon their comparatively limited resources and frequently pressing human development needs, and numerous developing countries have raised it in their submissions. It is intriguing that the Maldives does not raise human rights in its submission to the UNFCCC. *See* Views regarding the work programme of the United Nations Framework Convention on Climate Change, Ad Hoc Working Group on Long Term Cooperative Action under the Convention, *Submission of the Maldives on behalf of the Least Developed Countries*, UNFCCC/AWGLCA/2008/MISC.1 (Mar. 3, 2008) at 31.

523. Ideas and proposals on the elements contained in paragraph 1 of the Bali Action Plan, United Nations Framework Convention on Climate Change, Ad Hoc Working Group on Long Term Cooperative Action under the Convention, *Submission of Argentina*, UNFCCC/AWGLCA/2008/MISC.5 (Oct. 27, 2008) at 13.

524. United Nations Framework Convention on Climate Change, Ad Hoc Working Group on Long-Term Cooperative Action, *Ideas and Proposals on the elements contained in paragraph 1 of the Bali Action Plan, Submissions of Parties, Addendum (Part II)*, UNFCCC/AWGLCA/2008/MISC.5/Add.2 (Dec. 10, 2008) at 111.

525. For suggested substantive and political parameters for the progressive insertion of human rights within international climate change negotiations *see* Limon, *supra* note 83, at 466-8, suggesting *inter alia*: "First, it will be necessary to secure a formal entry point. While, as has been noted, the opening preambular paragraph to [Human Rights Council] Resolution 7/23 may, to some, have been startling in its timidity, the words "climate change . . . has implications for the full enjoyment of human rights" were nevertheless of the utmost importance ... That climate change has implications for the full enjoyment of human rights is now taken as given, as is the understanding that

the Council must move to assess the options for addressing this fact. What was true of the state representatives sitting in the Council is almost certainly true of state representatives sitting in the Conference of Parties to the UNFCCC and its subsidiary bodies. What is needed, therefore, in order to kick-start an organic assessment of the value, utility, and possible application of human rights principles in the context of climate change policy, is official wording in the agreed outcome document of COP 15 (whatever form it takes) recognizing that climate change has significant negative implications on the lives and livelihoods of individual people (especially vulnerable people) around the world, that climate change policy must therefore be premised on the need to protect and rehabilitate such individuals, and that human rights policy offers an important way of understanding the former and informing and facilitating the latter."

526. For illustrations *see* World Bank, *Realising Human Rights through Social Guarantees: An Analysis of New Approaches to Social Policy in Latin America and South Africa* (Feb. 2008), *available at* http://www-wds.worldbank.org/external/default/WDSContentServer/WDSP/IB/2008/03/27/000333037_2 0080327040951/Rendered/PDF/400470WP0P10371gh0Social0Guarantees.pdf; WORLD HEALTH ORGANIZATION & OFFICE OF THE HIGH COMMISSIONER ON HUMAN RIGHTS, HEALTH, HUMAN RIGHTS AND POVERTY REDUCTION STRATEGIES (2009), *available at* http://www.ohchr.org/Documents/Publications/HHR_PovertyReductionsStrategies_WHO_EN.pdf; United Nations Office of the High Commissioner for Human Rights, *Claiming the MDGs: A Human Rights Approach* (2008), *available at* http://www.ohchr.org/Documents/Publications/Claiming_MDGs_en.pdf; and United Nations Office of the High Commissioner for Human Rights, *Principles and Guidelines on a Human Rights Approach to Poverty Reduction Strategies* (2006), *available at* http://www.ohchr.org/Documents/Publications/PovertyStrategiesen.pdf. Query author.

527. Seymour, Daniel & Jonathan Pincus, *Human Rights and Economics: The Conceptual Basis for their Complementarity*, 26(4) DEV. POL. REV. 387 (2008), and Caney, *supra* note 536 (2006).

528. Charter of the United Nations, Preamble.

529. UNFCCC Article 2. Reference is made to this objective in the preamble to the Kyoto Protocol as well.

530. At the same time the environment can be argued as having independent worth and value on ethical grounds, even if this is reflected unevenly and imperfectly in MEAs. And there are obvious tensions between human rights claims and environmental policy objectives, including those concerning mitigation and adaptation to climate change, as we have seen.

531. *See* United Nations Intergovernmental Panel on Climate Change, *Climate Change 2007: Synthesis Report* 64 (Nov. 12-17, 2007). *See also* Australia's submissions to the AWG-LCA, United Nations Framework Convention on Climate Change, Ad Hoc Working Group on Long-Term Cooperative Action under the Convention, *Submission of Australia*, UNFCCC/AWGLCA/2008/MISC.1/Add.2 (Mar. 20, 2008) at 3 (noting that "social and economic conditions, including access to financial and investment flows, and other factors will be relevant" to such a value judgment "as will be the availability of affordable low emissions technologies").

532. *Id.*

533. Sachs, Wolfgang, *Climate Change and Human Rights*, WORLD ECON. & DEV. SPECIAL REPORT 3 (2007) at 3.

534. This view is held by Iceland, the European Community, Norway, Panama, Costa Rica, El Salvador, Honduras, Nicaragua, and Madagascar. By contrast, the small island States have proposed stabilization of GHG concentrations well below 350ppm CO_2 eq, temperature increases limited to below 1.5º C above the pre-industrial level, and reduction of CO_2 emissions by 85% below 1990 levels by 2050. *Submission by the Alliance of Small Island States* on Views Regarding the Work programme.

535. *See supra* Chapter IV.

536. Caney, Simon, *Global Justice, Rights and Climate Change*, 19 CAN. J. L. & JURISPRUDENCE 255, 262-3 (2006). For arguments along similar lines, drawing from ideas about minimum thresholds or benchmarks, *see* Caney, Simon, *Cosmopolitan Justice, Responsibility and Global Climate Change*, 18 LEIDEN J. INT'L L. 747 (2005); Shue, *supra* note 584; and Shue, Henry, *The Unavoidability of Justice*, in THE INTERNATIONAL POLITICS OF THE ENVIRONMENT 397 (Andrew Hurrell & Benedict Kingsbury eds., 1992).

537. Caney (2006), *id.* at 262-3.

538. *See e.g.* Craven, *supra* note 414, at 145-6 (arguing that a focus on minimum survival rights might divert the Committee's attention disproportionately towards developing countries); Porter, Bruce, *The Crisis of ESC Rights and Strategies for Addressing It*, in ROAD TO A REMEDY: CURRENT ISSUES

in Litigation of Economic, Social and Cultural Rights 55 (John Squires et. al. eds., 2005) (objecting to unclear philosophical foundations and risks of what Porter characterised as a "misguided search for universal, transcendental components of ESC rights"); Toebes, Brigit, *The Right to Health*, in Economic, Social and Cultural Rights: A Textbook 176 (Asbjörn Eide, Catarina Krause & Allen Rosas eds., 2001) (reducing socio-economic rights to an essential core may pretend a determinacy that does not exist and undermine broader human rights goals); and Young, Katherine, *The Minimum Core of Economic and Social Rights: A Concept in Search of Content*, 33 Yale J. Int'l L. 113 (2008) (critically reviewing the theory and practice around this concept, rejecting the goals of fixture and determinacy and the search for content, and urging instead a fresh inquiry into new concepts to facilitate rights' content, operating as law).

539. Langford, Malcom and Jeff King, Committee on Economic, *Social and Cultural Rights: Past, Present, Future*, in Social Rights Jurisprudence: Emerging Trends in International and Comparative Law (Malcolm Langford ed., 2009) at 478, 492-5.

540. Langford ed., *supra* note 59, at 22-4, commenting that those courts which have engaged explicitly with the idea of a minimum core of human rights entitlements have generally been those in jurisdictions where social rights are construed as forming part of civil and political rights guarantees.

541. Jonah Gbemre v. Shell Petroleum Development Co. (Nigeria) Ltd. et. al., Unreported Suit No. FHC/B/CS/53/05 (Nov. 14, 2005) (Benin).

542. *Id.*

543. See *e.g.* Massachusetts v. EPA, 549 U.S. 497 (2007).

544. Australian Conservation Fund v. Minister for Planning, [2004] VCAT 2029 (Oct. 29, 2004).

545. Bund für Umwelt und Naturschutz Deutschland e.V. & Germanwatch e.V. v. the Federal Republic of Germany, VG 10 A 215.04, 10th Chamber of the Administrative Court (Jan. 10, 2006), *available at* http://www.climatelaw.org/cases/country/germany/exportcredit/2006Feb03/.

546. See http://www.climatelaw.org/cases/country/us/eca/settlement.

547. Native Village of Kivalina v. ExxonMobil Corp. (N.D. Cal. Feb. 26, 2008) on the right to property, *available at* http://www.climatelaw.org.

548. Kingsbury, Benedict et. al., *The Emergence of Global Administrative Law*, 68 L. & CONTEMP. PROB. 15 (2005).

549. For an argument for integrating human rights and environmental impact assessments *see* de Boco, Gauthier, *Human Rights Impact Asssessments*, 27(2) Neth. Q. Hum. Rts. 139 (2009).

550. This methodology has been developed by the International Finance Corporation, the UN Global Compact Office and the International Business Leaders Forum to assist business enterprises in undertaking *ex ante* assessments of investment projects. *See* International Finance Corporation, *Guide to Human Rights Impact Assessment and Management: Road-Testing Draft*, 62-4 (June 2007) [hereinafter IFC Guide].

551. United Nations Framework Convention on Climate Change, *Compendium of methods and tools to evaluate impacts of, and vulnerability and adaptation to, climate change* (2005), *available at* http://unfccc.int/files/adaptation/methodologies_for/vulnerability_and_adaptation/application/pdf/200502_compendium_methods_tools_2005.pdf.

552. The IPCC guidelines are technical guidelines for the scientist that do not prescribe a single preferred method but rather a range of methods some of which may be more suitable than others to particular tasks, but which yield comparable results across regions and sectors. The guidelines aid users in assessing the impacts of potential climate change and in evaluating appropriate adaptations. The Guidelines outline a seven step process: (1) definition of the problem; (2) selection of the methods; (3) testing of the methods; (4) selection of the scenarios; (5) assessment of biophysical and socio-economic impacts; (6) assessment of autonomous adjustments; and (7) evaluation of adaptation strategies. A range of methods is identified at each step, *available at* http://unfccc.int/files/adaptation/methodologies_for/vulnerability_and_adaptation/application/pdf/ipcc_technical_guidelines_for_assessing_climate_change_impacts_and_adaptations.pdf.

553. United National Environment Programme, *Handbook on Methods for Climate Change Impact Assessment and Adaptation Strategies* (Feenstra et. al., 1998).

554. The IFC guide, *supra* note 550, refers explicitly to UN human rights treaties and to ILO instruments.

555. For an illustrative account of human rights impact assessment methodology in the context of trade policy assessments surveying the wider field of social and human rights-impact assessments in the development field, *see* Walker, Simon, Human Rights Impact Assessment of Trade Agreements: Adding Value? (forthcomming 2009).

556. *See e.g.* ELSON, DIANE, BUDGETING FOR WOMEN'S RIGHTS: MONITORING GOVERNMENT BUDGETS FOR COMPLIANCE WITH CEDAW (2006). For an overview of this and other tools for more effective monitoring of ESCR obligations *see* United Nations Office of the High Commissioner for Human Rights, *Report of the high-level task force on the implementation of the right to development on its fifth session,* U.N. Doc A/HRC.12/WG.2/TF.2 (June 17, 2009).

557. *See* www.cesr.org.

558. *See e.g.* Anderson, Edward & Marta Foresti, *Assessing Compliance: the Challenge for Economic and Social Rights,* OXFORD J. HUM. RTS. PRAC. (Sept. 11, 2009).

559. Lawson-Remer, Terra et. al., *An Index of Economic and Social Rights Fulfilllment: Concept and Methodology,* Working Paper (June 15, 2009), *available at* http://papers.ssrn.com/sol3/papers.cfm?abstract_id=1361363. For more detailed discussion on quantitative assessments *see* Felner, Eitan, *A New Frontier in Economic and Social Rights Advocacy? Turning Quantitative Data into a Tool for Human Rights Accountability,* 9 SUR: INT'L J. HUM. RTS. 109 (Dec. 2008), *available at* http://www.surjournal.org/eng/conteudos/pdf/9/felner.pdf.

560. Agrawala, Shardul, *A Development Cooperation Perspective on Mainstreaming Climate Change,* OECD Environment Directorate, Presentation to the Asia Pacific Gateway on Climate Change and Development (Apr. 23, 2008), *available at* http://www.climateanddevelopment.org/pdf/kick-off_2-1-1_OECD.pdf.

561. Ratha, Dilip et. al., *Beyond Aid: New Sources and Innovative Mechanisms for Financing Development in Sub-Saharan Africa,* in INNOVATIVE FINANCING FOR DEVELOPMENT 146 (Suhas Ketar & Dilip Ratha, eds., 2009).

562. For definitions of official and private flows, FDI and ODA *see* World Bank, *World Development Indicators* (2008) at 361 and for an outline of recent trends in financing for development taking into account the global financial crisis *see* World Bank, *Global Monitoring Report: A Development Emergency* (2009).

563. SCHUCHARD, RYAN AND WESTON, NICKI, *The Nexus of Climate Change and Human Rights Emerging Issues for Global Companies* BSR (2009) *available at* http://www.bsr.org/reports/leading-perspectives/2009/LP_Spring_2009_Nexus.pdf.

564. *See* United Nations Global Compact, *Overview of the UN Global Compact,* June 30, 2009, http://www.unglobalcompact.org/AboutTheGC/index.html.

565. *See The Equator Principles,* http://www.equator-principles.com.

566. For indicative content of human rights policies in extractive industries *see* Australian Human Rights Commission, *The Australian Mining and Resource Sector and Human Rights: 2009 Good Practice, Good Business, Fact Sheet No. 3* (2009), *available at* http://www.humanrights.gov.au/pdf/human_rights/corporate_social_responsibility/factsheet3.pdf.

567. *See e.g.* HSBC Climate Partnership, http://www.hsbccommittochange.com/environment/climate-partnership/index.aspx. On the IFC's support for private sector initiatives connected with climate change *see* IFC News, *Helping the Private Sector Address Climate Change,* http://www.ifc.org/ifcext/media.nsf/Content/Climage_Change_Dec07.

568. International Finance Corporation, *Guide to Human Rights Impact Assessment and Management: Road-Testing Draft* (June 2007), *available at* http://www.unglobalcompact.org/docs/news_events/8.1/HRIA_final.pdf.

569. For a description of the UN Human Rights Council's business and human rights mandate *see* United Nations High Commissioner for Human Rights, *Special Representative of the Secretary-General on human rights and transnational corporations and other business enterprises* (June 18, 2008), *available at* http://www2.ohchr.org/english/issues/trans_corporations/index.htm.

570. *See infra* note 587.

571. *See* United Nations Human Rights Council, *Promotion and Protection of all Human Rights, Civil, Political, Economic, Social, and Cultural Rights, Including the Right to Development,* U.N. Doc. A/HRC/8/5 (Apr. 7, 2008).

572. United Nations Human Rights Council, *Promotion and Protection of all Human Rights, Civil, Political, Economic, Social, and Cultural Rights, Including the Right to Development,* U.N. Doc. A/HRC/11/13, para. 3 (Apr. 22, 2009), *available at* http://www2.ohchr.org/english/bodies/hrcouncil/docs/11session/A.HRC.11.13.pdf. The consultation period closed on 31 January 2011 — for further information on the Principles or the mandate of the SRSG, *see* http://www.srsgconsultation.org.

573. *The Nexus of Climate Change and Human Rights: Emerging Issues for Global Companies* http://www.bsr.org/reports/leading-perspectives/2009/LP_Spring_2009.pdf at page 1. Last visited on 1/1//2010.

574. For example, the announcement of Canada's export credit agency's new "Statement on Human Rights" referenced the framework and said the agency would monitor the Special Representative's work to "guide its approach to assessing human rights." The United Kingdom's National Contact Point (NCP) for the OECD Guidelines for Multinational Enterprises found against a company for failing to exercise adequate human rights "due diligence" – using the term as defined in the Special Representative's report to the Council in 2008 (A/HRC/8/5) – and drew the company's attention to that report in recommending how to implement an effective corporate responsibility policy. *Id.* para.3.

575. For a useful and practice discussion of mechanisms worthy of support and potential replication *see* Sherman, John, *Embedding a Rights Compatible Grievance Process for External Stakeholders with Business Culture*, Corporate Social Responsibility Initiative Report No. 36 (Aug. 2009).

576. As the fourth assessment report of the IPCC remarked: "Technological adaptation can serve as a potent means of adapting to climate variability and change. New technologies can be developed to adapt to climate change and the transfer of appropriate technologies to developing countries forms an important component of the UNFCCC." IPCC, *supra* note 4, at 734.

577. *See e.g.* Burleson, Elizabeth, *Energy Policy, Intellectual Property, and Technology Transfer to Address Climate Change*, 18 TRANSN'L L. CONTEMP. PROBS. 69 (2009).

578. STERN, NICHOLAS, CLIMATE CHANGE AND THE CREATION OF A NEW ERA OF PROGRESS AND PROSPERITY (2009), cited in McKibben, *supra* note 15, at 39.

579. *Supra* note 31. The Bali Plan of Action also calls for: "Effective mechanisms and enhanced means for the removal of obstacles to, and provision of financial and other incentives for, scaling up of the development and transfer of technology to developing country Parties in order to promote access to affordable environmentally sound technologies; Ways to accelerate deployment, diffusion and transfer of affordable environmentally sound technologies; Cooperation on research and development of current, new and innovative technology, including win-win solutions; [and] The effectiveness of mechanisms and tools for technology cooperation in specific sectors."

580. Oliva, Maria Julia, *Promoting Technologies for Adaptation: A Role for the Right to Food?*, International Council on Human Rights Policy, Review Meeting (July 2009) at 1.

581. *Supra* Chapter I, note 27 and accompanying text and *see* the UNFCCC website, http://unfccc.int/2860.php for detailed information.

582. Musungu, *supra* note 352, at 13.

583. *Id.*

584. *Id.*

585. *Supra* note 244.

586. Oliva, *supra* note 580 at 2.

587. *Id.* at 7-9. The role of the private sector in technology transfer is critical as a generator of new technologies in light of the market-based nature of the channels for technology transfer such as trade, foreign direct investment and technology licencing. The question of the human rights obligations of the private sector is a perennially vexing one given the State-centric nature of international human rights law. However, there are increasing signs of corporate sensitivity to the human rights impacts of environmental harms in general, witnessed through such initiatives as the IFC Guide human rights impacts assessment tool discussed earlier and corporate social responsibility initiatives including the UN Secretary-General's Global Compact. While not legally binding in formal terms, full account should be taken of these processes from the standpoint of mitigation, adaptation, and technology transfer. The mandate and approach of the SRSG on Business and Human Rights, John Ruggie, may offer inspiration for how to most effectively engage the business sector on the human rights dimensions of climate change. For further information *see* http://www2.ohchr.org/english/issues/trans_corporations/index.htm.

588. For a more detailed exploration of this and other "implementation options," *see* STIFTUNG, FRIEDRICH EBERT & CENTER FOR INTERNATIONAL ENVIRONMENTAL LAW, HUMAN RIGHTS AND CLIMATE CHANGE: PRACTICAL STEPS FOR IMPLEMENTATION (2009).

589. Prott, Lyndel V., *Cultural Rights as Peoples' Rights in International Law*, in THE RIGHTS OF PEOPLES 106 (James Crawford ed., 1988).

590. Myers, Norman, *Environmental Refugees: An Emergent Security Issue*, 13th Economic Forum, Prague (May 23-7, 2005); Intergovernmental Panel on Climate Change, *Climate Change 2007: Third Assessment Report* (2001). Such estimates are to a great degree speculative. However, Stern describes Myer's assumptions as "conservative:" Stern Review, *supra* note 13, at 77 and more generally at 111

– 14. *See also* McAdam, Jane, *Climate Change "Refugees" and International Law*, South Wales Bar Association address (Oct. 24, 2007); and Christian Aid, *Human Tide: The Real Migration Crisis* 50 (May 2007), suggesting even higher estimates.

591. Crouch, Brad, *Tiny Tuvalu in Save Us Plea Over Rising Seas*, SUNDAY MAIL (Oct. 5, 2008).

592. Revkin, Andrew C., *Maldives Considers Buying Dry Land if Sea Level Rises*, N.Y. TIMES, Nov. 10, 2008.

593. *Supra* note 591.

594. Saul, Ben & Jane McAdam, *An Insecure Climate for Human Security? Climate-Induced Displacement and International Law*, Legal Studies Research Paper 08/131 (Oct. 2008).

595. *See e.g.* United Nations High Commissioner for Human Rights, *Executive Committee Conclusion No. 105 (LVI), Conclusions on Women and Girls at Risk* (Oct. 6, 2006). As the CEDAW noted: "Displacement, whether internal or international, weakens existing community and family protection mechanisms and exposes refugees and internally displaced women and girls to a range of human rights violations including sexual and gender-based violence, abuse and exploitation." Even before a woman or girl seeks to migrate, there are many human rights factors that can prevent her from reaching her destination including "restrictions on the freedom of movement of women in her country of origin, lack of access to necessary documentation, such as passports, because she is female, legal requirements for permission from husbands to travel, or cultural factors that put women travelling alone or without male family members at risk of harassment and violence." Edwards, Alice, *Summary of a background paper entitled: Displacement, statelessness and questions of gender equality and the Convention on the Elimination of All Forms of Discrimination against Women*, prepared for a joint seminar between UNHCR and CEDAW, U.N. Doc. CEDAW/C/2009/II/WP.3 (July 16-7, 2009).

596. This option is considered in Glahn, Benjamin, "Climate Refugees?" *Addressing the International Legal Gaps*, 63(3) INT'L BAR NEWS 17 (June 2009).

597. Falstrom, Dana Zartner, *Stemming the Flow of Environmental Displacement: Creating a Convention to Protect Persons and Preserve the Environment*, 6 COLO. J. INT'L ENVT'L. L. & POL'Y 1 (2001). Following the framework of the Convention Against Torture and Other Cruel, Inhuman and Degrading Treatment or Punishment, Falstrom argues that a treaty could be drafted offering both temporary protections for those displaced due to environmental problems and requiring the State parties to work towards ensuring that similar types of environmental problems do not recur.

598. Williams, Angela, *Turning the Tide: Recognizing Climate Change Refugees in International Law*, 30 L & POL'Y 502 (2008).

599. Docherty, Bonnie & Tyler Giannini, *Confronting a Rising Tide: A Proposal for a Convention on Climate Change Refugees*, 33-2 HARV. ENVTL. L. REV. 349, 372 (2009).

600. *Id.* at 384. The authors argue that the international community should provide three types of assistance: 1) assistance to host States to help cover the costs of remedial measures; 2) assistance to home States to support preventive measures; and 3) assistance to the refugees themselves via a coordinating agency or other aid organization.

601. The UNFCCC's Subsidiary Body for Scientific and Technological Advice (SBSTA) is composed of "government representatives competent in the relevant field of expertise" (Article 9(1) UNFCCC); however, Docherty and Giannini argue (*Id.* at 389) for an independent body.

602. Hodgkinson et. al. argue for the establishment of a structured international research capacity on climate change displacement which would generate *en masse* regional designations and *ex ante* risk analyses of "climate change displaced persons" with a dedicated secretariat and global fund to facilitate adaptation and migration as a substitute for the individual rights assessment framework of the 1951 Refugee Convention. Hodgkinson, David et. al., *Towards a Convention for Persons Displaced by Climate Change: Key Issues and Preliminary Responses*, The New Critic, issue 8 (Sept. 2008), *available at* http://www.ias.uwa.edu.au/new-critic.

603. The UNHCR claims that amendment of the 1951 Convention may undermine the international legal protections for refugees and present a potentially misleading link between climate change and migration. Glahn, *supra* note 596, at 18.

604. To similar effeict *see* Moberg, Kara, *Extending Refugee Definitions to Cover Environmentally Displaced Persons Displaces Necessary Protection*, 94 IOWA L. REV. 1107, 1135 (2009).

605. Stephen Castles, *Environmental Change and Forced Migration: Making Sense of the Debate*, UNHCR New Issues in Refugee Research, Paper No.70, 10 (Oct. 2002).

606. For example, in the context of the environment it can be difficult to demonstrate a link between a specific action causing the migration and a *specific* characteristic of the persons migrating (race, religion, nationality, political opinion, or membership in a particular social group). *See* Falstrom, *supra* note 597.

607. McAdam, Jane, *Climate Change "Refugees" and International Law*, South Wales Bar Association address 4-5 (Oct. 24, 2007); Williams, Angela, *Turning the Tide: Recognizing Climate Change Refugees in International Law*, 30 L & Pol'y 502, 508-9 (2008).

608. United Nations Commission on Human Rights, *Report of the Representative of the Secretary General, Mr. Frances Deng, submitted pursuant to Commission on Human Rights Resolution 1997/39*, U.N. Doc. E/CN.4/1998/53/Add.1 (Feb. 11, 1998) noted in Commission on Human Rights res. 1998/50. For further information *see* Brookings, *The Guiding Principles on Internal Displacement*, Brookings-Bern Project on Internal Displacement (2009), http://www.brookings.edu/projects/idp/gp_page.aspx.

609. Roger Zetter, Director of the Refugee Studies Centre, University of Oxford, *quoted in* Glahn, *supra* note 596, at 19. The former UN Commission on Human Rights and the General Assembly in unanimously adopted resolutions have taken note of the Principles, welcomed their use as an important tool and standard, and encouraged UN agencies, regional organizations, and NGOs to disseminate and apply them. Individual governments have begun to incorporate them in national policies and laws, international organizations and regional bodies have welcomed and endorsed them, and some national courts have begun to refer to them as relevant restatements of existing international law. *See* Brookings, *The Guiding Principles on Internal Displacement*, Brookings-Bern Project on Internal Displacement (2009), http://www.brookings.edu/projects/idp/gp_page.aspx.

ECO-AUDIT
Environmental Benefits Statement

The World Bank is committed to preserving endangered forests and natural resources. The Office of the Publisher has chosen to print World Bank Studies and Working Papers on recycled paper with 30 percent postconsumer fiber in accordance with the recommended standards for paper usage set by the Green Press Initiative, a non-profit program supporting publishers in using fiber that is not sourced from endangered forests. For more information, visit www.greenpressinitiative.org.

In 2009, the printing of these books on recycled paper saved the following:
- 289 trees*
- 92 million Btu of total energy
- 27,396 lb. of net greenhouse gases
- 131,944 gal. of waste water
- 8,011 lb. of solid waste

*40 feet in height and 6–8 inches in diameter